"Is your marketing team frustrated at losi
at birth by your Board? If so, then this bc
it lays out how to win over the minds, he
so that your plans are not just approved
in-market turbulence. It works – as one marketing star recently said of Ruth:
'I have learnt more in two hours than I have in fifteen years'."

Hugh Burkitt, CEO, The Marketing Society, 2003–2016

"Ruth's book is one of the most actionable management books that I have
read in a long time. Her easy to follow approach to engaging with the Board
will enable you to nail your pitch when it matters most."

Mark Evans, Marketing Director, Direct Line Group

"Boards are often populated by smart, left-brained, financially literate thinkers, whereas the best marketers bring at least as much right-brained intuitive and creative thinking. Ideas are often 'lost in translation'. Ruth's unique
background, as an Agency Strategist, Client Marketer and Management Consultant, enables her to help marketers interpret and articulate those ideas by
speaking the language of the Boardroom. She is bi-lingual. Read her book
and she can help you to be too."

Nigel Gilbert, Chief Marketing and Communications Officer,
TSB Bank PLC

"Ruth Saunders has built a successful consultancy business by teaching marketers how to communicate their strategic proposals more convincingly to
their company's Board. Against my advice she's decided to reveal her trade
secrets in this book . . . so I suggest you buy it if you're a marketer who wants
to improve their strike rate when pitching to the Board."

Hamish Pringle, Director General, Institute of Practitioners
in Advertising, 2001–11

"There are few moments as daunting for any CMO than entering a boardroom with the aim of getting buy-in to ideas that require a leap of imagination. Ruth Saunders has superbly captured the vortex in which the analytical
mindset of a commercial board meets the entrepreneurial creativity of marketing. Ruth provides the tools and advice needed to handle the challenges
from more logical minds with confidence. She knows what she is talking
about. I have seen her do it."

Jan Gooding, Global Brand Director, Aviva

"In the boardroom, it is marketing's responsibility to ensure that the voice of the
customers that the company and its board are serving is heard and acted upon,
to help guide the company to success. Having a plan to win in the boardroom is
fundamental to achieving this. Ruth's book gives you a great plan of how to win
in the boardroom – which you, your consumers and board will be grateful for."

Michael Inpong, Chief Marketing Officer, Muller Group

"This book is a must read for any marketer wishing to break out of their silo and impress in the Boardroom. Full of real-life case study examples, tips that I now know really work, and insights that I wish I had had earlier in my career, Ruth's book will help you understand the language of the business and Boardroom, and be successful at the top table."

Pete Turner, SVP Sales & Marketing, Avast

"I always knew I didn't know something, now I know what it is, and now I know why I need Ruth."

David Magliano, managing director, membership, marketing and consumer revenue, Guardian News and Media

Marketing in the Boardroom

It's tougher than ever before for companies to grow and survive.

The lower barriers to entry have made it easier for new, more risk-taking competitors to launch innovative products and services that better meet customer needs.

If a company invests at the minimum level, the business is likely to decline as competitors outpace them. Instead, if a company wants to grow, the Board must invest for growth – with marketing's ability to create customer-led growth clearly pivotal to delivering this.

To achieve this growth, marketers need to demonstrate to the Board why their projects are worth investing in, over and above other projects.

Yet it's no secret that marketing punches below its weight in the boardroom. CEOs and other board members perceive that marketers lack commercial credibility when compared with their peers, resulting in much needed breakthrough ideas not getting approved.

Marketing in the Boardroom helps marketers to be more commercially credible and thereby more successful in the Boardroom.

Ruth Saunders explains the importance of marketing in the Boardroom, and why marketers often struggle to engage the Board.

She then shows how to develop compelling marketing strategies that the Board will buy into, offering a mix of practical solutions and varied case studies drawn from her years of industry experience.

In the final section, she helps marketers better understand the Board mindset and language, demonstrating how to win over the Board members' hearts, minds and confidence.

Marketing in the Boardroom is an important book for any aspiring marketers who are moving up the career ladder, particularly those who are writing or giving presentations to the Board. It is also an important book for their organizations, particularly those that struggle to give marketing the support it needs to create customer-led strategies that will drive business growth.

Ruth Saunders uses her years of experience as a strategy consultant, marketer, advertising planner and market researcher to help clients develop, get Board buy-in to and implement innovative marketing strategies that deliver tangible business growth. Her work includes developing commercially actionable customer segmentations, streamlining brand portfolios, creating innovative brand positionings, conducting brand migrations, optimising the customer experience, and increasing marketing spend effectiveness. She is also a trainer, speaker and coach.

Ruth is currently a managing partner of her own strategic marketing and branding consultancy, Galleon Blue. Prior to this, she was a

- Marketing and branding consultant at McKinsey & Co and Prophet
- Strategic advertising planner with Saatchi & Saatchi and Mustoes
- Marketer and market researcher with packaged goods companies, Procter & Gamble and Mars Inc.
- Graduate from Birmingham University, with a Bachelor's degree in Statistics, followed by a post-graduate Diploma in Marketing.

Marketing in the Boardroom

Winning the Hearts and Minds of the Board

Ruth Saunders

First published 2017
by Routledge
2 Park Square, Milton Park, Abingdon, Oxon OX14 4RN

and by Routledge
711 Third Avenue, New York, NY 10017

Routledge is an imprint of the Taylor & Francis Group, an informa business

© 2017 Ruth Saunders

British Library Cataloguing-in-Publication Data
A catalogue record for this book is available from the British Library

Library of Congress Cataloging-in-Publication Data
Names: Saunders, Ruth (Marketing consultant), author.
Title: Marketing in the boardroom : winning the hearts and minds
   of the board / Ruth Saunders.
Description: Abingdon, Oxon ; New York, NY : Routledge, 2017. |
   Includes bibliographical references and index.
Identifiers: LCCN 2016036340 | ISBN 9781138281790 (hardback) |
   ISBN 9781138281813 (pbk.) | ISBN 9781315270944 (ebook)
Subjects: LCSH: Marketing. | New products. | Boards of directors.
Classification: LCC HF5415 .S2778 2017 | DDC 658.8—dc23
LC record available at https://lccn.loc.gov/2016036340

ISBN: 978-1-138-28179-0 (hbk)
ISBN: 978-1-138-28181-3 (pbk)
ISBN: 978-1-315-27094-4 (ebk)

Typeset in Garamond
by Apex CoVantage, LLC

Printed and bound in the United States of America by Publishers Graphics,
LLC on sustainably sourced paper.

Contents

PART THREE
Getting the Board on-board   155

Summary

Figures

Acknowledgements

My first book has been a long time in the making. It goes as far back as 1998 when I started to pull together some of the core ideas to which I've been adding ever since. Many thanks to all of my colleagues and clients who have helped shape those ideas over the years, as well as given me the opportunity to do work that I love. A particular thank you to Hamish Pringle, who some years ago encouraged me to focus my book more single-mindedly on 'helping marketers be successful in the Boardroom'.

Over the past year, there have been a number of clients and colleagues who have generously helped me to complete my first book, whom I would like to single out for praise.

These include the people who kindly took the time to read my book and endorse it, namely Hugh Burkitt, Mark Evans, Nigel Gilbert, Jan Gooding, Michael Inpong, David Magliano and Pete Turner.

They also include the people who gave me information and insights that enhanced specific sections and case studies within the book, most notably Chris Barnham, Ged Brannan, Alex Cheatle, Julie Davidson, Mark Evans, Sam Gilbert, Gemma Greaves, Nathaniel Greywoode, Philip Hanson, James Harman, Tony Isaacs, David Lethbridge, Fenella McVey, Steven Mendel, Michael Moszynski, Tim Perman, Paul Say, Paul Screawn, Chris Strange, Eamon Tuhami, Pete Turner and Karl Weaver.

Finally, I would like to thank my writing coach, Jill Daamen; my publisher, Jonathan Norman; John Smythe who made the introduction; and my fabulous family – all of whom have encouraged me along the way and helped to make this book a reality.

Part one

The importance of marketing in the boardroom

Summary

An unfortunate but familiar scenario frequently plays out in the boardroom.

A marketing team comes up with a breakthrough idea that could not only drive short-term growth but also ensure long-term financial stability. But once in the boardroom it all falls apart, with members exposing cracks in the investment strategy where outcomes have not been clearly outlined or supported with adequate financial projections or relevant data.

Defeat hangs heavy in the room, offset with blank stares and the demand to rewrite plans.

It's obvious when you think about it.

The Board, charged with the responsibility to protect and manage the company successfully, tends to be analytical, focusing on shareholder value. Optimising the net present value (NPV) of new initiatives, while minimising the risk of projects failing, leads to Board members being risk-aware. Pressure to grow the business now and over time means a more short- to medium-term mindset.

Marketers often enter the boardroom with a naïve appreciation of this, presenting and behaving in ways that reflect their own mindset. They believe a more creative approach is needed to build strong brands, drive successful innovation and create effective marketing campaigns. Risk-taking is important to them – in fiercely competitive markets, they believe risks have to be taken to reap rewards. And brands need time to deliver breakthrough innovation and step-change growth. In the boardroom, this attitude can cost them dearly.

Who's right and who's wrong? Should Boards be more appreciative of marketing's creativity? Should marketing be more appreciative of the need to be commercially credible?

No one is right or wrong – but both parties need to better appreciate and adapt to each other.

The Board needs to understand the importance and value of marketing in driving both short- and longer-term business growth – and in turn cash flow and shareholder value. It needs to applaud marketing's creativity and risk-taking approach, its ability to think outside of the box to develop marketing campaigns that resonate with both existing and new customers, and its drive to continually innovate with new products and services that delight customers.

Marketers must recognise that the boardroom is not regarded as their territory. Within the boardroom, marketers need to be commercially credible, by thinking and talking more like the Board. They need to demonstrate how their marketing strategies will build shareholder value by delivering profitable returns – and build compelling Board recommendations that the Board will buy into.

Making the most of this book

This book is designed to help marketers have more impact – both in the boardroom and among those that they need to influence as part of their day-to-day business, including upwards within their own managerial line and sideways with cross-functional teams.

It is divided into three parts, each of which can be read as an individual sub-book to hone specific skills, or can be read together in its entirety.

In Part one, we look at why marketers struggle in the boardroom, and what it takes to be a successful marketer and build a successful marketing team.

- In Chapter 1, we address the marketing issue – why marketing is increasingly important to business success and the underlying reasons why marketers underperform in the boardroom.
- In Chapter 2, we look at what it takes to be a successful marketer – including the need to behave in an entrepreneurial way, by building both creative skills and business acumen.
- In Chapter 3, we assess how to build a high-performing marketing team – by working with the business to define what it needs from marketing and building a day-to-day marketing team that incorporates the many and varied marketing skill sets required to meet today's business challenges.

In Part two, we focus on how to develop marketing strategies that the Board will engage with and buy into, using the 5W framework (Who, What, Why, Where, When) to help the Board choose where to focus their scarce resources to deliver higher returns.

- In Chapter 4, we look at *who* we should target – specifically which customers will deliver the greatest return for the company.
- In Chapter 5, we focus on *what* products and brands we should support for growth.
- In Chapter 6, we look at the importance of defining *why* we are in business – including which attributes we should invest our scarce innovation and communication resources in to build a customer-centric business.

- In Chapter 7, we address *where* we should sell – defining which distribution channels will enable us to manage and grow our brands as efficiently and effectively as possible.
- In Chapter 8, we look at *when* we should engage with people – by identifying which touch points and communication channels will have the greatest influence on our core target audience and therefore should be prioritised for growth.

Each of the five chapters explains why the relevant strategies are important to the Board – and includes key questions marketers should consider, as well as one-page analysis frameworks and relevant case study examples, to give marketers practical ideas on how to engage the Board.

In Part three, we look at how to win over the Board's mind, heart and confidence.

- In Chapter 9, we focus on how to win over the Board members' minds – by creating a strong Board recommendation with a succinct storyline, a compelling presentation deck and a robust business case.
- In Chapter 10, we look at how to win over the Board members' hearts – by engaging Board members throughout the problem-solving process from day one, assessing how to handle challenging Board-level conversations, and presenting with the end in mind on the day itself.
- In Chapter 11, we focus on how to win the Board's confidence and thereby keep the Board on-board once in-market – by learning how to embrace failure as much as success.

So let's get started.

Chapter 1

The marketing issue

"Success in dealing with people requires a sympathetic grasp of the other person's viewpoint."

Dale Carnegie, *How to Win Friends and Influence People*

It's tougher than ever before for companies to grow and survive.

In the past decade alone, we've witnessed a number of companies crashing and burning – some of them the bedrocks of our global business landscape – with statistics suggesting that this trend is likely to continue.

To navigate this ever-evolving landscape, it's not enough for companies to 'just stand still'. To survive and thrive, companies need to be innovative, while simultaneously protecting their core business. Marketing's ability to create customer-led growth is clearly pivotal in delivering this.

But it's no secret that marketing punches below its weight in the boardroom. Almost all of the senior managers in Galleon Blue's 2011 survey said that to be impactful in the boardroom, it was 'very important' for marketers to be commercially aware, yet only three-quarters of senior marketing managers, half of middle managers and less than a quarter of junior managers are perceived to be.

In this chapter, we assess:

A   Why it's getting tougher for companies to grow and survive.
B   The increasing importance of marketing to business success.
C   Why marketers underperform in the boardroom.

In the next chapter, we bring to the fore what it takes to be a successful marketer.

A: Why it's getting tougher for companies to grow and survive

The statistics speak for themselves. In today's competitive market, many top companies do not survive.

Of the twenty-two UK companies that performed most strongly each year between 1980 and 2001, only four still exist profitably in their original form today. Seven of them have collapsed and eleven have been acquired (Figure 1.1).[1]

Across the water, in 1982, Tom Peters and Robert H. Waterman Jnr famously talked about forty-three excellent companies in their book *In Search of Excellence*. But according to Richard Pascale, only six (or 14 percent of them) were still 'excellent' only eight years later.[2]

Year	Britain's top company	Performance
1979	MFI	Collapsed
1980	Lasmo	Acquired
1981	Bejam	Acquired
1982	Racal	Acquired
1983	Polly Peck	Collapsed
1984	Atlantic Computers	Collapsed
1985	BSR	Profitable
1986	Jaguar	Acquired
1987	Amstrad	Acquired
1988	Body Shop	Acquired
1989	Blue Arrow	Collapsed
1990	Maxwell Communications	Collapsed
1991	ICI	Collapsed
1992	Wellcome	Acquired
1993	Asda	Acquired
1994	TSB	Acquired
1995	BT	Profitable
1996	British Steel	Collapsed
1997	BA	Profitable
1998	Natwest	Acquired
1999	Marconi	Acquired
2000	M&S	Profitable

Figure 1.1 Of the twenty-two top-performing UK companies, only four still exist profitably today

Likewise, Richard Foster, in his book *Creative Destruction*, writes about how difficult it is for today's companies to retain their supremacy. Of the top one hundred American companies listed by Forbes in 1917, only thirty-nine still existed seventy years later in 1987 – of which only eighteen still remained in the top one hundred. And these eighteen surviving companies all significantly underperformed the market, achieving a 20 percent lower return during the 1917–1987 period.

Additionally, Foster notes that in the 1920s, the average turnover rate of companies in the S&P 90 was 1.5 percent, with companies expecting to remain in the list for more than sixty-five years. But by 1998, the average turnover of companies in the S&P 500 had increased to 10 percent, implying that companies could only expect an average lifetime of ten years in the list. Extrapolating from past patterns, this rate of change is predicted to continue – illustrating just how quickly established companies can expect to underperform and drop from the top tier elite.[3]

Why do successful companies go on to fail?

One reason for a company's demise tends to be a lack of customer-led innovation – a failure to find ways to make the 'breakthrough leaps' needed to achieve the level of step-change growth necessary for survival.

New companies typically launch with a radical, market-changing idea, finding new, innovative ways to better meet customer needs. These companies tend to be passionate, driven by a 'nothing-to-lose' attitude – comfortable with taking the necessary risks to cut through the market clutter.

These new ideas might centre on new technologies. Take Dyson, with its 'bag-less' vacuum cleaner, or Intel's highly efficient and effective core processors, or Apple with its more 'flexible' computer technology.

Or perhaps they offer strong brand propositions, such as Ella's Kitchen with its range of 100 percent natural food for babies, or Starbucks with its pledge to make coffee just the way you like it, or Vitabiotics' range of vitamins that are proven to help prevent and treat specific health issues.

Or maybe they make disparate products and services more accessible. For example, Confetti, the online wedding company that offers an array of products and services for recently engaged couples planning a wedding. Or Amazon, originally launched as the 'world's largest bookstore', which made it possible for people to buy any book they choose 24–7. Or HomeServe, the home emergency repairs business that makes it easy for people to buy insurance cover for, and quickly repair, household appliance breakages.

Or perhaps they find new routes to market that better meet customer needs. For example, EasyJet removing the frills of flying to create a low-cost airline. Or Honda's lean manufacturing that helps make its production processes more efficient. Or Zara's trim supply chain that makes it easier to bring in new clothing lines and quickly eliminate those that sell less well.

In *Creative Destruction*, Foster showed that new companies are increasingly important to overall market growth – with annualised growth rates that are much higher than both the growth rates of older companies within the top one hundred, and their predicted future annualised growth rates. In essence, the proportion of growth generated by these new companies is greater than ever – with the digital age making it increasingly easy for them to break into traditional markets cost-efficiently.

The paradox

As a company grows and becomes successful, it becomes increasingly important to the Board to protect the existing business and share price.

So, how does this play out?

The Board typically protects its existing business by setting up strict 'financial accounting' processes for all to adhere to. People are tasked with ensuring that this month's sales targets are delivered. The company creates growth by leveraging existing technology and business models rather than by investing in new ones. And people need strong business cases and compelling data to justify future capital expenditure. As the company becomes more and more constrained by the existing technologies and business models that it has already invested in, it becomes increasingly tough to develop radical product ideas that require significant investment.

Over time, this tightly controlled decision-making, unwillingness to take risks and inability to embrace new technologies effectively kills innovation – leaving the market wide open for more innovative established players in the market, or new, more risk-taking competitors. Think about it, where was Hoover when Dyson launched its 'bag-less' technology? Where was Waterstones when Amazon launched its online bookstore? Where was Blockbuster when Netflix starting streaming video over the Internet? And where were the big high street banks when Zopa launched peer-to-peer lending?

B: The increasing importance of marketing to business success

In the wake of the banking crisis, one school of thought is that it's time for companies to move away from short-term value creation to an increasing focus on mid- to longer-term value creation that is beneficial to society as a whole.

As Dominic Barton, Global Managing Partner of McKinsey & Company, wrote in his 'Capitalism for the Long Term' article: "The nature of the deep reform that I believe business must lead, is nothing less than a shift from what I call quarterly capitalism to what might be referred to as long-term capitalism (at least five to seven years). . . . This means changing how we view business's value and its role in society."[4]

Marketing's ability to create customer-led growth – by delivering both mid- and long-term growth while simultaneously protecting the core business – is pivotal to delivering this shift.

Let's look at how this can be done.

In the short term, marketers need to protect the core by developing and launching a range of new, evolutionary products, services and marketing activities that continuously keep the brand fresh. For example, these could include the 'new, latest and greatest must try' variants (such as Max Factor's 2000 Calorie mascara or Pot Noodle Bombay Bad Boy), or 'only available for a short time' limited editions (such as Mars Bar Dark or Walkers Crisps Pulled Pork in a Sticky BBQ Sauce), or 'they must be crazy' annual sales (such as RyanAir's £1 sale, or HSBC's January mortgage sale, or Asda's 'When It's Gone, It's Gone' Sale), or 'what a compelling combination' joint brand exclusives (such as H&M's guest designer collections, featuring Karl Lagerfeld, Stella McCartney and Jimmy Choo, or promotions combining McCain's Jacket Potatoes with Cathedral City cheese).

In the longer term, marketers need to deliver step-change growth by building strong, distinctive brands that people are willing to pay more for – supported by a range of revolutionary new products and services that better meet consumer needs. Examples of this include Dove's 'Real Beauty' campaign that revolutionised the way women feel about beauty. Or Lurpak's launch of premium cooking ingredients supported by its 'Good Food Deserves Lurpak' campaign that enabled Lurpak to become the pre-eminent butter. Or M&S's Simply Food range that offers people 'competitively priced, restaurant quality food', supported by a steady stream of new recipes to try. Or Santander's 1–2–3 account that offers customers the chance to earn interest and cash back on their current account.

A study conducted by the Product Development Institute (PDI) and the American Productivity and Quality Center (APQC) demonstrated the importance of strong product innovation to company success. Top-performing companies enjoy a higher percentage of new product successes (62 percent) than bottom performers (45 percent) – with 50 percent fewer new product failures post-launch.[5]

With this in mind, Boards need to recognise the importance and value of marketing in delivering both mid-term and long-term customer-led growth while, at the same time, protecting the core business. By doing this, marketing can help to drive sales and profit growth, cash flow and shareholder value – which in turn helps the company to grow and survive.

Why marketers need to be commercially impactful in the boardroom

As we've seen, if a company wants to grow, the Board must invest for growth.

But, by and large, most Boards are nervous of making large investments unless there is a strong business case and rationale to do so. Instead, the

Board is likely to invest its money in areas which are proven to deliver a strong return – for instance, in improving the performance of the sales force, or reducing factory inventory, or sourcing cheaper ingredients, or entering new overseas markets.

It is up to marketing to demonstrate the value of the project *over and above other cross-functional projects available to the company*, by pulling together robust market insight and data that will build the Board's confidence – and communicating their recommendation to the Board in a way that the Board will buy into.

In essence, to drive growth, marketing has an indispensable role, both in the company and at the boardroom table. But to deliver this, marketers need to be *commercially impactful* in the boardroom.

Which brings us to the crux of this book . . .

Marketers are not seen to be as commercially aware as they need to be.

C: Why marketers underperform in the boardroom

It's no secret that marketing punches below its weight in the boardroom.

Let's review the figures. Galleon Blue's 2011 survey revealed that 93 percent of senior managers said it was 'very important' for marketers to be commercially aware – yet only 78 percent of senior marketing managers, 49 percent of middle managers and 18 percent of junior managers are 'perceived' to be (Figure 1.2).

This 'perceived' lack of commercial awareness has in part contributed to chief marketing officers (CMOs) having the lowest tenure of any boardroom member. According to latest industry data, CMOs have a typical tenure of only forty-eight months compared to chief executive officers (CEOs) at

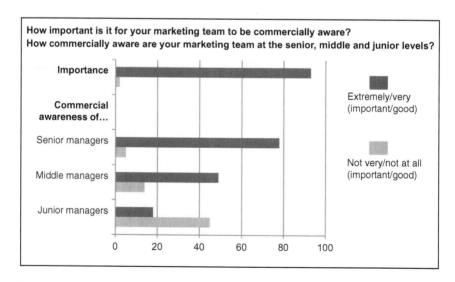

Figure 1.2 Galleon Blue's 2011 commercial awareness survey

eighty months, chief finance officers (CFOs) at seventy months and chief information officers (CIOs) at sixty months.[6]

Given this, it's not surprising that less than one-third of marketers aspire to the CMO role and more than two-thirds are drawn to general management. Yet, only 14 percent of all UK CEOs come from a marketing or advertising background.[7]

Of greater concern, a 2012 study conducted by the Fournaise Marketing Group among 1,200 CEOs worldwide reported that 80 percent of CEOs do not really trust and are not very impressed by the work done by marketers, while, in comparison, 90 percent of the same CEOs trust and value the work done by CFOs and CIOs. In essence, CEOs believe that marketers are "disconnected" from business results and focus on the wrong areas, with 78 percent saying that marketers "too often lose sight of what their real job is" – namely to increase demand for goods and services in a quantifiable way. The research concluded that "marketers would have to transform themselves into true ROI-driven business people if they are to earn the trust of CEOs and if they want to have a bigger impact in the boardroom." Otherwise, they will forever remain in what 65 percent of CEOs call "marketing la-la land".[8]

To summarise:

- The Marketing Society's Manifesto for Marketing states, "Many chief executives believe that their marketers are not stepping up to the challenge as they lack the discipline and capabilities to drive profitable growth."[9]
- A senior finance director stated, "Strategy and Finance are usually integrally linked but unfortunately Strategy and Marketing are often not."
- David Packard, co-founder of Hewlett Packard, famously said, "Marketing is too important to be left to the marketing department."[10]

Clearly, there's work to be done.

So, why is marketing seen to lack 'commercial awareness'?

Most business functions behave in a rational and commercial way.

Take finance, for example; accountants need to be numerically and commercially strong – or the sales team, which needs to be able to build mutually beneficial and profitable relationships.

The function of marketing is typically more complex.

Marketing needs to be *creatively strong* to generate new creative products and advertising that will attract customers. But it also needs to be *rationally and commercially strong* to ensure that their innovative ideas can be turned into a profitable, successful business, and that the investment money is spent in a financially responsible way that will deliver a profitable return.

In isolation, if marketers lack business acumen, they can come up with a radical idea – but struggle to make it a commercially viable proposition or prove the commercial case to take it to market. Conversely, if marketers lack creativity, they can err towards safe and commercially sound ideas that perform well in research – but fail to revolutionise the world.

In practice, this *need to be creative* can cause friction with the Board.

To be innovative, it's important that marketers possess:

- A creative mindset, honing strong brand propositions and generating breakthrough innovation and distinctive marketing campaigns.
- A risk-taking mindset, with the bigger the innovation or creative leap, the bigger the rewards – but also the bigger the risk.
- A mid- to long-term mindset, taking the time to build and deliver truly breakthrough ideas that will lead to step-change growth.

Yet to protect and manage the company successfully, Board members possess:

- An analytical mindset focused on growing shareholder value through profitable growth.
- A risk-aware mindset, optimising the performance of new initiatives, whilst minimising the risk of them not delivering.
- A short- to mid-term mindset, looking for ways to grow the business in a steady, sustainable way.

On a day-to-day basis, these differing approaches can divide marketing and the Board, with CEOs and Boards often feeling 'frustrated' by what they perceive as marketing's:

- *Lack of financial rigour* – for example, in proving the likely return on investment (ROI) of new product ideas and in-market activities.
- *Desire to take risks* – committing huge sums of money to seemingly unproven marketing campaigns and new product ideas.
- *Longer-term mindset* – often expecting marketing campaigns to take a while to 'take off', rather than deliver the quick wins that the business demands.

These can be exacerbated by what is regarded as marketing's lack of commercially rigorous measurement tools, across three key areas.

Firstly, marketers often struggle to measure the overall return on investment of various marketing activities, as well as isolate the ROI of specific marketing mix elements – and so can still be relatively backward in justifying their commercial contribution in the boardroom. As marketing pioneer John Wanamaker famously said, "I know that half my investment in advertising is wasted, but the trouble is I don't know which half." In reality, this creates two major challenges for marketers:

- How to justify the 'black hole' of marketing spend – showing how it directly impacts short- and longer-term sales and thus generates a valuable return.

- How to identify those activities that are really working and therefore should be prioritised for growth, versus those that are not paying out and therefore should be dropped.

Secondly, marketers often have difficulty in accurately measuring the net present value (or NPV) of new product launches. Traditional market research techniques, many of which have an accuracy range of plus or minus 50 percent, can produce very unreliable sales estimates. Additionally, truly revolutionary ideas – the types that reshape how we think about the world – can often take some 'getting used to'.

In research, consumers inherently choose the option that they feel most familiar with – which is often the one that is most like their current product. In essence, it's easier and quicker for our brains to relate to something that fits within our 'known present' than to take the time to consider something more radical that fits within an 'unknown and yet to be defined future'. This can lead to companies dismissing great ideas while in development – due to poor research results denting team confidence – and consequently not achieving the levels of revolutionary growth that they are looking for.

To illustrate, the 1972 qualitative research report on Heineken's famous UK advertising campaign, "Reaches the Parts That Other Beers Cannot Reach", initially concluded that the campaign shouldn't be developed as it was 'too surreal' for people to understand. When Olay's game changing "Proven Effective" campaign was launched in the UK in the mid-1990s, it was so radical that it took three months to get any traction with consumers. Sales were flat for the first three months, but then shot upwards, delivering a significant increase in sales and market share over the next three years. Similarly, when Mars Bar ice creams were launched in 1989, it was thought that its forty-nine pence price point was 'outrageous' compared with the more modestly priced Cornetto at nineteen pence. Consumer research indicated that demand for the ice cream bar at forty-nine pence would be small. But when it was launched, people couldn't get enough of this 'revolutionary' new ice cream bar – and the factory was unable to meet the high levels of unforecasted demand.

Instead, companies can be tempted to water down radical new product ideas to ones that seem more in keeping with today's world – and thus safer. Yet, in essence, this often results in the type of 'me too' product and service launches that fail to deliver the step-change growth needed to survive. In Chapter 6, we look at ways to counteract this.

Thirdly, once a new product or service has launched, marketers can be slow to track in-market performance.

No new product launch is perfect. A team, based on what it knows, launches what it thinks is the optimal product or service. But, in reality, not even the most lauded marketing team in the world can get everything right on day one of the launch – there are always aspects that can be improved.

These may be issues that were in the team's control. For example, poor display units that hide the most attractive products, or advertising that is poorly branded, or frontline staff who don't know how to sell a new product. Or they may be issues beyond the team's control; for example, competitors might come into the market to deliberately spoil the launch by loading people up with their brand, using three for ones (as Fairy did in the Persil Washing Up Liquid launch) or dropping free full-size bottles through people's doors (as Creamsilk did during the Pantene launch test market in Carlisle). Or people might respond differently to what was predicted in market research, where they said that they would be "interested in buying a product within the range" yet, in the real world, lack the incentive to switch.

If marketers are slow to track in-market performance and fix any launch issues, the majority of marketing investment could well be spent before the team realises that it's not working as well as it should be, with little left to successfully course correct.

The inability to accurately predict how well a new product or service will sell is so endemic that it is estimated that only 15 percent to 25 percent of all new product launches within consumer packaged goods are successful. The remaining 80 percent to 85 percent generally fail, due to a low sales rate causing them to lose their distribution as more new products take their place.[11]

Over time, this high level of unreliable sales estimates and lack of robust metrics can create a downward spiral, causing Boards to not feel confident in the proposed marketing strategies – and thereby not invest in them at the level that is required.

This can result in advertising campaigns that make promises that the company (outside of marketing) can't deliver, or small-time 'me too' innovations that don't give consumers a real reason to switch, or launch campaigns that are pulled before they have had a chance to be successful. These in turn don't work, making the Board more risk-averse. In Chapter 11, we look at ways to keep the Board on-board, once in-market.

Why it's getting tougher

And it doesn't stop there.

In today's fast-paced, ever-changing marketing landscape, it's tougher than ever to uncover ideas that are truly innovative.

- Power is moving from the manufacturer to the customer, and in the case of fast-moving goods also to the retailer, due to the wealth of choice and ease of comparing offers online.
- The lower barriers to entry have made it easier for new, more risk-taking competitors to enter the market – which in turn makes it harder to deliver something that's truly better than the competition.
- Increased customer segment and channel fragmentation makes it tougher to create a new product or service that can be successful at scale, with companies increasingly needing to choose where to focus.

To counter this, marketers need to not only be more creative in finding ways to drive sustainable, organic growth, but also more commercially aware and financially rigorous in how to take these ideas to market – a subject we will look at in more detail, in the next chapter.

In summary

It's tougher than ever before for companies to grow and survive, with the lower barriers to entry making it easier for new, more innovative, risk-taking competitors to enter the market.

To grow and survive, companies will need to be increasingly innovative, while simultaneously protecting their core business.

Marketing's ability to deliver both mid- to long-term growth – by launching revolutionary products and services – while simultaneously protecting the core business, is clearly pivotal to delivering this.

But it's no secret that marketing punches below its weight in the boardroom. The marketer's need to be creative can cause friction – with Boards often feeling 'frustrated' by what they perceive as marketing's lack of financial rigour, desire to take risks and longer-term mindset.

Great marketers need to be able to demonstrate to the Board why their project is worth investing in, over and above other projects – and so need to be commercially impactful in the boardroom.

So, in the next chapter, we will look at what it takes to be a successful marketer.

And then, in Chapter 3, we will look at how to build a high-performing marketing team that incorporates the many and varied marketing skill sets required to meet today's business challenges.

Notes

1 Malcolm McDonald, Brian D. Smith and Keith Ward, *Marketing Due Diligence* (Oxford: Elsevier Ltd., 2007), 9–10, leveraging the analysis conducted by Professor Peter Doyle of Warwick University on Britain's top-performing companies, with analysis updated to reflect today's situation.

2 McDonald, Smith and Ward, *Marketing Due Diligence*, 9.

3 Richard Foster, *Creative Destruction* (London: Pearson Education Ltd., 2001), 7–13.

4 Dominic Barton, "Capitalism for the Long Term," *Harvard Business Review*, March 2011.

5 Scott J. Edgett, "Latest Research: New Product Success, Failure and Kill Rates," www.stage-gate.com. Accessed April 2016.

6 Spencer Stuart, "Chief Marketing Officer Tenure Climbs to 48 Months," March 2015, www.spencerstuart.com/who-we-are/media-center/chief-marketing-officer-tenure-climbs-to-48-months; Spencer Stuart, "CFO Route to the Top 2015," September 2015, www.spencerstuart.com/research-and-insight/cfo-route-to-the-top-2015; Maryfran Johnson, "What It Takes to Improve CIO Tenure," *www.cio.com*, October 2012, www.cio.com/article/2391383/data-center/what-it-takes-to-improve-cio-tenure.html.

7 Jerry Noonan, "How to Make the Move Up to General Manager," *AdAge* citing Spencer Stuart data, March 2008, http://adage.com/article/talentworks/make-move-general-

manager/125430/; Robert Half, "Company Lifer, Sector Specialist or Career Chief Executive? Routes to Britain's Top FTSE Jobs Revealed," 18th May 2015, www.roberthalf.co.uk.

8 Fournaise Marketing Group, "80% of CEOs Do Not Really Trust Marketers (Except
If They Are 'ROI Marketers')," July 2012, www.fournaisegroup.com/ceos-do-not-trust-
marketers/.

9 Hugh Burkitt, "Marketing Excellence," *the.chiefexecutive.com*, March 2007, www.the-chief
executive.com/features/feature901/.

10 Steve Tobak, "7 Marketing Truths Every Business Leader Should Know," www.entrepre
neur.com/article/229822, accessed October 2016.

11 Elaine Watson, "Why Do 85% of New CPG Products Fail within Two Years?" citing
Nielsen data, July 2014, www.foodnavigator-usa.com/Markets/Why-do-85-of-new-CPG-
products-fail-within-two-years); Joan Schneider and Julie Hall, "Why Most Product
Launches Fail," *Harvard Business Review*, April 2011.

Bibliography

Barton, Dominic. "Capitalism for the Long Term." *Harvard Business Review*, March 2011.

Burkitt, Hugh. "Marketing Excellence." *the.chiefexecutive.com*, March 2007. www.the-chief
executive.com/features/feature901/.

Edgett, Scott J. "Latest Research: New Product Success, Failure and Kill Rates." Accessed
April 2016. www.stage-gate.com.

Foster, Richard. *Creative Destruction*. London: Pearson Education Ltd., 2001.

Fournaise Marketing Group. "80% of CEOs Do Not Really Trust Marketers (Except If They
Are 'ROI Marketers')." www.fournaisegroup.com/ceos-do-not-trust-marketers/. Last
modified July 2012.

Half, Robert. "Company Lifer, Sector Specialist or Career Chief Executive? Routes to Britain's
Top FTSE Jobs Revealed." 18 May 2015. www.roberthalf.co.uk.

Johnson, Maryfran. "What It Takes to Improve CIO Tenure." *www.cio.com*, October 2012. www.
cio.com/article/2391383/data-center/what-it-takes-to-improve-cio-tenure.html.

McDonald, Malcolm, Brian D. Smith and Keith Ward. *Marketing Due Diligence*. Oxford: Elsevier
Ltd., 2007.

Noonan, Jerry. "How to Make the Move Up to General Manager." *AdAge*, March 2008. http://
adage.com/article/talentworks/make-move-general-manager/125430/.

Schneider, Joan and Julie Hall. "Why Most Product Launches Fail." *Harvard Business Review*,
April 2011.

Stuart, Spencer. "CFO Route to the Top 2015." September 2015. www.spencerstuart.com/
research-and-insight/cfo-route-to-the-top-2015.

Stuart, Spencer. "Chief Marketing Officer Tenure Climbs to 48 Months." March 2015. www.
spencerstuart.com/who-we-are/media-center/chief-marketing-officer-tenure-climbs-to-
48-months.

Tobak, Steve. "7 Marketing Truths Every Business Leader Should Know." Accessed October
2016. www.entrepreneur.com/article/229822.

Watson, Elaine. "Why Do 85% of New CPG Products Fail within Two Years?" *www.
foodnavigator-usa.com*, July 2014. www.foodnavigator-usa.com/Markets/Why-do-85-of-new-
CPG-products-fail-within-two-years.

Chapter 2

The ideal marketer

"In the modern world of business, it is useless to be a creative, original thinker unless you can also sell what you create."

David Ogilvy

In the last chapter, we saw that it's tougher than ever for companies to grow and survive. To counter this, companies need to be increasingly innovative while simultaneously protecting their core business – and marketing is key to helping companies deliver this customer-led growth.

Yet it's no secret that marketing punches below its weight in the boardroom, which hampers it from having the Board-level impact it needs.

In this chapter, we explore what it takes to be a successful marketer, by focusing on:

A   The importance of being entrepreneurial.
B   Becoming more entrepreneurial by building creative skills.
C   Becoming more entrepreneurial by building business acumen.

Then, in the next chapter, we look at how to build a high-performing marketing team that incorporates the dissonant skill sets required to meet today's business challenges.

A: The importance of being entrepreneurial

Successful marketers need to be creative to drive sustainable, organic growth – as well as possess the commercial acumen and skills to deliver strong business performance.

That is, they need to be both creative *and* analytical.

Entrepreneurs naturally behave this way. They identify a gap in the market, develop new products and services to fill that gap, and launch a business that produces and supplies those products and services profitably.

For some people, 'entrepreneur' is a provocative word, conjuring up images of 'non-conformists' upsetting the natural order of things – challenging the status quo in a way that's neither helpful nor trustworthy.

For others, it's aspirational, describing a courageous career path that enables these 'intrepid adventurers' to take control of their lives and build something of value.

Entrepreneurs primarily achieve success in the marketplace by combining creativity with commercial accountability. In a sense, these 'mavericks' start out with a natural advantage – it's often their own money that they are spending, or that of an equity partner, which compels them to act accountably to ensure superior returns.

Because it's their money, entrepreneurs typically only launch brands that they genuinely believe have a high chance of success – the type that offer truly innovative products and services that will better meet the customer's need at a price they're willing to pay.

And, because it's their money, they tend to spend it in bite-size tranches, testing the effectiveness of the various activities to quickly identify those that work and cull those that don't. Which means that entrepreneurs tend to be strong at 'cost-efficiently' focusing their scarce resources (both money and time) on those activities that are more likely to drive profitable growth.

Entrepreneurs: The 'lifeblood' of business

Entrepreneurs have historically been, and continue to be, the lifeblood of business. Think of any credible company and almost undoubtedly there's an entrepreneur or two behind it. Some of today's biggest players were set up by one or two visionary people who applied creativity (by identifying an opportunity to develop and launch cutting-edge products and services to better serve the customer) with commercial acumen (by driving the business in a commercially savvy way to deliver strong sales and profit performance).

Procter & Gamble: William Procter and James Gamble

Take Procter & Gamble, the multinational consumer goods company founded in 1837 by William Procter, a candle maker, and James Gamble, a soap maker's apprentice.

As a boy, Procter worked as a general store apprentice, learning to dip candles – a skill that would later prove useful when developing innovative products.

But Procter's first entrepreneurial venture was a disaster. The day after opening his dry goods shop, it was robbed, leaving him $8,000 in debt, a huge sum in 1832. Determined to rebuild, Procter worked in a bank, absorbing the fundamentals of commercial moneymaking. He then combined his creative experience as a candle maker with his newly acquired commercial skills to manufacture, sell and deliver candles to his customers – taking advantage of the low-cost fat and oil by-products from Cincinnati's large meatpacking industry – and paid off his debt.

Gamble, meanwhile, was initially an apprentice with a local soap maker and then went on to open his own soap and candle shop. These two men married sisters Olivia and Elizabeth Norris, whose father Alexander Norris saw that his new sons-in-law were competing for the same raw materials and suggested a joint venture.

So in 1837, they pooled their total assets of $7,192.24 and launched Procter and Gamble, bringing together their innovative candle- and soap-making skills and the plentiful business efficiencies that Cincinnati's meat-packing centre provided in the form of its cheap and copious supplies of fat and oil, to produce and sell soap and candles across America. Remarkably, the struggling young firm was launched in one of the deepest nationwide depressions ever experienced, but it survived to become the thriving global conglomerate it is today.[1]

Microsoft: Bill Gates and Paul Allen

Bill Gates, one of the greatest entrepreneurs of our time, developed an early interest in software. He began programming computers at the age of thirteen, and so by the time he was a student at Harvard University, he was so proficient at programming that he wrote a version of the programming language BASIC, Microsoft's founding product, for the MITS Altair microcomputer.

In 1975, Gates left Harvard as an undergraduate to form Microsoft with his childhood friend Paul Allen. Together they developed software for the newly emerging personal computer market, sharing their inspired vision of 'getting a computer on every desktop and in every home'. Over time, they became famous for their state-of-the-art computer operating systems, such as MS-DOS which was launched in 1981, followed by the launch of Microsoft Windows 1.0 in 1985 – a next-generation operating system that revolution-ised the world.

Their mastery lay in combining cutting-edge programming skills with visionary thinking, bolstered by a canny ability to make killer business deals. For instance, a key move by Gates was to license software to numerous com-puter makers in 'partnerships', resulting in affordable machines being made available to the masses. Gates also talked IBM into letting Microsoft retain the licensing rights to MS-DOS, an operating system that IBM needed for its new personal computer, which he went on to make a fortune out of. By combining his huge vision with revolutionary products and a ruthless ability to commercialise them, Gates metamorphosed into one of the most success-ful and wealthiest men of all time.[2]

Google: Larry Page and Sergey Brin

Another giant to emerge from the digital age is Google which, although now a household name, began life as a Stanford University research project. In January 1996, Larry Page was a PhD student at Stanford, exploring the mathematical properties of the World Wide Web as his dissertation theme. Page joined forces with fellow PhD student Sergey Brin, whose focus was on data mining systems.

Together, they created a revolutionary search engine that listed results based on the popularity of pages visited, in the belief that the most popular result would often be the most useful. Initially, they called this search engine 'BackRub', because the system checked backlinks to estimate the importance of a site. But, in 1997, they registered the 'google.com' domain name, and in 1998, launched their company, 'Google' – named after the mathematical term 'googol', represented by the number one followed by a hundred zeros. Their mission was "to organise the world's information and make it universally accessible and useful".

Google's search engine performed well, with its simple, innovative design attracting a loyal following among the growing number of Internet users. But Google didn't make money. In 2000, in spite of Page and Brin's initial opposition, Google auctioned adverts to appear alongside the search engine. Keywords were sold based on a combination of price bids and click-throughs to create a profitable business model. Its first two advertising-funded search engines were flawed, and it wasn't until they launched their third advertising auction in 2002, AdWords Select, that they became commercially successful.

Ultimately, their success was borne out of combining their pioneering and innovative search engine thinking with a ruthless drive to commercialise it, creating one of the most widely used companies of all time.[3]

Virgin: Richard Branson

Richard Branson, another revered visionary, was still a teenager when he began carving out his entrepreneurial path. At sixteen, Branson launched a music magazine called *The Student*, as an alternative to the stale publications and school magazines of the day. It covered everything from pop culture and music to the Vietnam and Biafra wars, including published interviews with prominent personalities of the late sixties, such as Mick Jagger, as well as advertisements for vinyl records.

The Student became an overnight success.

In 1970, Branson (then aged twenty) set up a mail-order record business trading under the Virgin name (suggested by one of Branson's early employees because they were all new at business) that sold records for considerably less than the high street outlets. Two years later, Branson launched the Virgin Records music label, opened a chain of record stores under the Virgin Records name and set up a recording studio, signing controversial acts such as the Sex Pistols. The Virgin brand grew rapidly during the eighties and nineties, by challenging the market norms beyond the music industry, and creating a superior customer experience within airlines (Virgin Atlantic), transport (Virgin Trains), telecommunications (Virgin Mobiles) and financial services (Virgin Money).

By July 2015, Forbes listed Branson's net worth at almost $5 billion.[4]

Branson is clearly creative as well as commercially dynamic and highly driven, committed to bringing about real change on a large scale. For Branson, being an entrepreneur is about innovating and doing things better than what's currently out there. In his 'What Makes A True Entrepreneur' article, he says: "We really were out to disrupt the order of things. . . . We don't just want to carry out a simple moneymaking exercise, but to make a positive change in people's lives and give consumers a better deal. Whichever product or service we offer, we want it to be a lot better than all the rest."[5]

The Naked Chef: Jamie Oliver

Another celebrated British entrepreneur is Jamie Oliver, aka the Naked Chef.

Oliver left school at sixteen with just two GCSEs, refusing to let his lack of qualifications or dyslexia hold him back. Oliver trained at the Westminster Catering College before heading to France to further hone his culinary skills. After arriving back in the UK, he had a brief stint as a head pastry chef before moving to London's River Café where, in 1997, he made an unscripted appearance in a TV cookery documentary that set his career on a new trajectory. As a result, Oliver's TV show, *The Naked Chef*, debuted and his passion for cooking and his down-to-earth personality made him an instant hit.

But it was by combining his creative cookery skills with savvy business management that the TV chef also became one of the world's richest chefs. After becoming a TV phenomenon, a string of successes followed. Oliver set up his own production company, his many cookbooks regularly topped the weekly best-seller charts, he starred as the face of Sainsbury's supermarkets in their advertising campaign, he opened numerous restaurants – including the Fifteen Foundation that trains young, underprivileged people to work in his restaurant and Jamie's Italian restaurant chain that has been franchised globally – and his ongoing campaign for better food education is known worldwide. Perhaps one of the key reasons why Oliver has been successful where other celebrity chefs have failed is that not only is he a highly creative chef, but his cash management and business discipline is renowned for being tight, with each project run to strict targets.[6]

Facebook: Mark Zuckerberg

Facebook's Mark Zuckerberg is arguably one of today's finest examples of someone who managed to turn a seductively simple yet revolutionary idea into a highly successful commercial business. No company in history has ever achieved the sheer scale of Facebook, with an estimated 1.5 billion users logging in every month and the accolade of a billion users logging in on one single day.[7]

Zuckerberg became interested in programming when in elementary school and by the age of twelve he had created 'ZuckNet' – a messenger that connected all of the computers within his childhood home and his father's dental practice. Throughout high school, he enjoyed developing games and other communication tools, as well as an artificially intelligent media player 'Synapse' that carefully studied the playlist preferences of a user and 'guessed' which tracks they might want to listen to next.

Using his programming skills, Zuckerberg and three of his Harvard classmates invented Facemash, Facebook's predecessor, with Zuckerberg writing software that enabled fellow students to compare two student pictures side by side and vote on who was 'hotter'.

A year later, inspired by Facemash, Zuckerberg wrote code for a new website called 'thefacebook,' a social networking site for fellow Harvard students. On its first night, 'thefacebook' was launched to an online Harvard mailing list of 300 people, but within twenty-four hours, the idea had been so talked about that it had already attracted close to 1,500 registrants. Within its first month, more than half of Harvard's undergraduate population had registered.

Initially, the founders limited the site's membership to Harvard students, but within two months expanded it to colleges in the Boston area, other Ivy League colleges and Stanford University. It wasn't long before students across the United States and Canada were signing up. In 2005, the company changed the name to 'Facebook' after purchasing the domain name facebook.com for $200,000.

Facebook continued to expand globally, initially into UK and Latin American universities, then into universities further afield, and then into the public domain. By 2006, pretty much anyone over the age of twelve was on Facebook – and within ten years of launching, Facebook boasted more than one billion users, equivalent to one in seven of the world's population. In parallel, Zuckerberg made the Facebook site commercially viable by allowing advertisers to use Facebook's sufficiently detailed user profiles to better target their advertising.

In essence, Zuckerberg combined the creative vision of enabling people around the world to easily keep in touch with their friends by communicating online – something that was new – with a ruthless drive to launch and build Facebook into the huge, commercially viable business it is today.[8]

The rise of entrepreneurs

Today technology is making it easier than ever before to start a new business. So it's no surprise that there has been an upsurge in entrepreneurship around the world, with an estimated 300 million entrepreneurs across forty countries starting around 150 million new businesses, at a rate of 50 million new businesses a year or 137,000 each day.[9] Similarly, a report issued by Babson and Baruch Colleges suggests that in 2014, up to 14 percent of adults in the United States were involved in start-ups, a record high since the tracking of entrepreneurship rates began in 1999.[10]

In turn, entrepreneurs are the major creators of new, innovative ideas – and are thereby an important driver of global sales and employment growth, and of what the future will look like.

What marketers can learn from entrepreneurs

Marketers can behave 'entrepreneurially' whether they are working within an established organisation or within a start-up.

On the one hand, living and breathing 'entrepreneurially' means having the creative skills to champion 'the customer' – their needs, behaviours and mindset – and finding new and better ways to delight them. Marketers need to act 'radically' to create something truly groundbreaking that customers will want to buy.

On the other hand, it means having the analytical and commercial skills to transform their innovative ideas into a profitable, successful business. Marketers need to find commercially viable and profitable ways to take the idea to market – ways that the company can tangibly deliver and will generate a healthy return.

In isolation, however, if marketers lack creativity, they can create ideas that are commercially viable, but fail to make customers sit up and take notice. Or, conversely, if they lack business acumen, they can create a 'radical idea' but struggle to make it a commercially viable proposition to take to market.

To behave 'entrepreneurially', marketers need to immerse themselves in both sides of the industry – as entrepreneurs do – enabling them to not only be creative enough to come up with market-changing ideas, but also analytical enough to launch these ideas in a commercially viable and profitable way.

In essence, when in the boardroom, the role of the marketer is to *be the voice of the customer* – but to do so within the context of how the company operates. They need to help the Board better meet their customers' needs – and to do so profitably.

Which brings us to 'the marketing issue'.

It's rare to find people who can simultaneously come up with disruptive ideas *and* develop them into a commercially viable and profitable business – which in part explains why so many new businesses fail.

This either-or division starts as early as secondary school, where we are typically channelled into either the creative, art-based subjects (such as English, history, geography, languages, art) or towards the more analytical, science-based subjects (such as physics, chemistry, biology, mathematics).

This structure is reflected within the marketing community, which typically divides into, on one hand, the more creative types who thrive on creating innovative ideas and, on the other hand, the more analytical types who thrive on running a commercially strong business. The former are invariably drawn to the more creative end of the industry that prides itself on being revolutionary and disruptive – particularly agencies that specialise in creating innovative advertising, design, packaging and products. The latter are often attracted to the analytical sphere of the industry that relishes in being commercially savvy and insightful – such as management consultancies, quantitative research agencies and media agencies.

To be successful, it's important for marketers to hone both their intuitive, creative skills *and* their analytical, commercial skills – and in turn for their marketing teams to balance both skill sets. In conjunction, the two mindsets work in an effective and complementary way to drive market growth.

Now, let's look at how to build each of these two skill sets, in turn.

B: Becoming more entrepreneurial – Building creative skills

It has long been thought that creativity can be 'developed' in an individual. But creativity is not a 'set of skills' or a 'body of knowledge' that can be learnt in the classroom, it is a mindset.

Firstly, to develop a more creative mindset, it's important to set the team a creative problem that challenges the status quo – one that requires the team to think differently and look for new and better ways to do things. Without a problem, there is no intellectual challenge for the team to immerse itself in. These ideas might focus on the product or service offer itself, such as launching new products or services or innovative line extensions, or tweaking the existing products or packaging to improve them, or improving the customer experience. Or they might focus on how the products and services are taken to market, such as the distribution channels they are sold through, or the communication channels and messages that are used to engage people.

Secondly, it's about using that mindset to find the hidden connections that solve the problem.

To find those hidden connections, marketers should surround themselves with 'creative people' who look at the world differently – designers who think more visually, creatives who view the world through a different lens, semioticians who decode a brand's symbolism and messaging to identify what's really being communicated, researchers who understand what genuinely makes consumers tick, product development people who know which new technologies are emerging. All of these naturally creative people can encourage marketers to think more freely, imaginatively and inventively and provide fresh insights to draw upon that can lead to more innovative solutions.

They should get out of the office into the real world, and observe and talk with real people. People will tell you what they're looking for, what they're frustrated by, what excites them, what they wish they had that would make their life easier. Even if they can't articulate it, they will express this excitement or frustration while going about their daily routines, so just observing them can be insightful. Category experts such as journalists, shop assistants, bank managers, chemists, along with related experts such as GPs and playgroup owners, often know what people like and what gets them riled. Similarly, technology experts are often privy to the innovation trends about to hit the market that can be leveraged to create disruptive change.

A food company that I once worked with had a relatively large market research budget, yet none of the marketers had met a customer in the last year. No one went to the research groups – instead they let the researchers report back their findings. No one had visited a store to see how their customers shopped or what the competitors were doing. No one had tasted their own or competitor food products themselves in recent months. They were sitting in their ivory tower, reading reports and making 'me too' decisions that were divorced from the real world. No wonder sales were poor.

Marketers *need* to be out in the real world on a day-to-day basis, talking with people – be they customers, sceptics, category experts or technology experts – as well as regularly trying their own and competitor products or doing mystery shops, to see for themselves how appealing and differentiated their product or service actually is.

They should look for innovative ideas in relevant case studies within other industries. Perhaps there are companies in other sectors that have faced and overcome similar challenges by innovating in a fresh and daring way, which could inspire your company to do something similar. For instance, in the baby food market, Ella's Kitchen challenged the traditional incumbent brands by creating a range of 'good baby food that stimulates all five senses', using tasty, 100% organic ingredients in fun-to-play-with squishy, colourful packs. Within six years, it had become one of the UK's fastest-growing businesses with global sales of £60 million and a 14 percent share of the baby food market – and was ranked in the *Sunday Times* Top Fast Track 100 List for four consecutive years, between 2009 and 2012. This case study was used as one of the inspirations for the launch of Cussons Mum & Me – a range of baby toiletries designed to help mums through the ups and downs of becoming a mother, from Bump (supporting mums through pregnancy) to New Mum (helping new mums get the 'old you' back) to Baby. By assessing what had worked well for Ella's Kitchen, such as the recognition that having a new baby can be chaotic and the desire to use natural ingredients where possible, Cussons Mum & Me was able to replicate some of these drivers in the baby toiletries market to build a distinctive brand positioning.[11]

Thirdly, it's crucial to give the team 'permission' to fail. Truly revolutionary ideas, the sort that tend to reshape how we think about the world, can often take a significant length of time to develop.

For some, the time taken will result in something great. For instance, when I worked at Procter & Gamble we were tasked with turning around Olay. Whilst it was the UK's number one moisturising brand, it was suffering from flat sales and being circled by increasingly strong competitors, such as Nivea and L'Oréal. It took months of continuous creative development and testing to create the breakthrough "We can prove you can look younger" positioning. This painstaking work paid off and Olay restored itself as the UK's number one moisturising brand for many years to come.

For others, the time taken may result in failure. For example, when I worked at Mars Confectionary in the late 1980s, our brief was to launch Flyte – an extensive range of low-calorie chocolate bars of all shapes and sizes, each with a fraction of the calories and 'all of the taste'. Mars Confectionary proved that it could make delicious low-calorie chocolate bars. But the overall premise was flawed; when people eat chocolate they want to indulge, and the presence of 'low calorie' lessens that sense of indulgence. Eight years later, Mars Confectionary launched one type of low-calorie chocolate bar – Flyte – similar in taste and texture to Milky Way. In effect, while the years of work culminated in a new product launch, it didn't turn out to be the extensive launch that had been originally envisaged.

The lesson here is to not be too hasty. It's important to not give up on creating a truly disruptive idea too quickly – in favour of safer, smaller ideas – nor to berate marketers for admitting that an idea that has spent significant time in development turns out to be wrong.

For every good idea, there are hundreds of bad ones. Some will crash and burn at the starting blocks, others will take time to develop into successful propositions, while others can take up a lot of time and research only to be abandoned. Letting marketers 'waste time' by going down the wrong alleyways is an intrinsic part of the creative process.

C: Becoming more entrepreneurial – Building business acumen

Understanding the 'moving parts'

Success comes from more than just creativity – it involves not only coming up with the idea (the imaginative bit), but also having the commercial discipline to turn the idea into reality.

In their book *Will and Vision*, Gerard J. Tellis and Peter N. Golder identified that across sixty-six diverse sectors, only 9 percent of the pioneering companies who had invented a radically superior product or service ended up as the final winners, with 64 percent failing outright. As Jim Collins writes in his book *Great by Choice*: "Gillette didn't pioneer the safety razor, Star did. Polaroid didn't pioneer the instant camera, Dubruni did. Microsoft didn't pioneer the personal computer spreadsheet, VisiCorp did. Amazon didn't pioneer online bookselling and AOL didn't pioneer online Internet service." And from my own personal experience, Procter & Gamble's (P&G's) Wash & Go wasn't the first two in one shampoo to be launched, Unilever's Dimension was. Jim Collins concludes: "It seems that pioneering innovation is good for society but statistically lethal for the individual pioneer."[12]

So, why was the success rate so low?

While creativity motivates a team to generate new ideas and turn them into reality, on its own it's not sufficient. Business acumen and commercial discipline are also required to transform these ideas into a strong, sustainable, profitable business – by finding ways to manufacture, supply, launch, sell and manage an idea profitably.

Marketers who are commercially strong understand how an investment will deliver tangible value to the total company – or, to put it another way, commercially strong marketers think in a similar way to the Board.

Kevin Cope, in his 2012 work titled *Seeing the Big Picture, Business Acumen to Build Your Credibility, Career and Company*, proposed that "an individual who possesses business acumen views the business with an 'executive mentality' – they understand how the moving parts of a company work together to make it successful and how financial metrics like profit margin, cash flow, and stock price reflect how well each of those moving parts is doing its job."[13]

A marketer needs to not only understand how much incremental sales and profit will be generated by the brand, but also how it fits within the overall company strategy, company cash flow and company risk profile, as well as how it might impact the stock market price.

It's the job of the finance team to ensure that any business targets that have been promised to shareholders and investors are delivered and that stock market levels are managed. Similarly, finance people are charged with managing the overall company cash flow and risk profile and will be drawn to projects that fit within this. A commercially savvy marketer will take the time to grasp what the current company thinking is and how their own role in the business is perceived within this.

Like the Board, marketers must think holistically in terms of how the product or service launch will affect the entire business and spend time assessing 'incremental sales value'. The launch may bring additional sales, but if this adversely impacts another area of the business, it may weaken overall company value. For example, it may cannibalise another product, resulting in little, or negative, added value. Or it may antagonise a trade channel that's important to the core business, resulting in a loss of overall sales. Or it may eat up a lot of production, sales or call centre time that prevents those teams focusing on the core business. Sometimes, a new idea might be strong in its own right, but not make sense for the overall business today. If this happens, it's better that marketers accept the decision and step aside, rather than continue to push their own agenda.

Marketers must also spend time assessing 'cost' – namely where to spend more and where to cut costs. For example, it may be important to spend more on a particular product feature to ensure that it truly *is* distinctive versus competitors – and thus will encourage customers to switch. Or, it may be possible to cut costs on the basis that the new product feature (and additional cost) will not produce a significant increase in customers buying the product, and thus will not add value.

From a trade perspective, it may be important to pay higher trade fees to ensure that the product is sold prominently in an influential trade channel. Or it may be possible to challenge the status quo and sell through more cost-efficient channels, much as First Direct and Direct Line did when they launched.

From a communications perspective, it may prove beneficial to advertise on traditional media channels, such as TV, to appear 'mainstream' and 'reputable'. Or it may be possible to use more cost-efficient communication channels, such as social media and community-based marketing, to reach a discrete target audience in a more personalised way.

Being commercially savvy

Savvy marketers combine creativity with commerciality and financial responsibility, to relentlessly work at solving the creative problem and make it an in-market success.

Creatively, they don't accept that something won't work because they can't find the solution. On the contrary, they continuously look for the hidden connections until they find one that works.

They never accept mediocrity – both in the idea and in its execution. They're hungry to make a genuine difference to people's lives, and so they identify what's important to consumers and fight for it in the boardroom. They're hungry to be a commercial success in the real world, continually looking for cost-efficient yet effective ways to break through the market clutter and get noticed by people who matter.

They don't accept that something will work because market research suggests it will. On the contrary, they get out into the market and check if it's working and, if it isn't, challenge the current thinking to come up with new ways to drive growth.

Commercially, they ensure that the proposed ideas are viable and profitable.

They spend time with (and perhaps work alongside) people in other business functions – particularly finance, given that their innate, risk-aware mindset is often at odds with marketing thinking, but also with more commercially driven functions such as sales and production.

This enables them to better understand how the moving parts of the company work together to be successful, and, in turn, appreciate some of the issues that are relevant to other functions that marketing may not naturally consider.

Financially, they spend the investment money responsibly as if it was their own – ensuring that none of it is wasted.

They continually ask themselves questions like: Would I personally invest in this launch? Could the ideas be bigger or more disruptive? Would I invest in the proposed distribution and communication channels? Are there more cost-efficient and effective ways to connect with my target audience? Knowing where to invest for success and where to cut costs is key to a successful business model.

They invest the money in tranches, to ensure that each tranche is optimised and has a good chance of success. They are quick to find out which activities are performing well and should be invested in more, and those that are not and should be killed off. They adopt a test-and-learn attitude and approach from day one, acknowledging that part of the launch plan and product and service offer will not hit the mark, and therefore will need to be optimised.

This combination of creativity, commerciality and financial responsibility sets great marketers apart.

In summary

Successful marketers need to be creative to drive sustainable, organic growth – as well as possess the commercial acumen to deliver strong business performance. That is, they need to be both creative *and* commercial.

To quote some marketing greats, Philip Kotler said, "Marketing is the science and art of exploring, creating, and delivering value to satisfy the needs of a target market at a profit."[14]

In their book *Marketing in the Boardroom*, Kevin Luscombe, Graeme Chipp and Peter Fitzgerald wrote, "The role of marketing is to bring know-how and discipline to the task of developing and delivering competitively superior products and services, profitably. It is the driver of demand and the company's cash flow."[15]

And as Jim Collins writes in his book *Great by Choice*: "The great task, rarely achieved, is to blend creative intensity with relentless discipline so as to amplify the creativity rather than destroy it. When you marry operating excellence with innovation, you multiply the value of your creativity."[16]

In this chapter, we looked at how entrepreneurs naturally behave this way – they identify a gap in the market, develop new products and services to fill that gap, and launch a business that produces and supplies those products and services profitably.

To get the Board on-board, marketers need to think and act like entrepreneurs, by building both their creative skills and business acumen. Creatively, they need to come up with disruptive ideas that will better meet customer needs. Commercially, they need to make projects viable and profitable, succinctly showing how their marketing strategies will build growth and shareholder value.

Likewise, Board members need to understand and value marketing's role and importance to the business, in developing strong brands and break-through innovation that delights customers – and marketing's creativity, risk-taking approach and ability to think 'outside of the box' to deliver this.

The best relationships between marketing and the Board are invariably built over time, with marketers consistently proving their worth in terms of business performance, and the Board increasingly appreciating the customer-driven mindset and fresh, innovative thinking that marketing contributes to the business. This in turn should help to encourage Boards to become more customer-centric in their thinking and decision-making, thus building an even more successful business.

In the next chapter, we will look at how to put this into practice – by enabling senior marketers to assemble a high-performing marketing team that incor-porates the dissonant skill sets required in today's competitive marketplace.

Notes

1 Procter & Gamble, "Our History – How It Began," https://www.pg.com/en_US/downloads/media/Fact_Sheets_CompanyHistory.pdf, accessed October 2016.
2 Claudine Beaumont, *The Telegraph*, June 2008, http://www.telegraph.co.uk/technology/3357701/Bill-Gatess-dream-A-computer-in-every-home.html; Entrepreneur "Bill Gates," https://www.entrepreneur.com/article/197526, accessed October 2016; Glenn Chapman, "Bill Gates to Sign Off at Microsoft," *The Sydney Morning Herald*, June 2008, http://www.smh.com.au/world/bill-gates-to-sign-off-at-microsoft-20080627–2y8l.html; Mary Bellis, "Putting Microsoft on the Map," February 2016, http://inventors.about.com/od/computersoftware/a/Putting-Microsoft-On-The-Map.htm; Wikipedia, "History of Microsoft," https://en.wikipedia.org/wiki/History_of_Microsoft, accessed October 2016; Wikipedia, "Bill Gates," https://en.wikipedia.org/wiki/Bill_Gates; Wikipedia, "MS-DOS," https://en.wikipedia.org/wiki/MS-DOS, accessed October 2016.
3 Peter Coy, "The Secret to Google's Success," *Bloomberg*, March 2006, http://www.bloomberg.com/news/articles/2006-03-05/the-secret-to-googles-success, accessed October 2016; Will Oremus, "Google's Big Break," *Slate*, http://www.slate.com/articles/business/when_big_businesses_were_small/2013/10/google_s_big_break_how_bill_gross_goto_com_inspired_the_adwords_business.html, accessed October 2016; "Larry Page and Sergey Brin," *www.entrepreneur.com*, October 2008, https://www.entrepreneur.com/article/197848; Google, "Company website," https://www.google.co.uk/about/company/, accessed October 2016; Google, "Our history in depth," https://www.google.co.uk/about/company/history, accessed December 2016; Wikipedia, "History of Google," https://en.wikipedia.org/wiki/History_of_Google, accessed October 2016; Wikipedia, "Sergey Brin," https://en.wikipedia.org/wiki/Sergey_Brin, accessed October 2016.
4 Wikipedia, "Richard Branson," https://en.wikipedia.org/wiki/Richard_Branson, accessed October 2016; Mark Darcy, "Rags to Riches: How Richard Branson Became a Billionaire," April 2015, https://blog.bancdebinary.com/2015/04/14/rags-to-riches-richard-branson/; "The World's Billionaires," *Forbes*, http://www.forbes.com/profile/richard-branson/, accessed October 2016.
5 Richard Branson, "Entrepreneur: A Bold Brand," December 2013, http://www.thenassauguardian.com/index.php?option=com_content&view=article&id=44046&Itemid=2.

6   Magareta Pagano, "Jamie Oliver's Recipe for Success," *The Independent*, May 2012, http://www.independent.co.uk/news/business/analysis-and-features/jamie-olivers-recipe-for-success-7767011.html, accessed October 2016; *www.culinaryschools.org*, http://www.culinaryschools.org/famous-chefs/jamie-oliver/, accessed October 2016; Wikipedia, "Jamie Oliver," https://en.wikipedia.org/wiki/Jamie_Oliver, accessed October 2016.

7   Dave Lee, "Facebook Has a Billion Users in a Single Day, says Mark Zuckerberg," *BBC News*, August 2015, http://www.bbc.co.uk/news/world-us-canada-34082393

8   "Mark Zuckerberg Biography; Success Story of Facebook Founder and CEO," *Astrum People*, https://astrumpeople.com/mark-zuckerberg-biography-success-story-of-facebook-founder-and-ceo/, accessed October 2016; Rob Williams, "Revealed: The Third Largest 'Country' in the World – Facebook Hits One Billion Users," *The Independent*, October 2012, http://www.independent.co.uk/life-style/gadgets-and-tech/news/revealed-the-third-largest-country-in-the-world-facebook-hits-one-billion-users-8197597.html; Wikipedia, "History of Facebook," https://en.wikipedia.org/wiki/History_of_Facebook, accessed October 2016; Wikipedia, "Facebook," https://en.wikipedia.org/wiki/Facebook, accessed October 2016; Wikipedia, "Mark Zuckerberg," https://en.wikipedia.org/wiki/Mark_Zuckerberg, accessed October 2016.

9   Moya K. Mason, "Worldwide Business Start-Ups," 2016, http://www.moyak.com/papers/business-startups-entrepreneurs.html, accessed October 2016.

10 Babson College, "U.S. Entrepreneurship Hits Record Highs According to Researchers at Babson College and Baruch College," http://www.babson.edu/news-events/babson-news/Pages/2015-babson-issues-2014-united-states-gem-report.aspx, accessed December 2016.

11 Natalie Brandweiner, "Food for Thought: The Success Behind Ella's Kitchen," *Business Zone*, December 2011, http://www.businesszone.co.uk/do/customers/food-for-thought-the-story-behind-the-success-of-ellas-kitchen, accessed October 2016; Will Smale, "The Man Who Built the UK's Largest Baby Food Firm," *BBC News*, December 2014, http://www.bbc.co.uk/news/business-30411724, accessed October 2016.

12 Jim Collins and Morten T. Hansen, *Great by Choice* (London: Random House Business Books, 2011), 74.

13 Kevin Cope, *Seeing the Big Picture, Business Acumen to Build Your Credibility, Career and Company* (Austin, TX: Greenleaf Book Group Press, 2012).

14 "Dr. Philip Kotler Answers Your Questions on Marketing," *www.kotlermarketing.com*, www.kotlermarketing.com/phil_questions.shtml, accessed October 2016.

15 Peter Fitzgerald, "Introduction," in *Marketing in the Boardroom*, ed. Kevin Luscombe, Graeme Chipp and Peter Fitzgerald (Melbourne: Growth Solutions Pty Ltd., 2007), xii.

16 Collins and Hansen, *Great by Choice*, 78.

Bibliography

Babson College. "U.S. Entrepreneurship Hits Record Highs According to Researchers at Babson College and Baruch College." Accessed December 2016. http://www.babson.edu/news-events/babson-news/Pages/2015-babson-issues-2014-united-states-gem-report.aspx.

Beaumont, Claudine. "Bill Gates's Dream: A Computer in Every Home." *The Telegraph*, June 2008. www.telegraph.co.uk/technology/3357701/Bill-Gatess-dream-A-computer-in-every-home.html.

Bellis, Mary. "Putting Microsoft on the Map." *About.com*, February 2016. http://inventors.about.com/od/computersoftware/a/Putting-Microsoft-On-The-Map.htm.

"Bill Gates." *Entrepreneur*. Accessed October 2016. www.entrepreneur.com/article/197526.

Brandweiner, Natalie. "Food for Thought: The Success Behind Ella's Kitchen." *Business Zone*, December 2011. Accessed October 2016. www.businesszone.co.uk/do/customers/food-for-thought-the-story-behind-the-success-of-ellas-kitchen.

Branson, Richard. "Entrepreneur: A Bold Brand." *Nassau Guardian*, December 2013. www.thenassauguardian.com/index.php?option=com_content&view=article&id=44046&Itemid=2.

Chapman, Glenn. "Bill Gates to Sign Off at Microsoft." *The Sydney Morning Herald*, June 2008. www.smh.com.au/world/bill-gates-to-sign-off-at-microsoft-20080627-2y8l.html.

Collins, Jim and Morten T. Hansen. *Great by Choice*. London: Random House Business Books, 2011.

Cope, Kevin. *Seeing the Big Picture, Business Acumen to Build Your Credibility, Career and Company*. Austin, TX: Greenleaf Book Group Press, 2012.

Coy, Peter. "The Secret to Google's Success." *Bloomberg*, March 2006. Accessed October 2016. www.bloomberg.com/news/articles/2006-03-05/the-secret-to-googles-success.

Darcy, Mark. "Rags to Riches: How Richard Branson Became a Billionaire." *Banc de Binary*, April 2015. https://blog.bancdebinary.com/2015/04/14/rags-to-riches-richard-branson/.

"Dr. Philip Kotler Answers Your Questions on Marketing." *www.kotlermarketing.com*. Accessed October 2016. www.kotlermarketing.com/phil_questions.shtml.

Fitzgerald, Peter. "Introduction." In *Marketing in the Boardroom*, edited by Kevin Luscombe, Graeme Chipp and Peter Fitzgerald, xii. Melbourne: Growth Solutions Pty Ltd., 2007.

Google. "Company." Accessed October 2016. www.google.co.uk/about/company/.

Google. "Our history in depth." Accessed December 2016. https://www.google.co.uk/about/company/history.

"Jamie Oliver's Career, His Chef Education and His Cuisine." *www.culinaryschools.org*, October 2016. www.culinaryschools.org/famous-chefs/jamie-oliver/.

"Larry Page and Sergey Brin." *www.entrepreneur.com*, October 2008. www.entrepreneur.com/article/197848.

Lee, Dave. "Facebook Has a Billion Users in a Single Day, says Mark Zuckerberg." *BBC News*, August 2015. www.bbc.co.uk/news/world-us-canada-34082393.

"Mark Zuckerberg Biography; Success Story of Facebook Founder and CEO." *Astrum People*. Accessed October 2016. https://astrumpeople.com/mark-zuckerberg-biography-success-story-of-facebook-founder-and-ceo/.

Mason, Moya K. "Worldwide Business Start-Ups." Accessed October 2016. www.moyak.com/papers/business-startups-entrepreneurs.html.

Oremus, Will. "Google's Big Break." *Slate*. Accessed October 2016. www.slate.com/articles/business/when_big_businesses_were_small/2013/10/google_s_big_break_how_bill_gross_goto_com_inspired_the_adwords_business.html.

Pagano, Magareta. "Jamie Oliver's Recipe for Success." *The Independent*, May 2012. Accessed October 2016. www.independent.co.uk/news/business/analysis-and-features/jamie-olivers-recipe-for-success-7767011.html.

Procter & Gamble. "Our History – How It Began." Accessed October 2016. www.pg.com/en_US/downloads/media/Fact_Sheets_CompanyHistory.pdf.

Smale, Will. "The Man Who Built the UK's Largest Baby Food Firm." *BBC News*, December 2014. Accessed October 2016. www.bbc.co.uk/news/business-30411724.

Wikipedia. "Bill Gates." https://en.wikipedia.org/wiki/Bill_Gates.

Wikipedia. "Facebook." Accessed October 2016. https://en.wikipedia.org/wiki/Facebook.

Wikipedia. "History of Facebook." Accessed October 2016. https://en.wikipedia.org/wiki/History_of_Facebook.

Wikipedia. "History of Google." Accessed October 2016. https://en.wikipedia.org/wiki/History_of_Google.

Wikipedia. "History of Microsoft." Accessed October 2016. https://en.wikipedia.org/wiki/History_of_Microsoft.

Wikipedia. "Jamie Oliver." Accessed October 2016. https://en.wikipedia.org/wiki/Jamie_Oliver.

Wikipedia. "Mark Zuckerberg." Accessed October 2016. https://en.wikipedia.org/wiki/Mark_Zuckerberg.

Wikipedia. "MS-DOS." Accessed October 2016. https://en.wikipedia.org/wiki/MS-DOS.

Wikipedia. "Richard Branson." Accessed October 2016. https://en.wikipedia.org/wiki/Richard_Branson.

Wikipedia. "Sergey Brin." Accessed October 2016. https://en.wikipedia.org/wiki/Sergey_Brin.

Williams, Rob. "Revealed: The Third Largest 'Country' in the World – Facebook Hits One Billion Users." *The Independent*, October 2012. www.independent.co.uk/life-style/gadgets-and-tech/news/revealed-the-third-largest-country-in-the-world-facebook-hits-one-billion-users-8197597.html.

"The World's Billionaires." *Forbes*. Accessed October 2016. www.forbes.com/profile/richard-branson/.

Chapter 3

Creating the ideal marketing team

"None of us is as smart as all of us."

Ken Blanchard, *The One Minute Manager*

As we saw in Chapter 1, CEOs and Boards can feel frustrated with their marketing team's perceived lack of financial rigour, desire to take risks and longer-term mindset. This plays some part in CMOs having the shortest tenure in the Boardroom – only forty-eight months versus CEOs at eighty months, CFOs at seventy months and CIOs at sixty months – and for the Fournaise Marketing Group's claim that "80% of CEOs do not really trust and are not very impressed by the work done by marketers."[1]

Yet when asked what it is that marketing *isn't delivering*, few CEOs know.

This is in part due to few CEOs and Boards knowing what it is that they want from their marketing teams – compounded by a failure to set clear objectives or reasonable levels of expectation.

It's also in part due to marketing, unlike other functional areas, being a broad church of activities, requiring both highly analytical *and* creative thinking – which in practice makes it difficult for any marketer to cover all aspects well.

To create a successful marketing team, the CMO needs to align with the Board on what marketing expertise the company requires and the business objectives that marketing is expected to achieve. Then the CMO needs to create a team with the right breadth and balance of creative and analytical skill sets needed to deliver these objectives.

In this chapter, we look at how to build a high-performing marketing team, by focusing on:

A   Defining what the company needs from marketing.
B   Assembling a marketing team that can deliver what the business needs.
C   Building day-to-day project teams that will deliver a great outcome.

A: Defining what the company needs from marketing

To deliver the company objectives, the CMO needs to ensure that the Board understands and agrees on what the marketing team should focus on and achieve. This entails defining what the business needs and determining marketing's role in delivering this.

To elaborate, there are times when a company will be more focused on growth, requiring creative skills to build a strong brand or innovation skills to develop a steady stream of new products and services – and times when it will be more focused on cost, requiring commercial skills to choose where to play or analytical skills to find ways to 'do more with less' spend.

And there are times when it will be focused on both, simultaneously.

Given the broad scope of creative and analytical skills that marketing covers, it can be hard for the Board to know precisely what it needs marketing to achieve – which can lead to unrealistic expectations.

Additionally, the required focus for marketing can quickly shift, in line with changing business needs. I saw this in action when a financial services company hired in senior marketers, with a proven track record in building strong brands, to help the company create great advertising campaigns. Within the year, however, the company had unexpectedly acquired another company, and consequently the Board's emphasis moved away from growth to cost optimisation. The marketing team had to suddenly refocus its attention away from growth, onto optimising its new portfolio of brands to drive out costs.

Similarly, when two food companies merged, the Board spent a year aligning teams and processes across the business to drive out costs. However, at the end of the year, the Board realised that its focus on cost reduction had resulted in both the company's brand performance and innovation pipeline being unacceptably weak. Consequently, the marketing team had to quickly shift its focus away from cost optimisation, and back onto brand and innovation growth.

Concerningly, these shifts seem to be happening more than ever before. Increasingly, marketers are being asked to build their commercial, digital and data capabilities as their roles expand, beyond classic brand management and communications development, into helping all areas of the organisation to create and deliver a superior customer experience at each and every touch point.

For this reason, it's crucial that CMOs work together with the Board to define where the business emphasis lies and to agree on the role that marketing is playing to help the company achieves its objectives. For example, does the Board need marketing to focus on growth creation, calling for more creative or innovation skills – or on cost optimisation that requires more commercial or analytical expertise?

Additionally, CMOs need to build marketing teams with the range of skill sets to cover all business issues – and the versatility to flex and adapt in line with changing business needs.

To illustrate, let's look at four activities that the Board may ask the marketing team to prioritise, and address each in turn. All of these require great strategic capability, but some call more for creative skills while others demand more analytical expertise.

At the more creative end of the scale, marketers may need to:

1   Build a strong brand – using creative skills to develop compelling brand positionings and inspirational communications campaigns.
2   Deliver breakthrough innovation – using innovation skills to deliver a steady stream of new product and service ideas, profitably.

At the more analytical end of the scale, marketers may need to:

3   Choose 'where' to focus scarce resources – using commercial skills to define where to play in the market to drive profitable growth.
4   'Do more with less' – using analytical skills to select which marketing activities to focus on to maximise return on investment.

I. Building a strong brand

Building a strong brand – one that people are willing to pay more for – typically falls at the more creative end of the marketing spectrum. This is often called for when the brand is stagnant and needs to be 'turned around'.

Perhaps the brand is the market leader but is suffering from flat sales or market share and needs to reassert itself. Or, worse, the brand is losing sales or market share, with every pound spent on advertising and sales promotions producing an increasingly poor investment return – usually evidenced by weak brand health metrics, such as brand awareness, brand consideration and brand preference.

To build a strong brand, the marketing team needs strong creative skills, collaborating with creative agencies to develop both a compelling brand proposition and a market-leading communications campaign, as well as with cross-functional teams to bring the brand to life across the most important customer touch points.

Let's look at how global skincare brand Olay did this in the mid-1990s. Global Olay sales were flatlining. The existing campaign focused on wrinkle prevention, yet featured a girl in her early twenties who was perceived to know little about the trials and tribulations of skin ageing. This left the market wide open for brands like Nivea and L'Oréal to take the anti-ageing high ground.

To combat this, local P&G teams from around the world (including in the UK, Germany, France, Italy and Japan) were asked to create the next Olay campaign. The goal was to restore the brand to its pre-eminent status.

The local P&G teams worked individually with their local creative agency teams to develop new advertising campaigns. This included conducting their own qualitative research to generate new customer insights, briefing creative teams to use these insights to develop new campaign ideas and testing the campaigns qualitatively and then, for those that performed well, quantitatively. Months went by and advertising test results in all markets were weak.

Meanwhile, one of Olay's products, New Skin Discovery, was tested by an independent skin institute, that demonstrated that the product visibly reduced wrinkles and was superior to competitors at doing so.

The UK team grabbed the endorsement with open arms – recognising its power as independent proof that a moisturiser can visibly reduce the signs of ageing. They created the revolutionary "Proven Effective" campaign with the unique "Try the product and your skin will look noticeably softer and smoother within fourteen days" money back guarantee, supported with the highly assertive end line, "We can prove you can look younger."

While the campaign may seem mainstream today – partly due to the length of time it's been on-air and the extent that competitors have copied it – it was so bold back then that it took three months to get traction with consumers. Sales stayed flat for the first three months. But, as people began to assimilate these 'bold' claims, sales rose sharply, both for the premium New Skin Discovery product and the brand as a whole, including the lower priced pink Olay Beauty Fluid that made up the majority of the brand sales at that time.

Within six months, Olay was again the clear number one moisturiser brand in the UK, and over the next three years, both sales and profit margin had significantly increased. Interestingly, the "Proven Effective" campaign was so successful that it became one of the first (if not the first) international campaigns to be run in the United States, P&G's homeland.

Other examples of strong brand turnarounds are Lea & Perrins and HP Sauce.

In the late 1990s, brands like Lea & Perrins and HP Sauce had been in steady sales decline for ten years or more, causing margin pressure due to the high cost of the advertising spend.

A review of consumer data directly linked this decline to the decline in the host foods that these condiments were used with. For example, HP Sauce was seen as the ultimate 'greasy spoon' brand due to people's love of it with a good old English fry-up. But 'fried-egg-and-bacon breakfasts' had been in slow, steady decline over the past couple of decades, taking HP Sauce with it. And people were unsure what to use Lea & Perrins with – it was seen as more of an old-fashioned cooking ingredient than a sauce that was relevant for today's market.

Using qualitative research to talk with people who loved Lea & Perrins and HP Sauce, the marketing team was able to 'reframe' each of the brand's markets, by identifying more modern everyday meals and snacks that Lea & Perrins and HP Sauce complemented perfectly – in Lea & Perrins' case, foods such as cheese on toast and spaghetti bolognaise, and in HP Sauce's case, bacon sandwiches, beans on toast, and scrambled eggs.

From this came new advertising campaigns, supported with in-store promotions and on-pack recipe suggestions – all focused on the yummy foods that people could dress with Lea & Perrins and HP Sauce. The result? For both brands, a reverse of the years of sales decline, into a significant sales boost.

2. Delivering breakthrough innovation

Developing a steady stream of innovative and profitable new products and services is another more creatively led activity that the marketing team may be asked to focus on.

This often occurs when the Board has a 'high growth mindset' and is looking to significantly grow existing brands, either within existing or new adjacent categories, or launch new brands. Or when the category competitors are offering a similar range of products or services, causing our brand's sales and market share to stagnate or, worse, be driven by price wars.

In response, the marketing team needs to work with the product development team to create new product and service propositions that will both delight customers as well as deliver a strong margin. This way, the brand can reassert itself and shake up the category.

Let's look at a couple of real-life examples.

Prior to the 1990s, Seven Seas enjoyed a relatively unchallenged UK market leadership position within vitamins. But, in the 1990s Vitabiotics (a privately owned UK company) started to build its UK presence.

Vitabiotics developed a steady stream of product innovations. Unlike the more ingredient-led Seven Seas range, Vitabiotics' innovations were primarily life-stage led (for example, Wellkid, Wellwoman, Wellwoman 50+, Pregnacare, Menopace) or benefit led (for example, Jointace, Cardioace, Immunace, Visionace, Osteocare).

Vitabiotics supported each launch with highly efficacious claims. These included category leadership accolades (such as "The UK's number one vitamins company"), research claims (such as "90% of women reported a significant benefit"), expert endorsements (such as "Bupa Approved"), business awards (such as "Boots Award for Number One Overall Supplier of the Year") and testimonials from leading sports people (such as the cricketer, James Anderson).

By creating and focusing on a steady stream of life-stage and benefit-led innovation – and supporting these with compelling efficacy claims – Vitabiotics was able to topple the category incumbent to become the UK's number one vitamins brand.[2]

Another example is Lurpak Butter.

Lurpak was under pressure due to people switching to what they perceive to be 'healthier' and cheaper spreads and margarines. Clearly, Lurpak needed to reassert itself to regain the high ground.

Lurpak responded by identifying a big, profitable and growing customer segment – foodies – who love cookery shows and books. Lurpak's premium status and natural credentials gave it credibility to engage with this segment and join in the food debate. Its "Good Food Deserves Lurpak" campaign celebrated the joy that food brings to life, the importance of quality ingredients and what Lurpak adds to them. This was followed by a range of higher price-per-kilogram spin-off innovations such as The Cook's Range (for example, Clarified Butter and Cooking Mist) and flavoured butters (for example, garlic).

The new advertising campaign and innovation pipeline enabled Lurpak to reassert its premium credentials and return the brand to volume and value growth. This in turn enabled Lurpak to overtake Flora to become the number one spread brand in the UK.[3]

3. Choosing 'where' to focus scarce resources

On the more analytical side, the Board may call on the marketing team to help define where to focus the company's scarce resources to maximise profitable growth. For instance, which brands and geographies are likely to deliver the highest growth – both today and in the future – and should be allocated the most innovation resources and marketing spend? Or which products and services are most likely to deliver the greatest growth and therefore should be prioritised?

The need to decide 'where' to prioritise resources can arise when company growth is low and resources (including spend and people) are scattered across too many initiatives, resulting in 'mass market', rather than breakthrough, thinking. Or following a merger or acquisition when a company has a number of new brands and products to assimilate.

To address this, the marketing team needs to leverage its commercial skills, to create a customer-focused marketing strategy and work closely with cross-functional teams to select which brands, products and geographies to invest in for current and future growth.

A good example of this was when Lloyds TSB combined with HBOS to form Lloyds Banking Group that had upwards of fifteen brands. Some of these were large, well-known banks on the high street (such as Lloyds TSB, Halifax and Bank of Scotland), some were well-known brands but with a less visible presence (such as Scottish Widows, Clerical Medical and Birmingham Midshires) and some were highly specialist and therefore less well known (such as Black Horse, Lex and Insight Investment).

As part of the merger, the marketing team assessed which brands to prioritise for future growth and how to position them alongside each other to maximise group market share and minimise group cannibalisation. Given the financial impact of these decisions, and thus the Board's desire to be involved at each stage, pressure was on the team to do this in a commercially robust way.

Hence the marketing team reviewed existing data and conducted bespoke quantitative research to assess the health of each brand today – including its size, growth trend, how well the brand was known and loved by its customers, its image and its ability to tap into future growth trends. The team combined this with the company growth vision to recommend which brands to prioritise for future growth.

Then, for the priority brands, the team conducted bespoke qualitative research to assess where the heartland of each brand lay – including its core target customer, what the customer was looking for, and what the brand was known for that made it attractive.

They then pulled the analysis and 'so whats' into a robust Board presentation deck that the Board could engage with and buy into.

By doing this, the team was able to demonstrate a robust financial argument to the Board, as to which brands to prioritise. It was also able to create compelling brand positionings that both the heritage Lloyds TSB and HBOS teams could buy into, as well as demonstrate the power of pulling the brands apart to create broader market coverage and less brand overlap.

4. 'Doing more with less'

Similarly, the primary focus of the marketing team might be to 'do more with less', engaging its analytical skill set to identify, for instance, which customer touch points the team should focus on to best influence people, or which media activities it should prioritise to successfully drive awareness, consideration and trial.

This situation typically arises when the company is under cost pressure and looking for ways to deliver the same sales as last year at a lower cost, or more sales than last year at no extra cost.

To achieve this, the marketing team needs to set up a 'test & learn' programme that systematically tests each marketing and communication activity – to identify which are the highest performing and thus should be continued, and which are underperforming and thus should be eliminated.

It then needs to engage in more rapid campaign testing, with the aim of generating faster feedback loops that enable marketers to identify and optimise the best-performing activities more quickly.

A classic example of 'doing more with less' involved Direct Line Group, which was tasked with significantly reducing its cost base following its separation from RBS. To help the company achieve its objective, the marketing team, led by Mark Evans, invested in building a team of marketing effectiveness experts and data analysts, supported by a leading-edge marketing effectiveness agency.

This underpinned the creation of a robust AB testing and econometrics regime that supported a systematic 'test & learn' programme which enabled the marketing team to focus on those marketing activities that were performing well and culling those that weren't. This generated faster feedback loops, enabling the team to more quickly and more accurately identify and optimise the best-performing communications activities. This in turn gave the team confidence to re-balance communication spend away from traditional above-the-line channels (such as television) into emerging channels (such as digital, social media, affiliates and paid search) in a very measured and knowing way.

Within three years, the team had generated a significant improvement in efficiency as measured by ROI and cost per acquisition, improving its sales performance despite a third less marketing spend – making it one of the biggest contributors to the company's overall cost reduction programme.

Defining which areas marketing should focus on

As we've seen, there are times when a business may need to prioritise more creatively driven activities (such as a brand turnaround or a focus on high growth), and times when it may need to prioritise more analytical activities (such as a merger and acquisition, or a focus on cost reduction) – and even times when it needs to focus on both. Consequently, the CMO needs to work together with the Board to understand the goals of the business, and the time period that these need to be delivered in – thereby ensuring that the business and marketing priorities are aligned.

They then need to work closely with the Board to define marketing's role within the team – setting clear marketing objectives that both the Board and marketing can buy into, with clearly laid out milestones to assess whether marketing is on track.

To prioritise which activities marketing should focus on, CMOs can systematically work through the various options with the Board using a diagnostic tool (such as the one shown in Figure 3.1.) in which the Board and marketing rate each of the activities based on (i) how important they are to today's business needs and in the corresponding column (ii) how well they perceive marketing to be delivering on each activity today.

This way, the CMO gives the Board ideas and a common language to work with when deciding which activities marketing should focus on – helping the Board members to clearly pinpoint what they need marketing to achieve as well as articulate what's really on their minds.

In practice, this enables each Board member, including the CMO, to compare notes to define and agree what the business priorities are and what aspects marketing should focus on over the coming year to achieve them – setting clear objectives and milestones that everyone buys into.

Whatever the short-term focus is, CMOs should encourage the Board to keep some people focused on delivering the longer-term business objectives. For example, if the short-term Board focus is to drive out costs during a company merger, it makes good business sense for some marketers to focus on

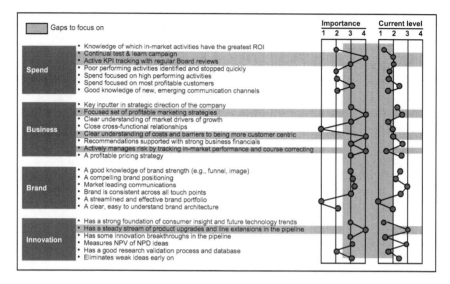

Figure 3.1   Diagnostic tool to help marketers and the Board define what marketing should focus on

the likely longer-term growth agenda of developing strong brand campaigns and innovation pipelines.

B: Assembling a marketing team that can deliver what the business needs

Once marketing's objectives are defined, the next step is to pull together a high-performance team to deliver these objectives. Ideally, at the top of the marketing team, there should be at least one senior marketer whose experience and expertise is a good fit with the business needs. This person should then be supported with a team of marketing experts who can deliver the other facets.

The differing characteristics of marketers

Given the breadth of creative and analytical skills that marketing covers, the characteristics and skill sets of senior marketers can vary widely, primarily based on their experience profile to date.

Firstly, all senior marketers combine creative expertise with commercial expertise – these two skill sets are key to being a great marketer.

But, some senior marketers are more analytically minded by nature, with a strong commercial bias and a sharp financial sense – that is, they naturally think and talk like the Board. Others are more creatively minded by nature, with an explicit sense of what delights customers now and the emerging trends that might shape their needs and behaviour in the future.

Few senior marketers are equally strong at both. Their leaning tends to depend on whether they've learnt their trade in a more brand- and creative-orientated environment, where intuition and breakthrough thinking are more highly valued, or in a more commercial and analytical environment, where commercial awareness and business acumen are more prized.

Both play their part. But, a more commercial, analytical mindset is needed to address business and spend issues, such as developing profitable marketing strategies, prioritising investment and driving business decision-making, while a more visionary, creative mindset is needed to address brand and innovation issues, such as developing a category leading brand, or breakthrough advertising and innovation.

Secondly, some senior marketers are highly politically astute, while others are more entrepreneurial.

Politically astute marketers are strong at influencing senior managers, peers and teams to achieve consensus and deliver strong results – and so typically flourish in a large global company, either in the global team responsible for global profit and loss (P&L) performance, or in a local team with local P&L responsibility.

Entrepreneurial marketers prefer to spend their time finding new ways to cost efficiently drive business growth, rather than on influencing others – and so typically flourish in a locally run company with local P&L responsibility.

Thirdly, some marketers are innately highly decisive, leading from the top by being quick to make, and stick to, commercial business decisions – and then galvanising the team to deliver them. A decisive mindset is essential for marketers in a leadership role, such as a CMO who is on the Board with global P&L responsibility.

Others marketers are more collegial, preferring to make decisions and guiding the business as a team with others' input and direction. A more collegial mindset is important for a marketer in a business support role – for instance, someone in a global marketing team supporting local marketing teams to deliver their local P&Ls, or someone supporting sales in a sales-led business-to-business (B2B) organisation.

Playing to your strengths

Ideally, senior marketers should place themselves in roles and business environments that play to their strengths. This will primarily depend on whether the business challenges are more analytical or creative – and whether the company is a matrix organisation with many people to influence or more of an entrepreneurial organisation where people work in small teams.

Based on this, there are five types of roles that senior marketers could consider (see Figure 3.2).

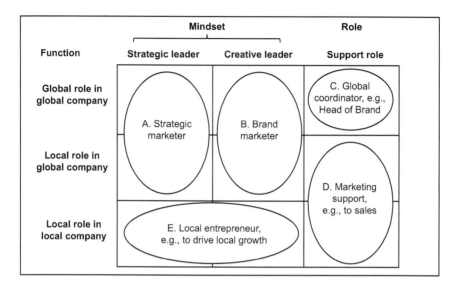

Figure 3.2 Five types of senior marketer roles

A *strategic marketer* drives commercial decision-making from the top by being decisive on where to invest for growth, influential at bringing the Board with them, and inspirational across the business. They tend to be more analytically and commercially strong, as well as politically astute, and are not afraid to make, sell in and stand by the tough decisions.

These people are likely to have a more commercial background, often having trained within a marketing team with strong commercial responsibility, such as Procter & Gamble or Mars, or within a management consultancy. These marketers are often being mentored for a senior Board role.

Companies tend to recruit a strategic marketer when decisive, strategic directions need to be made on where to focus their business for growth.

A *brand marketer* tends to drive growth by building a strong brand supported by a steady stream of innovation. They tend to be more creatively strong at developing compelling brands and communication campaigns, inspirational at bringing the Board and creative agencies with them and visionary in identifying bold new product and service ideas for the future.

Brand marketers are likely to have a more creative background, often having trained as a marketer within a company that is highly creative, innovative and futuristic, such as Apple or L'Oréal, or within a creative agency or brand consultancy. These people are often being groomed for a senior marketing position.

Companies tend to recruit a brand marketer to turn a declining brand around or reposition it for growth, supported by a strong advertising campaign and a steady stream of innovation.

An *entrepreneurial marketer* tends to grow a local brand into a category leader by identifying new, non-traditional ways to build a brand, making tough choices on where to focus scarce resources and convincing the Board of the need for marketing investment.

They tend to be entrepreneurial, rather than politically astute, and unafraid to challenge the status quo. They also tend to be a strong self-starter.

Companies tend to recruit an entrepreneurial marketer when they need to turn a declining local brand around (with little need for global alignment) or to build a local brand from scratch.

A *global brand coordinator* helps local teams build a compelling and consistent brand worldwide by defining what the brand should look and feel like across all touch points and helping local markets deliver this.

They tend to be empathetic at understanding local needs, as well as persuasive influencers, encouraging local teams to adopt the global model. They are also fuelled by a love of brands and are most likely to stay within the marketing arena.

Global brand coordinators often exist within global companies with strong global brands, such as Experian, Zurich Financial Services and AMEX, as these organisations typically need help to build a robust, consistent global brand across all markets.

A *supporting marketer* supports the sales team by developing strong brand and customer communications that the sales team can use.

They tend to be commercially minded, with a good understanding of what the sales team needs to be effective, as well as empathetic and supportive of the sales team's point of view. They are comfortable making decisions collectively as a team.

Companies that are highly sales led, rather than advertising led, tend to need a supporting marketer, particularly those operating within the business-to-business space.

Building a marketing team that has the skills to deliver

Now that we've done the groundwork, let's put this all together.

Most businesses focus on multiple business issues at any one time. So, when recruiting the marketing team, it's important that it contains marketing experts representing all key creative and analytical skill sets – both at the top of the team and throughout – with the emphasis on those areas that are critical to the company's future success.

For instance, at the top of the team, if the CMO is more of a creative brand marketer, the number two should ideally be a strong analytical thinker – someone who naturally thinks and talks like the Board. Similarly, if the CMO is more of a strategic marketer, the number two should ideally be more of a creative thinker – someone who is naturally good at building strong brand campaigns and being innovative. By pooling skills, together they can handle any issue that the Board throws at them.

Then when recruiting the rest of the team, the CMO should consider bringing in a broad range of skill sets, including:

- More creative brand-oriented marketers who can help build a compelling brand positioning and deliver strong advertising campaigns. They are likely to have a classic marketing background with a history of creating strong brands and advertising campaigns or to have worked within a creative agency.
- More innovative marketers who can develop a steady stream of new, breakthrough products and services. These marketers are likely to have a creative mindset, having worked either within a marketing team or product development team that was responsible for innovation or within an innovation or design house.
- More commercial marketers who can help decide which brands, products and geographies to prioritise and thus where to focus scarce resources. Like strategic marketers, they are likely to have a more commercial background, having trained within a marketing team that has strong commercial responsibility, such as in Procter & Gamble or Mars, or within a management consultancy.
- More analytical marketers who can assess how effective the marketing spend is and help decide which marketing and communication activities to prioritise in the coming year. These marketers are likely to have a more statistical or data background, often trained within an analytics or market research team or within a media agency.

The CMO needs to have a broad understanding of each of these functions and the leadership skills to focus the right people within their team on the right business priorities. They then need to ensure that the various disciplines work together harmoniously as a team – and flex the balance over time as needed, in line with the changing business needs.

In this way, CMOs can be sure that the depth of team expertise and experience exists whatever the business issue and whatever the Board asks of them.

C: Building day-to-day project teams that will deliver a great outcome

Turning our focus to individual project teams, it's important for a new brand, product or service launch team to consist of the 'right people'.

Team members should be encouraged to challenge each other and bounce ideas around so that the launch plan and its execution are fully optimised. The ideal launch team consists of people with differing attitudes and beliefs – such as *passionate thinkers*, *disruptive challengers*, *objective doubters* and *pragmatic doers*. This diversity is critical.

Ideally, some team members should be more visionary and optimistic, passionate about the opportunity and potential that the team can achieve and driving the team to deliver it in all of its glory. In most launch teams, there are marketers who are passionate about the idea that is being launched. Often they have worked on the idea from scratch, identifying the opportunity, developing the idea, nurturing it into what it is today, seeing customers talk positively about it, and championing it through the organisation. These types of *passionate thinkers* engender team energy, enthusiasm, drive and a desire for perfection – keeping the team moving forward at pace and with vision.

Others should be *disruptive challengers*, challenging the status quo to come up with new and better ways to go to market. These people are often ideas driven, flitting from one idea to the next until one takes root. They tend to view things differently – as well as accept the risk of doing things differently – in an effort to achieve a better outcome. They can be tricky to work with day to day – challenging what others accept as the norm – but over time, will help drive the team to bolder outcomes.

In contrast, it's important for some team members to be *objective doubters*, namely more cautionary and risk-averse. Their sceptical nature makes them slower to believe the upside until it's proven to them. In this way, they are good at challenging the agreed wisdoms to identify any flawed assumptions – keeping the plans realistic and grounded.

To ensure that the proposition is delivered, the team needs to include *pragmatic doers*, focused on doing what it takes to ensure that the new brand, product or service is launched successfully in-market. They help to ensure that the team are launching in a simple yet impactful way, delivering what the business needs without creating high levels of internal complexity. Additionally, they help to ensure that the team stays on track, delivering a successful launch on time and to cost.

A team that combines the traits of passionate thinkers with disruptive challengers, objective doubters and pragmatic doers has a good chance of optimising the launch from all angles, especially if they are at ease when bouncing ideas around together. The doubters will raise questions and issues that the optimists might have overlooked, rousing the team to sort out any major issues prior to launch. The passionate thinkers will look for answers to make sure that their 'baby' survives. The disruptors will find new ways of doing things that challenge the market norms, giving the team a meaningful competitive advantage. The pragmatic doers will ensure that any launch plans are simple yet impactful – and that the team delivers the launch on time and to cost.

By the same token, it's important that no team member be so passionately involved that they take every challenge and rejection personally, resulting in the team not doing the right thing for the business.

Similarly, it's vital that no team member is so dispassionate that they purely want to make a 'quick buck', so that they miss the opportunity to understand the market well enough to invest in something truly appealing and differentiated.

In summary

To build Board confidence, it's imperative that CMOs and Boards are aligned on what the business needs, the role that marketing needs to play to help the company achieve its objectives, and what success looks like.

To achieve this, CMOs need to work with the Board to:

- Understand the goals of the business, and the time period that these need to be delivered in.
- Define marketing's role within the team.
- Set clear marketing objectives that both the Board and marketing can buy into.
- Define clear marketing milestones that help ensure that marketing is on track.

Alongside this, CMOs need to build high-performing marketing teams that can deliver what the business needs. These should include:

- At least one senior marketer whose experience and expertise is a good fit with the business needs.
- A good balance of skill sets at the top. For example, if the CMO is more of a creative brand marketer, then their number two should ideally be a strong analytical thinker, and vice versa.
- Marketing experts across all key creative and analytical skills, with the emphasis on those areas that are critical to the company's success.

The CMO needs to have a broad understanding of each of these functions and the leadership skills to focus the right people within their team on the right business priorities. They also need to flex the balance of the marketing team over time, in line with the changing business needs.

Additionally, CMOs need to build high-performing project teams that can deliver a great project outcome – namely diverse teams that include passionate thinkers, disruptive challengers, objective doubters and pragmatic doers.

By doing this, the CMO can work together with the Board to ensure that the marketing team has what it needs to drive the level of success required, both for the company and for marketing.

Notes

1 Spencer Stuart, "Chief Marketing Officer Tenure Climbs to 48 Months," March 2015, https://www.spencerstuart.com/who-we-are/media-center/chief-marketing-officer-tenure-climbs-to-48-months; Spencer Stuart, "CFO Route to the Top 2015," September

2015, https://www.spencerstuart.com/research-and-insight/cfo-route-to-the-top-2015; Maryfran Johnson, "What It Takes to Improve CIO Tenure," *www.cio.com*, October 2012, http://www.cio.com/article/2391383/data-center/what-it-takes-to-improve-cio-tenure. html; Fournaise Marketing Group, "80% of CEOs Do Not Really Trust Marketers (Except If They Are 'ROI Marketers')," July 2012, https://www.fournaisegroup.com/ceos-do-not-trust-marketers/.

2 "IRI value sales for w/e 20 April, 2013," *Vitabiotics*, https://www.vitabiotics.com/ourhistory, accessed October 2016.

3 Arla, "Arla Butter Brand Lurpak Takes the Top UK Spot," July 2014, http://www.arlafoods.co.uk/overview/news–press/2014/pressrelease/arla-butter-brand-lurpak-r-takes-the-top-uk-spot-1034188/, accessed October 2016; Wieden+Kennedy, "Lurpak Cook's Range," March 2015, http://creativepool.com/wk/projects/cooks-range-for-lurpak, accessed October 2016.

Bibliography

Arla. "Arla Butter Brand Lurpak Takes the Top UK Spot." July 2014. Accessed October 2016. www.arlafoods.co.uk/overview/news–press/2014/pressrelease/arla-butter-brand-lurpak-r-takes-the-top-uk-spot-1034188/.

Fournaise Marketing Group. "80% of CEOs Do Not Really Trust Marketers (Except If They Are 'ROI Marketers')." www.fournaisegroup.com/ceos-do-not-trust-marketers/. Last modified July 2012.

"IRI Value Sales for w/e 20 April, 2013." *Vitabiotics*. Accessed October 2016. www.vitabiotics.com/ourhistory.

Johnson, Maryfran. "What It Takes to Improve CIO Tenure." *www.cio.com*, October 2012. www.cio.com/article/2391383/data-center/what-it-takes-to-improve-cio-tenure.html.

Stuart, Spencer. "CFO Route to the Top 2015." September 2015. www.spencerstuart.com/research-and-insight/cfo-route-to-the-top-2015.

Stuart, Spencer. "Chief Marketing Officer Tenure Climbs to 48 Months." March 2015. www.spencerstuart.com/who-we-are/media-center/chief-marketing-officer-tenure-climbs-to-48-months.

Wieden+Kennedy. "Lurpak Cook's Range". March 2015. Accessed October 2016. creativepool.com/wk/projects/cooks-range-for-lurpak.

Creating marketing strategies that the Board will buy into

Summary

As we saw in Part one, it's tougher than ever before for companies to grow, with marketing increasingly important in helping companies deliver the breakthrough innovation and compelling brand positionings needed to achieve this.

Yet, to convince the Board to invest, marketers need to demonstrate how their marketing strategies will build shareholder value by delivering profitable returns.

The importance of choosing where to play

The main players in a market often have similar resources – both similar levels of money to spend on advertising and innovation as well as similar levels of people available to work on a brand. If all companies spend those resources equally across everything, then they will behave similarly in a 'mass average' way and so won't be distinctive.

To develop marketing strategies that drive shareholder value, marketers need to focus their scarce resources on those areas that will deliver the highest returns. This includes which brands and products to support, which geographies to focus on for growth, which customer segments to attract and retain, which messages to communicate, which distribution channels to sell through, which customer touch points to use to influence people and which media and communication activities to focus on.

Some companies inherently choose where to focus their scarce resources. For example:

- P&G focuses its resources on delivering breakthrough innovation, as well as building a strong brand presence.
- Ryan Air drives out cost to offer low-price air travel.
- First Direct invests in its people to build a superior call centre service experience.
- Starbucks invests in building ubiquity on every street corner.
- Zara uses a highly efficient supply chain to keep stock production runs to a minimum.

- Amazon stocks a wide range of products, supported by fast and reliable delivery every time.

By focusing their resources in this way, companies such as these achieve a competitive advantage.

Why engage the Board

As we will see in the next five chapters, Boards have become increasingly interested in where to focus their scarce resources to deliver higher returns. They are increasingly realising that to create growth over and above competitors, they need to cut through the market clutter, by defining what business they are in, and what attributes they are investing in – as well as what they are not investing in – to make it customer-centric.

One way to do this is by addressing the questions raised by the '5W framework' (Figure P1) as outlined here:

- *Who* should we target?
  Which customers will deliver the greatest return for the company – and therefore which should we focus our scarce resources on recruiting and retaining?

- *What* should we support?
  Which products, brands and geographies will deliver the greatest return – and therefore which should we invest our scarce innovation and communication spend on growing and maximising?

- *Why* should we be in business?
  What are our customers looking for – specifically which attributes should we be investing our scarce innovation and communication resources in to build a customer-centric business?

- *Where* should we sell through?
  Which distribution channels will enable us to manage and grow our brands as efficiently and effectively as possible?

- *When* should we engage people?
  Which touch points and communication channels have the greatest influence on our core target audience – and therefore should be prioritised for growth?

Why should marketers engage the Board

To maximise shareholder return, it's imperative for marketers to engage the Board on where – and crucially where not – to invest to create a superior customer experience and hence growth, over and above competitors.

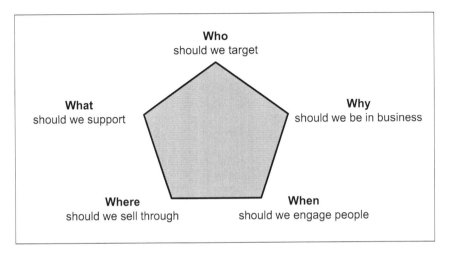

Figure P1 5W framework

For example, should they invest in twenty-year innovation programmes that revolutionise the market, or in shorter-term innovation programmes (such as new flavours, new designs or new packaging formats) that drive growth in a more evolutionary way? Should they invest in a superior customer experience across all customer touch points, or in driving out cost to create a low-cost option? And should they invest in big scale above-the-line advertising that dominates their sector, or in more entrepreneurial communication using creativity and flexibility to stand out in less expensive mediums?

Marketers should engage the Board for two reasons.

Firstly, the impact of these decisions is likely to be high – both on brand and company performance – so it's important that senior management agree that this is the right direction to take.

Secondly, once the decision has been made, marketing will most likely need cross-functional support to make the chosen strategy a reality – and so need their agreement on which direction to take and on how to deliver it. For example, it's likely that marketing will need to work closely with the innovation team to deliver superior products and services, or with sales and call centre teams to deliver a superior service experience, or with the digital team to deliver a joined up customer and brand experience across all channels, or with the production and supply chain team to create a low-cost option that drives out costs without damaging the customer experience.

How to engage the Board

To win the Board over, marketers need to engage the Board using thinking, rationale and language that the Board members will understand.

As discussed in Chapter 1, the Board's primary objective is to protect and manage the company successfully, so Board members naturally have a mind-set that is more analytical, risk-aware and short- to medium-term focused.

They are also invariably time-starved, and so need to be able to assimilate new, recommended strategies succinctly and quickly.

Therefore, to engage the Board, marketers need to develop marketing strategies that are:

- *Clear*, in what they are recommending and why this makes sense for the Board to consider.
- *Succinct*, ideally showing the recommendations in a one-page storyline and the analysis in a one-page framework.
- *Robust*, supported with a compelling fact base that builds the Board's confidence.
- *Jargon-free*, using the Board's language rather than marketing jargon to make the case.
- *Intuitive*, in what is being recommended and why this is good for the business.

Making the most of Part two

Part two comprises five chapters, each of which focuses on one of the 5Ws – namely, Who, What, Why, Where, When – to better understand how companies can apply each to create a competitive advantage.

These five chapters are designed to guide and inspire marketers on how to develop more compelling and robust marketing and brand strategies that the Board will buy into. Each includes:

- Key questions that marketers should consider when developing their marketing strategies.
- One-page analysis frameworks that can help marketers present their recommended strategies succinctly and quickly.
- Relevant case study examples that demonstrate how other companies have successfully put these strategies into practice.

The first three chapters – Who, What and Why – are primarily based on consulting work that I've done with Boards, on issues that they increasingly have a vested interest in – namely where they should invest their scarce resources for growth.

The last two chapters – Where and When – are primarily based on the work that I've done with entrepreneurs, on finding new, more cost-efficient and effective ways to go to market. By behaving in an entrepreneurial way, marketers can demonstrate to the Board that they are spending the company's money wisely.

So now, let's look at each of the 5Ws in turn.

Chapter 4

Choosing 'who' to target

"I cannot give you the formula for success, but I can give you the formula for failure, which is: Try to please everybody."

Herbert B. Swope, American journalist

When thinking about which customers to target, companies should not try to please everyone. Instead, they should focus their scarce resources on attracting and retaining those customers who will deliver the greatest return for the company – that is, those who will be most drawn to the brand, hence the easiest to recruit, and those who will buy the most products and therefore will be the most valuable.

By defining which customers to focus on – and crucially which *not* to focus on – Boards can ensure that more of their scarce resources are spent on creating a truly superior customer experience for their most valuable customers.

The most effective way to select 'who' to target is to use **customer segmentation**, a marketing technique that categorises customers into 'like groups' that share similar underlying patterns of attitudes, needs and behaviours that drive their purchase decisions. By doing so, marketers can determine:

- *Where to focus scarce resources* by identifying which customers generate the most value now – and which are likely to generate the most value in the future.
- *How to capture this value* by identifying what these customers are looking for and what they need to be offered *over and above* competitors to encourage them to switch so that the company can capture more than its fair share of business.

As we will see in this chapter, customer segmentation not only generates valuable insight that can help solve business problems, it can also transform companies, especially when used at Board level to help define the company strategy. Yet often it is used ineffectively, or not at all.

Therefore, in this chapter we focus on:

A   Why choosing 'who' to target is important to the Board.
B   Selecting the optimal customer segmentation approach.
C   Developing a commercially actionable segmentation.
D   Choosing where to play.
E   Bringing the segmentation to life.

A: Why choosing 'who' to target is important to the Board

To build compelling brands, companies should decide which customer segments to focus on – and crucially which *not* to focus on. By doing so, Boards can spend their scarce resources on creating a superior product or service experience that their most valuable customers will switch and stay loyal to – which in turn should deliver strong, sustainable growth.

When defining 'who' to target, there are a number of business scenarios in which it pays to engage the Board early on. These include brand turnaround, optimising a multi-branded portfolio, creating a brand's next wave of growth and delivering a personalised customer experience, among others.

Engaging the Board early on helps to build Board buy-in in two important ways.

Firstly, the impact that these decisions will have on brand performance and ultimately company performance is likely to be high. If the team gets it right, brand performance is likely to be strong. If the team gets it wrong, brand performance will suffer. So it's critical that everyone agrees that this is the right direction to take.

Secondly, recommendations can often extend beyond marketing per se, affecting all teams that have an impact on the customer experience. For example, they may affect how the sales team liaises with their customers, or how the digital team designs the online experience, or how the call centre and retail teams deliver the service experience, or how the innovation team designs new products and services. Therefore, marketers need to ensure that the segmentation approach and its recommendations are understood and bought into at the highest level – with all relevant cross-functional teams aligned on 'who' to target and how.

One criticism that I sometimes hear is that customer segmentations reflect the world as it is today – rather than how the world will be in the future. Yet, in my experience, the size of the customer segments themselves tend to stay relatively static over time. In the unlikely circumstance that the segment sizes will change, then customer segmentation serves as an effective way to accurately size the current market and form a robust basis on which to predict what the future might look like.

What *does* change is the way companies, in line with the latest technological solutions, meet the needs of the different customer segments.

To illustrate, I once had the privilege of referencing a customer segmentation that was conducted in 1970 within the financial services sector – as well as meet with the person who had created it. We found that the same customer segments existed in 1970 as they did today, and that the size of each of the customer segments was broadly similar. The one noticeable blip was a bigger 'self-directed' segment buying shares in the heady years of the dotcom boom, which quickly dropped back down to pre-boom levels, once the bubble had burst. However, while the segments themselves were similar, what had changed was how companies were meeting the needs of their target customer segments in the 1970s versus today, using the latest technologies of the day to offer relevant product, service and channel solutions.

Let's look at some real-life scenarios, where customer segmentations were used effectively to engage the Board and drive significant business growth, starting with brand turnarounds.

Brand turnarounds

Brands that are losing sales and market share – and thus need to be 'turned around' – are often doing so because they have lost their focus. This is typically due to either fragmenting their resources across multiple segments and so not building a distinctive brand positioning or offer, or by chasing successful competitors in territories where the brand has little credibility or permission to play.

In these cases, attitudinal segmentations can help form the basis of a successful and sustained brand turnaround by helping underperforming companies refocus their scarce resources on those customers that are most valuable to them. In essence, they can help to:

- Identify the customer segments that are most attracted to the brand and therefore are the easiest to recruit and will buy the most products.
- Define which territory the brand can credibly own and build a distinctive positioning in.
- Develop products and services that their priority customer segments will value and pay more for.
- Develop communication campaigns that tap into meaningful insights that reflect what their priority customer segments are thinking and looking for when choosing what to buy.
- Build a strong presence in the purchase channels that are most important to priority customer segments, as well as meet their customers' needs at each step of the purchase process.

Real-life case study: A savings and investments company

Many examples exist of how segmentations have formed the basis of a successful and sustained company revival. One such case is that of a building society that had been steadily losing market share, primarily due to a lack of business focus resulting in its scarce resources being fragmented across multiple customer segments – and thus not building a distinctive positioning or offer within any.

Segmentation revealed one customer segment that was especially attracted to the brand's heritage. Typically, they were actively planning for retirement but were risk-averse. They were older and thus needing to reduce their risk profile as they approached retirement, and had invariably been financially burnt by previous stock market crashes. They were therefore reluctant to invest in anything deemed 'too risky' that might result in a loss of retirement funds – and so preferred to invest in products with guaranteed returns.

Additionally, because many had borne the brunt of bad advice in the past, they preferred to make their own decisions rather than take advice from others. Above all, they sought peace of mind that their investments were safe, secure and suited to their needs.

This meant they were typically drawn to fixed rate savings accounts, guaranteed bonds and Cash Individual Savings Accounts (ISAs) – something that the building society was well known and respected for. They liked to select products themselves by reviewing the financial pages online or in the press to find the best rate – and then they bought them online, over the telephone or in-branch. Given their slightly more traditional attitude, they expected a more personalised service – one that treated them as individuals, got things right first time and resolved problems quickly and efficiently.

Armed with this information, the company decided to primarily refocus resources on this segment with the aim of developing a competitive range of guaranteed-rate savings accounts, bonds and Cash ISAs, building a strong presence in the 'best performing rate' league tables, and improving the in-branch, online and call centre experience to get things right first time. Once implemented, the company launched a compelling advertising campaign that, unlike its competitors, reassured its customers that they were in safe hands.

By focusing more resources on one customer segment, the building society was able to significantly reduce the number of projects it was working on – which enabled it to channel those scarce resources into creating a superior product range, in-branch, online and call centre experience, and advertising campaign for this priority customer segment.

Real-life case study: A food company

Similarly, a food company had for three years been steadily losing its market share. Two huge competitors had successfully innovated within the Italian food sector with a steady stream of new, innovative product launches that were backed up by high-spend advertising campaigns, prompting significant growth.

Lured by this growth, the food company had spent the past two years innovating within this particular sector – in spite of its lack of Italian heritage, as well as a lack of superior product innovation and significantly less money to spend than its two main competitors. Unsurprisingly, our client was getting killed in the market share ratings, as well as getting slammed as 'me too'.

Customer segmentation, however, showed that our client's brand was strong in another food sector, in 'good old family favourites', such as cottage pie, hot pot and stew – an area that the competitors were ignoring.

By going back to its roots and refocusing resources to come up with innovative 'family favourite' recipes, and supporting these with a new 'family favourites' advertising campaign, the company carved out a distinctive niche for itself and, in so doing, achieved significant double digit growth.

Incidentally, the same segmentation was conducted across Europe, even though our client was initially sceptical about being able to create a pan-European segmentation owing to the vast differences in eating habits that exist between countries, such as the UK and France. Interestingly, by creating one pan-European segmentation, the company was able to prove why the UK and France were so different, as well as size the gap. When it comes to eating with families, the Brits are significantly more convenience driven, grabbing meals when they can and often eating separately. In contrast, the French prefer to savour their family meals around the table, eating well-prepared, fresh-tasting food. This enabled the French team to convince the Board of the need to create its own range, rather than pursue pan-European innovation solutions.

Many companies use customer segmentation as a way to help them turn a brand around – but few talk publicly about it.

One that has spoken publicly is the office supply chain store Staples. Launched in 1986, Staples was the inventor of the 'office superstore' category. But over time, as retailers (such as Walmart and Best Buy) and new entrants (such as Office Depot) entered the category, its offer became increasingly undifferentiated. To counter this, Staples conducted customer segmentation research that identified a number of profitable customer segments that wanted a more 'hassle-free' shopping experience – something that no brand in the market was providing at that time. This insight led them to design a much simpler shopping experience – including new store layouts, clearly marked aisles and easy-to-access customer service, supported by a 'That Was Easy' advertising campaign. In doing so, Staple's turned its business and brand around, enabling it to overtake Office Depot and regain its position as the number one office superstore.[1]

Optimising a multi-brand portfolio

Another common business scenario in which customer segmentation can play a valuable role is when a company manages multiple competitive brands within a category. For example, P&G owns an array of competing brands within hair care – including Pantene, H&S, Herbal Essences and Aussie.

Customer segmentations can help multi-branded companies optimise their go-to-market portfolio strategy, by pulling competitive brands apart to maximise market coverage and minimise brand overlap.

In these cases, attitudinal segmentations can help Boards to:

- Identify which customer segments prefer each of their brands today.
- Assess where and how to pull brands apart to achieve greater market coverage and minimise brand overlap.
- Based on this, define which territory each of their brands should own and the products and services each should offer to best engage their customer segment.

Real-life case study: A hotel company

A hotel company with a number of hotel chains wanted to use each of its brands to better target the needs of a discrete customer segment so that collectively they maximised market coverage and minimised brand overlap.

An 'occasion-based' customer segmentation identified a number of segments. Some were more leisure based, with couples or families valuing restaurants, bars and children's activities, such as a games room or swimming pool. Others were more business based, with business travellers valuing the technology, facilities and services essential for them to work efficiently in their rooms, such as in-room menus with healthy options, power breakfasts and gyms to keep them fit.

Some segments were more basic in need with travellers (such as people staying over for a wedding) just wanting a comfortable bed to sleep in and bathroom to shower in. Others were making the stay more of an occasion, valuing more premium amenities such as a destination restaurant, a club lounge, a spa and a concierge service that could get hotel guests into the must-see shows and restaurants.

Some segments were more social, such as conferences, where companies host team workshops alongside golfing, to encourage team bonding. Others were more individual, where hotel guests value having a quiet pint and a read of the newspaper in the 'home from home' hotel lounge bar.

By understanding the distinct needs of each hotel occasion and where each of its brands best played, the company was able to define which occasion, or occasions, each of its brands should own going forward. It then identified which price point each of its brands should operate at in the market – and, for each brand, developed a number of signature hallmarks to invest in to deliver a competitively superior customer experience.

Many companies use customer segmentation as a way to help optimise their brand portfolio but, as with brand turnarounds, few discuss it openly.

One exception is Electrolux. When interviewed about the company's transformation, Electrolux CMO MaryKay Kopf talked about the power of having a strategic brand portfolio in which specific brands are targeted to specific customer segments. She goes on to say,

> Electrolux, for example, targets two different consumer segments and we know everything about those segments. We know our consumers demographically and typographically; we know her style, what's important to her at home, and what kind of relationship she wants to have with brands. We think about how she gets inspired, how she discovers what's right for her, how she shops, how she makes her selection, and then what happens when she gets her new appliance home. We look at pre- and post-purchase as one experience. We focus everything we do for her with that brand, and fill that positive consumer experience. We build products for her. We build shopping experiences for her. We build ownership experiences for her.[2]

Creating a brand's next wave of growth

A third business scenario involves using segmentations when a company is performing well, in order to drive further growth by increasing a brand's customer base. In these cases, marketers have helped to create the brand's next wave of growth by:

- Identifying the key attitudinal, demographic and behavioural differences between loyal users and non-users.
- Understanding why loyal users buy the brand, and why non-users don't.
- Identifying which non-user segment or segments are most open to persuasion.
- Assessing what to say or offer to non-users to overcome their reasons for not buying, perhaps by communicating the key benefits that the loyal users value, or by offering a tailored product or service that better meets their needs.

Real-life case study: A drinks company

While Boards tend to value the robustness of quantitative segmentations, qualitative segmentations can also be successfully used to build Board buy-in, as this example from the mid-2000s shows.

A drinks company selling an extensive range of specialty premium teas (such as Earl Grey, Lady Grey and Ceylon) was enjoying a stable market share, but was struggling to grow the category, in part due to consumers' preference for mainstream teas.

Qualitative research among mainstream tea drinkers and those who drank specialty teas revealed a stark difference between these two customer segments.

Those who drank *only* mainstream teas drank it to feel invigorated, particularly in the morning when they needed to wake up, but also as a 'kick' throughout the day. They didn't view tea as having any other role, preferring to move onto either water or Coca-Cola later in the day for a more refreshing drink.

Conversely, those who drank specialty teas often drank mainstream teas to wake them up in the morning. But some specialty tea drinkers went on to drink lighter teas (such as Earl Grey or Lady Grey) to 'refresh' or 'relax' themselves throughout the day, choosing tea instead of a cold drink to quench their thirst. Similarly, other specialty tea drinkers drank specialty teas during the day to enjoy experimenting with new tea flavours, such as a lemon tea in summer to cool them down or a chai tea in winter to warm them up.

Unlike mainstream tea drinkers, specialty tea drinkers recognised that tea is more than just a 'wake up' beverage – other specialty tea flavours can also be used throughout the day to satisfy other moods and occasions.

The company used this 'different teas for different moods' insight to segment and repackage its tea range into 'occasions' and 'moods' that people experience every day. They then developed a new advertising campaign for its specialty tea range, with the aim of introducing many new tea-drinking 'occasions' to mainstream tea drinkers and thereby encouraging them to try specialty teas.

The result?

This brand of tea has grown significantly in size over the last decade, with almost half of UK consumers now enjoying it as part of their repertoire.

A company that famously grew sales and market share over twenty years between 1993 and 2013 was Tesco. In part, this was due to the creation of bespoke sub-brands, designed to better meet the needs of discrete customer segments.

In 1993, at the height of the 1990s recession, Tesco was the first UK grocery retailer to launch a low-end 'Value' range for more price-conscious customers. Then in 1998, as the UK came out of recession, it was the first to launch a premium 'Finest' range for more discerning customers who were willing to pay more for freshness and provenance. These launches were so successful that by 2008, 'Tesco Finest' alone emerged as the UK's biggest grocery brand with sales of £1.2 billion, with 'Tesco Value' accounting for a further £1 billion.[3]

Delivering a personalised customer experience

A fourth business scenario illustrates how service-driven companies can use customer segmentations to deliver a superior customer experience every time the customer interacts with the brand – by identifying, where possible, which segment each customer belongs to and tailoring the service experience accordingly.

In these cases, service-driven companies have used attitudinal segmentations to:

- Target each customer with tailored direct marketing offers that they are likely to find appealing.
- Better predict, address and meet the needs of each customer when they call into the call centre.
- Train their sales force to adjust their sales style, language and which product and service offers to focus on, to match the needs of the customer segment they are talking with.

To illustrate, a financial services company successfully used customer segmentation to deliver a more personalised customer experience.

Its sales and call centre teams asked each customer and non-customer they talked with five questions, which categorised them into one of five segments. In tandem, the company trained financial advisors in how to use this same approach. They trained the sales and call centre teams and financial advisors to recognise 'who' each of the customer segments were and what each customer segment would be looking for, enabling them to tailor their questions, language and overall sales approach to each of their customer's individual needs.

For example, some customer segments wanted a more considered call centre experience, taking the time to talk through the pros and cons of all possible options before selecting which was right for them. In contrast, other customer segments wanted a more directional call centre experience, preferring a shorter conversation that led them to the one or two best options more quickly.

Similarly, a multi-branded B2B company ran a global customer segmentation to better understand the needs of its core customers. For instance, some of its customers were all about 'price' – preferring to buy from the manufacturer who offered good quality, low-priced products. Others prioritised 'convenience' – wanting reassurance that the products would be delivered quickly and on time. Others wanted 'basic products' – ones that were tried and true with no fancy add-ons. Others valued a 'business partnership' – preferring manufacturers who could give them the added support they needed to build a strong business. Once the company had identified the distinct needs of each of its customer segments, it trained its sales force to quickly assess which segment each of their customers belonged to, and tailor their sales approach to better meet each of their customer's needs, including which of the brands within the company portfolio to steer them towards.

One company that has publicly talked about using customer segmentation as a basis for delivering stronger customer propositions is Wolseley, the world's leading specialist distributor of plumbing and heating products. Group chief executive Ian Meakins stated, "Customer service is a key element to keeping customers happy for the long haul. And providing excellent customer service requires knowing your customers and how they want and need to be served. Across the group, we have basically found that there are fundamentally four to five different segments requiring different approaches to how to serve them."[4]

In the company's 2015 Annual Report, Meakins goes on to say, "We are continuing to roll-out new customer segmentation models to develop better targeted customer propositions than our competitors. This also enables us to better match our cost to serve customers – so a large national contractor that is often tendering for work may value competitive pricing whereas a local plumber doing regular repairs work may value immediate product availability over price."[5]

A drawback of this fourth scenario is that these segmentations rely on companies knowing which attitudinal segment each customer is in – when, in reality, companies often lack the attitudinal data needed to assign people to the appropriate segment, especially in the case of non-customers or new customers, for whom little data is known.

To mitigate this, companies should identify the five to ten attitudinal questions that most accurately predict which segment a person falls into, typically to a 75 percent to 80 percent accuracy level. Then, when interacting with a customer (be it in-store, when they call into the call centre or when a sales representative visits them) they can ask the customer these five to ten core attitudinal questions to define which segment they are in and record this on their customer database.

Over time, this segment allocation will slowly but surely build to a level that is actionable. To speed this up, companies can build an algorithm that allocates customers to segments by using the limited demographic or behavioural data that they have on each individual to best predict which segment they belong to. They can then update their 'best guess' as more data on that individual comes in, so that over time segment allocation becomes increasingly accurate and therefore predictive of an individual's behaviour.

Additionally, companies operating in the B2B space can incentivise their sales force to ask each of their customers the five to ten questions when meeting them. Similarly, companies in the business-to-consumer (B2C) space can send customers mail outs containing the five to ten questions, offering them a reward (such as entry into a free category draw) if they complete the questions.

So, now that we've looked at why Boards should consider investing in customer segmentation, let's look at how to create commercially actionable customer segmentations that Boards will buy into.

B: Selecting the optimal customer segmentation approach

When conducting customer segmentations, marketers need to start by selecting the optimal customer segmentation approach, based on the business issues that they are trying to resolve.

There are various ways to segment a market, each producing different types of customer segmentations that can be valuable in addressing differing business issues.

Using the ABCDE framework, customers can be segmented in five distinct ways:

Attitude

Attitudinal segmentations identify customer needs, desires and beliefs within a category, including what people are looking for when selecting which products or brands to buy and why, and thus which brands and products they prefer, as well as their preferred buying process.

These are typically used to identify which customers to focus on and how to capture most value, as they tend to best explain the underlying psychological reasons as to why customers behave as they do – and thus which products and services the company can offer to better meet their needs.

Behaviour

Behavioural segmentations typically focus on what the customer's relationship is with a brand; for instance, are they aware of it but have never thought to try it, or have they tried it once but never done so again, or are they a loyal user?

These are often used to identify the key differences between loyal users and non-users. For example, are there attitudinal or demographic differences that we can use to better identify those people who are most likely to buy our brand in the future, or do our loyal users have beliefs about the category or brand that we could use to convince non-users?

Channel

Channel segmentations typically focus on what people do when purchasing a category or brand, including which channels they prefer to use and what influences them when going through the purchase process.

These are often used to better identify the attitudinal and demographic differences of those who prefer to use one channel over another, for example, face-to-face versus online – as well as optimise the purchase process within each channel to better meet the needs of its priority segment, for example, the in-store layout, the on-shelf signage, the need for help and advice, and the role of promotions.

Demographics

Demographic segmentations typically focus on who the customer is, for example, in B2C categories, their age, sex, location and household structure, their life stage and lifestyle, and in B2B categories, which business type they are in, how big the company is and how long it's been in business for.

These are typically used to better define the brand's targeting, both in identifying any major differences in how different demographic groups view and shop the category or brand, as well as in helping the media agency better define which media types and programming to buy against in order to reach a specific demographic group.

Economics

Economic segmentations typically focus on what customers are worth to a brand or company; for example, how much of the category do they buy, how loyal are they to the brand, and how much does it cost to serve them?

These can be used to better identify those segments that will deliver the most profitable return for the brand and business in the future – as well as which existing customers are most profitable and should be the focus of future marketing and sales activity.

Thus, the first questions that marketers should ask are 'What is the business question that we're trying to solve?', 'What are the key differentiators in the market that are causing people to behave differently?' and then, 'What type of segmentation will best help us – Attitudinal, Behavioural, Channel, Demographic or Economic?'

C: Developing a commercially actionable segmentation

Once they've identified which type of customer segmentation to use, marketers need to develop a customer segmentation that is commercially actionable – namely, one that will help to resolve their business issues.

This is where companies often go wrong. We've probably all seen examples of customer segmentations that have ended up gathering dust on shelves, rather than being used day to day to drive business growth. This can be caused by a number of reasons – for example, the segmentation that has been developed is not commercially actionable, or people haven't understood how to interpret and implement it, or the segmentation hasn't 'stuck' over time.

To be commercially actionable, any attitudinal segmentation that is implemented needs to be both quantitatively robust and reflect the way consumers behave in the real world. Realistically, there is never a 'mathematically right' answer – therefore marketers need to apply both *science* and *art* when choosing which segmentation best suits their business needs. They should do this by adhering to five key rules:

1   It should be *statistically robust*, with each segment being:

- Of a reasonable size, with none so small that it's effectively irrelevant or difficult to analyse in more depth.
- Statistically stable, with each member of each segment being relatively similar to each other so that each segment has minimal statistical variation within, resulting in the majority of statistical variation explained by the differences between segments.

2   It should have *meaningful differences* in the types of products and services each segment prefers, in the way they shop the category and in the brands they are attracted to, and thus be commercially actionable. If there are no meaningful quantitative differences in the products, services, channels or brands that each segment prefers, the segmentation is not actionable, because it doesn't identify which segments will be most attracted to your brand, nor what products or services to offer the segment to better meet their needs, nor which channel to target them through. In essence, it can't help the company decide where to best focus its scarce resources for success.

3   It should be *linked with real-life economic data* to ensure that any segments chosen are both valuable and profitable. This analysis should assess the value of each customer segment to the company over time (based on trial, repurchase and loyalty rates) and then subtract the cost to attract and serve each segment, to determine their overall profitability. If the team does not take into account segment value and profitability when choosing which segment to focus on, then it cannot be certain that the company is focusing resources in the best way financially.

4   It should *make intuitive sense*, with frontline staff being able to easily recognise each of the segments in day-to-day life. If the segments are not identifiable in the real world, the segmentation is likely to fail because senior management and frontline employees will have difficulty remembering and buying into it. Additionally, it will be impossible to identify which segment real-life customers fall into – and therefore cannot be used to drive day-to-day business decision-making and frontline behaviour.

5   Where relevant, it should be *actionable globally*, with each country being able to size each of the segments and work through the 'so whats' for their individual market. If each country has its own individual segmentation solution, senior management are unlikely to remember it and more importantly use it for global decision-making. In reality, remembering ten global segments is manageable, but trying to recall ten from India, ten from the UK, ten from France and ten from China, with all segments being completely different from each other, is nigh on impossible. Additionally, a global segmentation solution can reveal where major country differences lie and consequently why two markets might behave very differently.

Before selecting which attitudinal segmentation solution to adopt, it's essential to review the segments in-depth – both quantitatively to ensure they are robust, contain meaningful product, service, channel and brand differences and can be valued economically, as well as qualitatively to ensure they exist and are identifiable in the real world.

Additionally, before finalising the solution, it's important to work through at a high level what it means for each brand to ensure that the results coming out are credible and actionable.

For instance, when we created a segmentation solution for a financial services company, the more we delved into one of the segments, the more we realised that it wasn't cohesive as a recognisable customer group. By analysing the segment further, it became clear that it combined two distinct groups of people. Both liked to delegate decision-making to a third party due to a lack of category involvement and interest. However, one group saved responsibly whereas the other 'lived for today', saving as little as possible. By doing this deeper analysis, we realised that we needed to move to a new segmentation solution that pulled the two segments apart.

D: Choosing where to play

Once the optimal customer segmentation solution is chosen, the next stage is to identify what it means for the business. To achieve this, marketers should identify the sweet spot between what customers want, and what the company's brands are known for and can deliver.

For example, when assessing which customer segments the company should focus on – and crucially not focus on – the marketing team is likely to use the customer segmentation to review:

- Who the different customer segments are – for example, what is their demographic profile, what are their needs and behaviours, and what differentiates them from the other customer segments?
- Where each of its brands plays today – for example, which is its core customer segment and which other customer segments is it also playing in?
- How strong each of its brands is within its core segment – for example, is it the number one brand within this segment, or are there stronger competitors?
- Which customer segment or segments each brand should play in, in the future – by assessing which customer segments are most attracted to the brand today, which are likely to be attracted to the brand in the future given any planned product or service launches, and which can be served profitably?
- What it would take to strengthen each brand amongst its most valuable customer segments – for example, how should each brand be positioned

to attract them, and what new products and services could be launched to better meet their needs?

To get Board buy-in, the team should take the Board through the answers to these questions, bringing the customer segmentation solution and a clear picture of each customer segment to life.

Once the customer segments are agreed, the customer segmentation can then be used to help the Board 'optimise the brand portfolio' and 'position brands for growth' – strategies we will look in greater depth in Chapters 5 and 6 respectively.

E: Bringing the segmentation to life

Once the marketing team is clear about which customer segments to focus on, it needs to get business buy-in, starting from the top to ensure that senior management is on-board with using the segmentation as a day-to-day decision-making tool, and to the recommendations that are being proposed.

To make this happen, the marketing team should present the overall customer segmentation to senior management, as well as bring each segment to life in a way that is:

- *Clear*, in terms of the analysis and recommendations, and what this means for the business.
- *Succinct*, with the customer segmentation analysis and 'so whats' summarised on one page.
- *Robust*, demonstrating the compelling fact base that the segmentation is built on.
- *Jargon-free*, using commercial and customer language, rather than marketing jargon.
- *Intuitive*, bringing each of the individual customer segments to life, to enable the Board to really understand their needs.

Ideally, the customer segmentation should be easy-to-understand and memorable, so that all Board members and cross-functional teams can understand it, buy into it and use it day to day. To achieve this, the marketing team should plot the customer segmentation on one page – thereby making it easy to visualise and remember, using:

- A memorable number of core (or primary) segments, ideally no more than seven – the maximum number of items that the short-term memory is said to be able to hold at any one time. If more segments are needed, then the core segments should be grouped into a manageable number at the higher level, with each group then broken down into a memorable number of sub-segments.

- Succinct, relevant and memorable segment names (ideally one word) that summarise *how* the individual segments think and behave, so that they are easy to use as part of everyday, business vernacular.
- A two-dimensional framework, containing the two dimensions that best describe *why* the segments think and behave differently.

Two dimensions that can be used in many categories to differentiate people are (i) people's desire for advice (with some preferring to make their own decisions and others wanting to delegate) and (ii) how involved they are with the category (with some being highly involved and others less so).

For example, within the wine category, four high-level segments can be plotted along these two dimensions, with each occupying one of the four quadrants, and each with a succinct name that captures the essence of what is different about them, making them easy to remember (see Figure 4.1).

For example, 'Enthusiasts' and 'Aspirers' are both highly involved in the category – enjoying both drinking wines that they know and experimenting with new wines. 'Enthusiasts' are fairly knowledgeable about wine and so prefer to do their own research and make their own decisions – by reading wine publications and wine reviews, belonging to wine clubs and shopping at specialist discount wine stores. 'Aspirers' are further down the learning curve, enjoying the process of learning about wines – and so refer to restaurant wine lists for ideas and high end specialist wine stores for advice.

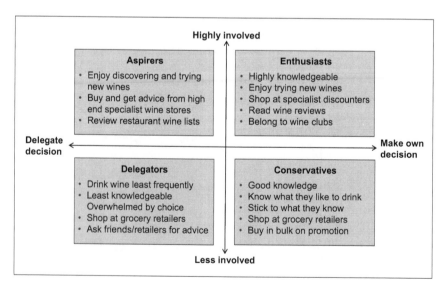

Figure 4.1 High-level wine customer segmentation example

In contrast, 'Conservatives' and 'Delegators' are less involved in the category – and so tend to enjoy a more limited repertoire of wines. 'Conservatives' have a good knowledge of wine, knowing what they like to drink and sticking with what they know – and so they tend to buy the wines that they know and love when doing their grocery shop, and buying in bulk when they are on promotion. 'Delegators' drink wine least frequently of any of the segments, and so are the least knowledgeable about wine. They tend to be overwhelmed by the high level of choice, and so buy tried and trusted wine recommended by their friends and family, or by the friendly person at the wine counter, when doing their grocery shop.

Another example from the food category uses two primary dimensions that segment people into different types of eating behaviour, namely:

- People's primary preference for convenience, health or taste.
- Whether there are children in the household.

In this example, time-starved parents (or 'Fixers') typically resort to frozen foods that can be cooked within twenty minutes, such as pizza, or fish fingers and chips. Parents who are more health-oriented but still time-starved ('Fuellers') might use cooking sauces along with fresh meat and vegetables as a faster way to cook a more nourishing and balanced meal for their children. Parents who are more taste-and health-driven rather than convenience driven ('Nurturers') might take the time to cook tasty, wholesome meals from scratch.

Conversely, time-starved singles (or 'Satisfiers') might focus on takeaways, ready meals and one-pot snacks as their main diet; health-oriented older couples ('Balancers') might ensure that they eat a healthy meal together each evening, such as marinated chicken and salad; while more taste-oriented couples ('Connoisseurs') might enjoy a good steak (see Figure 4.2).

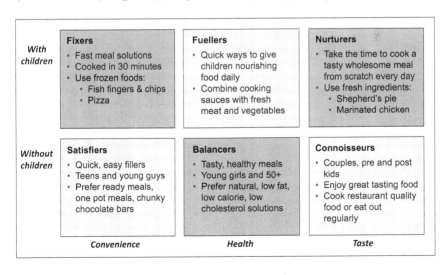

Figure 4.2 High-level food customer segmentation example

Once the customer segmentation is agreed, it should be rolled out across all cross-functional teams that need to understand and action it.

For example, sales and call centre people should be trained to quickly identify which segment each customer is in and how to adapt their communication and behaviour to best meet the customer's needs. Likewise, the innovation team should be trained in what each customer segment is looking for, helping them develop innovative products and services that each segment will love. Similarly, the customer loyalty team should be trained in the types of product offers, communication messages and media vehicles that are most likely to resonate with each group, to enable the team to develop more tailored loyalty packages.

It's helpful for each person in the company to be given a one-page segmentation summary that they can access easily and use on a day-to-day basis to help build their knowledge; for instance, this might be a laminated sheet that they can either put on their wall or in the top drawer of their desk, an online tool, or customer segment posters or rooms that bring each segment to life.

In summary

When done well, customer segmentation is an incredibly powerful tool, yielding valuable insight that helps solve business problems and transform company growth.

It does this by helping companies decide 'who' to target and 'how' to target them. For example:

- *Where to focus scarce resources* by identifying which customers generate the most value now and which are likely to generate the most value in the future.
- *How to capture this value* by identifying what these customers are looking for and what they need to be offered *over and above* competitors to encourage them to switch, so that the company can capture more than its fair share of business.

When conducting customer segmentation, it's important to ensure that the customer segmentation:

- *Uses the right segmentation approach* – to achieve this, marketers should ask: 'What is the business question that we're trying to resolve?' followed by 'Which type of segmentation will best help us resolve it – attitudinal, behavioural, channel, demographics or economic?'
- *Is commercially actionable* – by being statistically robust, by showing meaningful commercial differences in the types of products and services each

segment prefers, by being linked with real-life economic data to identify how valuable and profitable each segment is, by making intuitive sense in the real world, and by being actionable globally.

- *Helps choose where to play* – by identifying the sweet spot between what customers want and what the company's brands are known for and can deliver.
- *Is brought to life* – by containing a memorable number of core segments, each with succinct, relevant and memorable names, and visualising these on one page along the two dimensions that best describe why the segments think and behave differently.

It can be used as the foundation for resolving a myriad of business issues – including 'Optimising a brand portfolio' and 'Positioning brands for growth', which we will look at in more depth in Chapters 5 and 6 respectively.

Notes

1 Prophet, *www.prophet.com*, March 2016.
2 Joe Lazauskas, "How Electrolux's CMO Unified Her Global Marketing Efforts through Content," January 2016, https://contently.com/strategist/2016/01/29/how-electroluxs-cmo-unified-her-global-marketing-efforts-through-content/, accessed October 2016.
3 Zoe Wood, "Tesco Rebrands Value Range," *The Guardian*, April 2012, https://www.theguardian.com/business/2012/apr/04/tesco-rebrands-value-range, accessed October 2016; Simon Neville, "Tesco Revamps Finest," *The Independent*, October 2013, http://www.independent.co.uk/news/business/news/tesco-revamps-finest-range-in-bid-to-win-back-customers-8865166.html, accessed October 2016; Jemima Bokaie, "Tesco Finest Hits £1.2bn Sales to Become Top Grocery Brand," *Campaign*, April 2008, http://www.campaignlive.co.uk/article/803672/tesco-finest-hits-12bn-sales-become-top-grocery-brand, accessed October 2016.
4 Jenel Stelton-Holtmeier, "Wolseley's Customer Segmentation Strategy," *MDM*, September 2015, http://www.mdm.com/blogs/14-distribution-sales-marketing/post/34422-wolseleys-customer-segmentation-strategy, accessed October 2016.
5 Wolseley's Annual Report, 2015, http://www.wolseley.com/files/pdf/reports/annualreport/WOS-AR-2015.pdf.

Bibliography

Bokaie, Jemima. "Tesco Finest Hits £1.2bn Sales to Become Top Grocery Brand." *Campaign*, April 2008. Accessed October 2016. www.campaignlive.co.uk/article/803672/tesco-finest-hits-12bn-sales-become-top-grocery-brand.

Lazauskas, Joe. "How Electrolux's CMO Unified Her Global Marketing Efforts through Content." January 2016. Accessed October 2016. https://contently.com/strategist/2016/01/29/how-electroluxs-cmo-unified-her-global-marketing-efforts-through-content/.

Neville, Simon. "Tesco Revamps Finest." *The Independent*, October 2013. Accessed October 2016. www.independent.co.uk/news/business/news/tesco-revamps-finest-range-in-bid-to-win-back-customers-8865166.html.

Prophet. *www.prophet.com*, March 2016.

Stelton-Holtmeier, Jenel. "Wolseley's Customer Segmentation Strategy." *MDM*, September 2015. Accessed October 2016. www.mdm.com/blogs/14-distribution-sales-marketing/post/34422-wolseleys-customer-segmentation-strategy.

Wolseley's Annual Report. 2015. www.wolseley.com/files/pdf/reports/annualreport/WOS-AR-2015.pdf.

Wood, Zoe. "Tesco Rebrands Value Range." *The Guardian*, April 2012. Accessed October 2016. www.theguardian.com/business/2012/apr/04/tesco-rebrands-value-range.

Chapter 5

Choosing 'what' to support

"Say no to everything, so you can say yes to the one thing."
Richie Norton, *The Power of Starting Something Stupid*

At the end of the twentieth century, Boards believed that the more brands they had, the more their company would grow, with brand proliferation rife.

Between 1997 and 2001, figures show that the number of brands in the pharmaceutical industry increased by 79 percent, in white goods and travel and leisure by 60 percent, in the automotive industry by 46 percent and in food, household goods and beverages by at least 15 percent.[1]

Today, however, it's a different story.

Many Boards have since realised that this strategy was wrong and that the majority of company profit is generated by a small number of brands and products – reflecting the 'Pareto Principle' or '80–20 rule', where 'roughly 80% of the effects come from 20% of the causes'.

In response, many CEOs and Boards have done an about-turn, increasingly reducing complexity by choosing which brands and products to support for growth, based on those that deliver the greatest return for the company today, as well as those that are likely to grow and therefore be important for the future.

To quote Mark Gottfredson at Bain & Company: "A truly focused company – one that has cut complexity to the minimum – does not invest to win in every element of its business. It invests primarily in its core, the business in which it can outperform everybody else."[2]

In this chapter, we look at why it is important to engage the Board in choosing which brands and products to support, and we review marketing strategies that in recent years have increasingly interested Boards in their drive for growth through reduced complexity, by addressing:

A   Why choosing 'what' to support is important to the Board.
B   Prioritising which brands and products to focus on:

- A commercial view.
- A consumer view.

C   Considering whether to migrate to one brand.

A: Why choosing 'what' to support is important to the Board

Why fewer and bigger is better

Many companies earn the majority share of their profits from just a small number of brands – some as much as 80 percent to 90 percent of their profits from fewer than 20 percent of their brands – while they lose money or barely break even on many of the other brands in their portfolios.

Take Diageo, the world's largest spirits company. In 1999, eight (or 23 percent) of Diageo's thirty-five brands accounted for half of its sales and 70 percent of its profits.

Of Nestlé's eight thousand brands, the majority of its 1996 profits came from a mere two hundred (or 2.5 percent) of them.

Between 1992 and 2002, Procter & Gamble's ten biggest brands – a mere 4 percent of the company's total portfolio of over 250 brands – accounted for half of the company's sales, more than half of its profits, and 66 percent of its sales growth.

Similarly, more than 90 percent of Unilever's profits in 1999 came from four hundred (or 25 percent) of its 1,600 brands, with most of the other 1,200 brands either making losses or, at best, marginal profits.[3]

As A. J. Lafley, P&G's chief executive officer, said, "In retail the 80/20 rule normally applies, with 20% of the brands and products accounting for 80% of the sales."[4]

Understandably, the operational complexity and cost of running and supporting each additional brand is high. So, given that a small number of brands drive a high percentage of sales and profitability, it's not surprising that many companies have optimised company return by streamlining the number of brands in their portfolio.

For instance, in 1999, Unilever announced its 'Path to Growth' strategy. When Niall FitzGerald became co-chairman of Unilever in 1996, he commented on Unilever's attention being spread too thinly: "We weren't able to focus our innovation, our support – we were doing too many things and we had too many people."[5] Around that time, Unilever had acquired Bestfoods, with brands such as Hellmann's mayonnaise, Skippy peanut butter and Knorr soups swelling its brand portfolio to more than 1,600.

The management team decided that it would make higher profits if it focused on fewer, stronger brands to promote faster growth. So, just over a year later, Unilever had reduced its brand portfolio from 1,600 to 970 brands – with a further three hundred identified for 'delisting' and two hundred for 'merger and migration' – and had focused 94 percent of its advertising budget on its four hundred 'focus' brands. Since then, it has continued to consolidate, retaining a portfolio of around four hundred brands with a focus on its priority ones, thirteen of which now have global annual sales of more than €1 billion each.

In 2008, Hans Wohmann, P&G's Regional Manager for Asia-Pacific & Latin America, declared that "Our strategy has long been to focus on our big brands. Companies like us are interested in building classics and investing long-term." He went on to say, "fewer, bigger, better, remains the right thing to do."[6]

By 2014, P&G had reduced its brand portfolio from more than 250 brands to around 160. Then, by mid-2015, P&G divested a further ninety-three brands – collectively accounting for only 10 percent of P&G's total sales and less than 5 percent of its profits – leaving a portfolio of less than sixty-five brands to focus on.[7]

When analysts and reporters asked why P&G was doing this, Lafley replied, "This new streamlined P&G should continue to grow faster and more sustainably, and reliably create more value" – and it would make P&G "a much simpler, much less complex company of leading brands that's easier to manage and operate."[8]

In 2000, Reckitt Benckiser, the multinational consumer goods company, sold off more than a third of its non-core brands to focus on its core brands within household cleaning and health and personal care. Yet, the following year's sales increased by 6 percent and operating profits by 14 percent. Reckitt Benckiser's CEO, Bert Bech, commented, "2001 was a very good year for Reckitt Benckiser . . . By focusing on our growth strategy, increasing our rate of innovation and investing heavily behind our core brands we are gaining market share and delivering consistent growth."[9]

This focus on complexity reduction has also been prevalent outside of fast-moving consumer goods.

For instance, when Alan Mulally became CEO of the Ford Motor Company in 2006, he found himself at the helm of a company that was drowning in complexity.

By reversing its strategy to compete in every major segment within the automotive industry, Mulally reduced the company's complexity by cutting the number of brands it offered from eight to two, Ford and Lincoln, and the number of models it produced. This brand and product reduction was one of the catalysts spurring Ford's subsequent turnaround, resulting in a reversal of a $2 billion operating loss in 2007 to an impressive $20 billion profit in 2011. As John Felice, a Ford executive, told *Detroit Free Press* in 2010, "One of the things we realised is we just had too much complexity."[10]

Another example is the rationalisation of Electrolux's brand portfolio within the professional food service equipment market. In 1996, the company had fifteen brands in this market – mostly acquired when buying up local rivals. By 2001, it had just four pan-European brands – three of which already existed and one of which was new – each of which targeted a distinct customer segment: 'Basic', 'Performance', 'Gastronomy' and 'Prestige'. The resultant economies of scale helped to turn the business around. Although Electrolux deleted twelve brands, the division's sales never fell and it reported a profit of $37 million in 2001, up from an operating loss of around $8 million in 1996.[11]

This rule isn't just true for brands – It's true for products as well

In the 1990s, after decades of spinning out different variants of 'new and improved' this, 'lemon fresh that' and 'extra jumbo the other', P&G decided that enough was enough. By 1997, its product roster was a third lighter than it had been in 1990, with the number of products in its hair care range nearly slashed in half.

Intuitively, marketers are likely to be concerned that fewer products will mean that some customers will be unhappy at not being able to buy the product they want, triggering a decline in sales. Yet interestingly, over the same period, P&G's market share of the hair care market increased by five percentage points, reflecting a theory championed by Lafley that "giving consumers too many choices can hurt rather than boost sales."[12]

Since then, P&G has further simplified its global operations. In December 2010, P&G announced that it was "building a culture focused on simplifying our business and the processes that support it while simultaneously driving improved productivity – all designed to increase agility, reduce costs and free up resources for innovation and expansion."[13] This has resulted in fewer, more standardised products and packaging, innovations being rolled out across multiple brands and fewer new product launches, as was illustrated in December 2015 when P&G announced that it had eliminated a sixth of its Olay products, ones that didn't fit with the brand's anti-ageing message or weren't selling well.[14]

Many other successful companies both within and outside of fast-moving consumer goods have followed a similar path, choosing to reduce the size of their product portfolios.

In 2010, Unilever reduced its ranges by eliminating 1,200 stock keeping units (SKUs) as part of its bid to prioritise top sellers, cut its long tail, reduce supply chain overstocks and waste, and increase factory efficiency.[15] Then, in 2013, Unilever announced that it was pruning its product portfolio by up to 40 percent by the end of 2014, with the aim of driving down costs and in turn boosting operating margins.[16]

When facing fierce competition, a European supermarket chain responded by offering its customers more product choice and deeper price promotions. But this didn't work. Instead, the CEO was forced to reverse the company strategy – making it easier for its customers to find the right products – by eliminating many of the brands and SKUs that it stocked in-store (the latter by 40 percent) and initiating everyday low pricing. The result was an impressive drop in overhead costs and inventory days (the latter by 60 percent) and a 25 percent increase in revenues.[17]

Similarly in January 2015, Tesco announced that it was pulling up to a third of products off its shelves as "shoppers are left baffled by a choice of up to 90,000 products on their weekly shop," including "a bewildering array of 28 tomato ketchup SKUs". According to Dave Lewis, Tesco's CEO, doing so would enable Tesco to "cut prices, make shopping easier and improve on-shelf availability".[18]

B: Prioritising which brands and products to focus on

As with large brand portfolios, the cost of supporting all brands and products is high, particularly if *all* are being supported with the expectation of growth. Some brands and products are likely to deliver more return than others – and some customer segments are likely to be more valuable than others.

Therefore, it's vital that marketers focus their scarce resources on supporting those brands, products and customer segments that will deliver the highest returns for the company today – that is, those that account for a high level of today's sales or margin – as well as those that are likely to deliver the highest returns in the future.

Weaker performing brands and products should either be supported for maintenance rather than growth, or delisted or divested. By rationalising their brand and product portfolios, Boards can then concentrate their finite resources on growing fewer, bigger, more successful brands with less confusing product portfolios and a company structure that is easier and less costly to manage day to day.

To engage the Board in selecting which brands, products and customer segments to focus on, marketers should look at the issue from two perspectives – the commercial lens and the consumer lens.

Let's see how this can be done.

A commercial view: The five-stage portfolio prioritisation process

Portfolio mapping can be used to map the contribution that each brand, product and customer segment delivers to the company today, and what each is predicted to contribute in the future.

When done well, it helps to identify which brands, products and customer segments are likely to generate the highest return today, and over the next three to five years. This enables Boards to more confidently prioritise their scarce resources – most notably their sales, innovation and communications spend – on those areas that they believe will deliver the highest returns.

As outlined in previous chapters, Boards resonate with marketing strategies that are:

- *Clear*, in what they are recommending and why this makes sense for the Board to consider.
- *Succinct*, showing the recommendations in a one-page storyline and the analysis in a one-page framework.
- *Robust*, supported with a compelling fact base that builds the Board's confidence.
- *Jargon-free*, using the Board's language rather than marketing jargon to make the case.
- *Intuitive*, in what is being recommended and why this is good for the business.

With this in mind, the Five-Stage Portfolio Prioritisation Process is an effective way to engage the Board in assessing which brands and products to prioritise, using the following five steps:

- *Step 1*: Quantify the sales and profitability that each brand, product and customer segment contributes today.
- *Step 2*: Quantify the sales and profitability that each might contribute in three to five years' time.
- *Step 3*: Prioritise which brands, products and customer segments to focus spend on.
- *Step 4*: Assess how much of today's spend is allocated to these priority brands, products and customer segments.
- *Step 5*: Reallocate spend across the portfolio as required.

Let's look at this five-stage approach in more detail.

1   The first step in portfolio mapping is to assess which brands, products and customer segments generate the most sales and profit today. Figure 5.1 illustrates an example showing brand contribution by customer

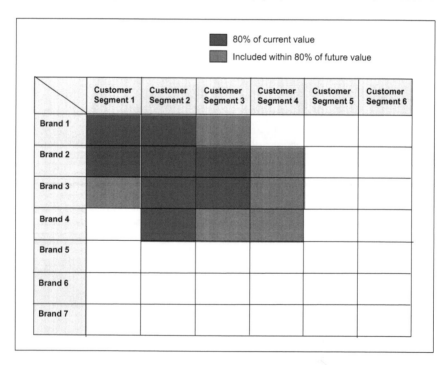

Figure 5.1 Example of brand versus customer segment portfolio mapping

segment. In this example, the team quantified the sales and profit that each brand and customer segment contributed. So, for example, how much sales and profit did Brand 1 contribute overall, and how did this break down for each of the customer segments? Similarly, how much sales and profit did Brand 2 contribute, overall and by customer segment? By doing this, the team was able to identify which brands and customer segments contributed most to today's business success and thus needed to be invested in.

2   The second step is to predict which brands, products or customer segments might generate the most sales and profit in three to five years' time, based on an analysis of future trends. This analysis should include anything that might affect the future category landscape, such as changes in consumer behaviour, technology, channels and competitor intervention. In this way, the team can identify which brands, products and customer segments may be important for future business success – and therefore should also be invested in going forward – as shown in Figure 5.1.

3   The third step is to prioritise spend. Obviously, some level of spend will be needed to support each brand and product in the portfolio. But the majority of spend should be focused on those brands, products and customer segments that make up 80 percent of the current and future business value. Given the '80–20 Pareto Principle', this typically accounts for a fraction of the total company portfolio. As Figure 5.1 illustrates in a real-life case study example, eight out of forty-two cells accounted for 80 percent of the current business value, and a further six were expected to be an important part of future business value.

4   The fourth step is to determine how much of today's communication and innovation spend is focused on these most valuable brands, products and customer segments. In theory, this may sound easy to do, but in practice getting accurate numbers can be difficult. However, even an approximate 'back of the envelope' audit of where today's spend is focused is likely to prove invaluable in revealing those resources that are being wasted today and could be repurposed for greater return.

5   The fifth step is to reallocate spend across the portfolio – away from the less valuable brands, products and customer segments – to those that are more valuable, namely those that make up 80 percent of current and future business value. When defining 'who' to focus spend on, marketers may have to use the more demographic-based customer segmentations that media buying companies typically use as a proxy for the attitudinal customer segments that are most attracted to the company's brands and products.

To make this analysis easy for the Board to understand and buy into, it should be presented on one page, similar to the example shown in Figure 5.1.

Marketers can then determine which brands, products and customer segments they should prioritise and, more importantly, deprioritise. To achieve this, they should assess where to:

- *Invest more than their fair share for growth*, by investing in those brands, products and customer segments that are both important for current and future business growth.
- *Invest in line with market share for maintenance*, by investing in those brands, products and customer segments that are unlikely to grow significantly but are important as they account for a high level of today's sales and profit.
- *Invest selectively* by testing ways to create future growth, for example, by investing in those brands, products and customer segments that could generate significant return, but are as yet unproven.
- *Stop investing*, due to lack of critical mass today and lack of future potential, thereby freeing up funds to better support the priority growth areas.

The recommendations can be summarised in a one page Investment Prioritisation Matrix, similar to the one shown in Figure 5.2.

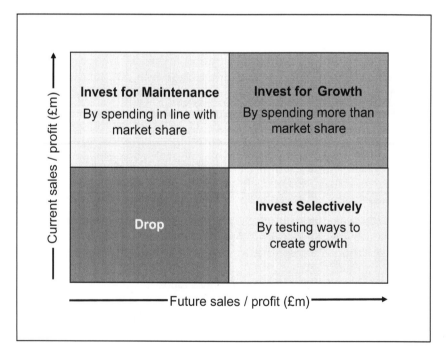

Figure 5.2 Investment Prioritisation Matrix

To illustrate, let's look at a real-life case study in which a business-to-business company mapped the current and future value of its seven brands and six priority customer segments – as shown in Figure 5.1. In doing so, it realised that two of its brands (Brands 1 and 2) and one of its priority customer segments (Customer Segment 2) were key to its current business success, yet only one-third of the company's sales and marketing spend was allocated to these brands and segments today. Looking forward, two additional brands (Brands 3 and 4) would become increasingly important to future business growth, yet more of the company's communications spend was focused on its other three less important brands (Brands 5, 6 and 7).

The company took the brave decision to move spend away from its non-priority products and customer segments – with the aim of giving them just enough spend to maintain their sales over time – and to reallocate this spend against the products and customer segments that were key to its current and future performance. As a result, the Board was better able to focus its resources on those areas that were likely to deliver steady, sustainable growth – which became an analysis that they conducted annually to help maintain the growth momentum.

A consumer view: Brand portfolio optimisation

When optimising a company's brand and product portfolio, it's also important to assess the issue through the consumer's eyes – namely which brands are successfully meeting their needs and resonating well and thus are most likely to drive future growth.

Brand Portfolio Optimisation is an effective way to identify the optimal number of brands a company should have within a category, with the aim of maximising market coverage while minimising brand overlap. Where possible, redundant or unprofitable brands should be eliminated and successful brands repositioned and stretched to take their place.

To achieve this, the marketing team should start with an attitudinal customer segmentation ideally grouped around two discriminating dimensions – such as those outlined in Chapter 4 and shown in Figure 5.3 – namely 'level of category involvement' and 'desire to make their own decision'. These can help to identify how many different types of customer segments there are with differing attitudes and needs that may require different brands.

When reviewing this, the marketing team should address a number of questions. For example, from a customer perspective, which customer segments are key? How are they different to each other, both demographically and behaviourally? How different are their needs? What drives their purchase behaviour, both overall and across the different product types?

From a brand perspective, can one brand stretch across the whole market to service all of their needs? Or do some segments require a different brand, either because they reject some of the brands in the market or because they are looking for a brand that stands for something specific?

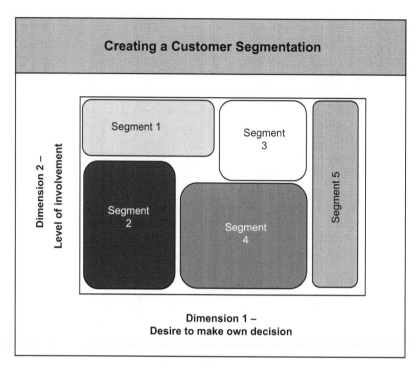

Figure 5.3 Creating a customer segmentation

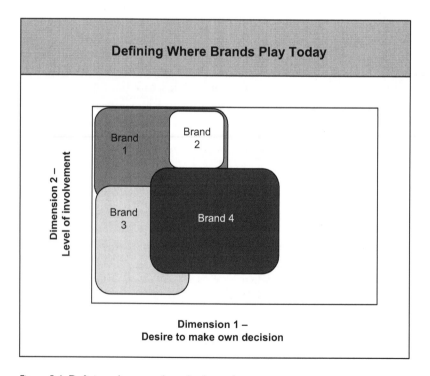

Figure 5.4 Defining where our brands play today

Once the customer segmentation is developed, it can be used to identify where the company's brands play today, as shown in Figure 5.4.

For example, where do our brands sit on the brand portfolio map? Are they on top of each other or spread out? Which customer segments use them and why? What does each brand stand for? Is it tapping into distinct customer needs?

How strong is each of the brands among its target audience – for example, how many of them are aware of the brand, or would consider it, or have tried it or are loyal to it?

How distinctive is each of the brands in terms of brand image? For example, what does each brand stand for, and how appealing, credible and distinctive is this? Who are the brand's true competitors – and is any brand particularly strong at containing a key competitor?

Once this is done, the marketing team needs to identify where future growth is most likely to come from. For example, which future technologies, customer segments, usage occasions and purchase channels are likely to grow most in the future? Which brands can best support these high-growth products, technologies and customer segments?

Next, it should assess how to best reposition the brands to tap into these trends (Figure 5.5). For example, are there brands that are on top of each other that are meeting similar customer needs and therefore can be merged?

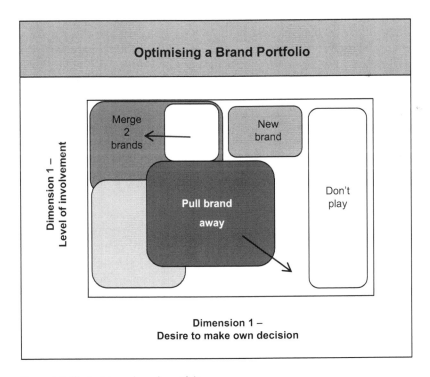

Figure 5.5 Optimising a brand portfolio

Or are there overlapping brands that are meeting different customer needs and therefore need to be pulled apart? Are there brands that are playing in an increasingly declining market that should be deprioritised? Or are there gaps that we could successfully fill?

By carrying out a robust segmentation analysis, marketers can demonstrate:

- Which brands to focus scarce resources on (both money and time) to drive both current and future growth.
- Which brands to support for maintenance by investing in line with market share, given that they have lower growth potential.
- Which brands to merge (due to their similar business profile), milk (due to their strong profitability but low growth profile), divest (due to being non-core), or kill (due to their future business performance expected to be poor) – thus enabling company resources to be focused on growing fewer, bigger brands.

This in turn helps to convince the Board why it makes commercial sense to proceed.

Optimising a company's brand architecture

As a company moves to fewer, bigger brands, optimising each brand's architecture becomes increasingly important.

A cohesive brand architecture helps consumers make sense of the brand portfolio, thereby making it as easy as possible for them to find the right product. Additionally, it helps to extend a brand across as many adjacent product categories as possible, increasing the effectiveness of every pound spent on advertising.

There are a number of levels that marketers need to consider when optimising their brand architecture, as shown in Figure 5.6. These include:

- *The Corporate brand* – the brand that is used when talking about the company as a whole, most frequently with employees, business partners, journalists and investors. Strong corporate brands have strong corporate brand propositions that are:
  - *True* to what the whole company does, reflecting how it is unique and distinctive to both the market as a whole and its competitors.
  - *Aspirational*, inspiring people to 'realise' a bold, exciting, innovative future vision.
  - *Appealing*, making life better for its customers day to day.
  - *Own-able*, so that anybody who reads it can recognise which company is being referred to.
  - *Inspirational*, building internal belief and pride in 'who we are' and 'what we do'.

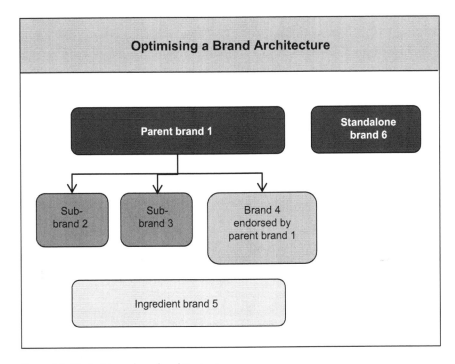

Figure 5.6 Optimising a brand architecture

An example of a strong corporate brand is Mondelez International, the confectionery division of Kraft Foods, with its "dream to create delicious moments of joy".[19]

- *The Parent brand* – the brand the company focuses its spend on in order to build credibility with consumers, as well as build an own-able property. The parent brand proposition should be:
  - *Relevant*, to a sizeable group of customers.
  - *Appealing*, meeting a real customer need.
  - *Distinctive*, demonstrating what the brand gives consumers over and above competitors.
  - *Credible*, given the brand's history and their perceived future capabilities.

An example of a strong parent brand is Cadbury, which operates within Mondelez International, with its "Promise of quality and commitment to continuous improvement".[20]

- *The Sub-brand* – the name that makes it easy for a customer to find the right range for them. This isn't a brand as such, more a sub-brand name or signpost that helps the customer identify the product range they're looking for, be it the more premium range (e.g., Excel, Advanced, Finest) or lower cost range (e.g., Economy, Value), the benefit that the product delivers (e.g., Luminesse, Radiance), who the product is for (e.g., consumer versus business) or the category in which the product is playing (e.g., iPod versus iPhone, hair colorant versus skincare).

It's important for the sub-brand to be:

- *Descriptive* of what the sub-range actually does, to help customers more quickly identify which product they should buy.
- *Distinctive*, so that it's more than just a variant name.
- *Meaningful*, addressing a large enough need to warrant a sub-brand of its own.

An example of a strong sub-brand within Cadbury is Dairy Milk.

- *The Variant name* – the name that helps the consumer select the right variant within the sub-brand that is most suitable for them. This is not a brand, more a descriptive name to make the purchase decision easier for the customer, for example, Cheese & Owen and Salt & Lineker crisps, or Shiny & Smooth versus Repair & Protect shampoo.

  An example of a strong sub-brand within Cadbury Dairy Milk is Bubbly, Caramel or Whole Nut.

- Finally, there may be an *Ingredient brand* that refers to additional technology, ingredients or expertise that is included in the range to make it superior to competitors – for example, Pantene Pro-V or Apple's Genius Bar.

  Examples of strong ingredient brands within Cadbury Dairy Milk are the much-loved Oreo or Daim Bar ingredient additions.

To optimise a brand's architecture, marketers should address questions such as:

- Should the corporate and parent brand be the same, or should we distance the corporate brand from the parent brand to minimise business risk?
- Do we need multiple parent brands to attract different customer segments, or to play in different distributor channels or at different price points?
- Is there a need for sub-brands and, if so, why and how many?
- How many distinct variants do we need to address the distinct needs of our customers?
- Is there a role and need for an ingredient brand to convey our superiority?

C: Considering whether to migrate to one brand

The ultimate Board-level question of any brand portfolio optimisation project is whether to migrate all (or most) of the existing brands within a company to one global brand.

Over the past thirty years, this topic has become more prevalent in the boardroom, in part because of the increase in merger and acquisition activity, but also because of the desire for more global synergies and the growth in brand asset value.

Mergers and acquisitions cause Boards to reassess how to assimilate the newly acquired brands into their existing brand portfolio, with the aim of driving out costs and creating growth.

The need for global synergies compels Boards to break down internal silos to eliminate duplicative costs and encourage greater levels of internal best practice sharing.

Additionally, the growth in brand asset value is not to be ignored – in 2015, Millward Brown's BrandZ's report valued global brands such as Apple at $247 billion, Google at $174 billion and Coca Cola at $84 billion.[21]

Making the brand migration case

Selling products and services under one global brand is obviously the most efficient way to go to market, as the company has only to pay the costs of supporting and running one brand worldwide. But, in reality, making the case to migrate to one global brand can be tough. It's likely to cost a significant amount of money that, most probably, will not deliver an immediate payback with few customers endorsing such a move in market research.

Take, for instance, the rebranding of Paine Webber and S.G. Warburg – two large, distinguished international financial services companies that had been acquired by UBS and were rebranded into the UBS stable in 2003.

While UBS was a sizeable, respected bank in its European heartland, its top-of-mind awareness was relatively low among international customers – particularly among corporate clients, wealthy individuals and institutions in the United States.

Paine Webber and S.G. Warburg, on the other hand, were two renowned and highly respected heritage brands in their local markets.

In situations like this, making the business case for such change can be hard to justify. To make the 'UBS' brand as strong as 'Paine Webber' and 'S.G. Warburg' combined – with all the top-of-mind awareness, brand strength and rich imagery they both enjoy – would undoubtedly take considerable money, resources and time, for no immediate or tangible reward. Similarly, customers will be mystified as to *why* a strong brand such as S.G. Warburg would even think of getting rid of its name to replace it with one that they've never heard of.

So, why should a company consider moving to one global brand?

In today's world of increasing globalisation, companies appear to be using brands to create growth in one of two ways – by being exceptionally locally tailored to meet distinct local needs or by being globally aligned to maximise global synergies. Let's look at some examples.

Model 1: Increasing local tailorisation

Some companies create growth by retaining a portfolio of bespoke local brands that resonate strongly with local customers – brands that are counter to the globalisation trend by being truly flexible to local needs.

Take Royal Sun Alliance or SAB Miller; their global brand portfolios are mostly made up of many locally based brands. For example, Royal Sun Alliance uses its RSA brand in some parts of the world, but uses well-known local brands, such as Codan, Trygg Hansa and Balta in Scandinavia and Eastern Europe, as well as more niche-direct brands, such as More Than and Aktsam, to maximise local resonance.

Similarly, SAB Miller follows a more locally based brand model, including Birell in the Czech Republic, Barena in Peru and Coors Light in the United States, driven by its history of acquiring locally based beer brands across the world. This is in contrast to Diageo's more global brand model, including global giants such as Guinness, Smirnoff and Johnny Walker.

Strong portfolios of local brands typically create value in five ways (Figure 5.7).

Companies should consider staying 'locally focused' if they have a broad portfolio of local brands, all of which stand for something different (for instance, a different product, sold to a different customer segment, with a

A portfolio of local brands generates value in five ways

1	Local brands	Retaining well-known, much loved local brands that appeal locally
2	Local advertising	Using locally resonant advertising to create cut-through
3	Segment expertise	Using segment specific brands to build credibility in areas where the parent brand is weak
4	Local talent	Attracting and retaining people who want to work autonomously, in a more entrepreneurial way
5	Flexibility	Dialling brands up or down in line with market trends

Figure 5.7 A portfolio of local brands generates value in five ways

different positioning) and have multiple brands in each major market that they can dial up or down. For example, Direct Line Group targets the UK insurance market with a number of different brands – Privilege, Churchill, Direct Line – aimed at different customer segments with local advertising, making it hard for more global brands to penetrate this market.

Model 2: Increasing global alignment

Some companies create growth by moving to one brand worldwide that, across countries, shares the same name, brand positioning, customer target and innovation.

Consider HSBC, UBS or Aviva – all have migrated their major incumbent brands to one brand worldwide, resulting in all markets occupying a similar brand positioning to attract a similar set of customers with a similar product set.

Companies that move to one global brand typically create value in five ways, with the greatest growth realised when combined with back-office integration (Figure 5.8).

Companies that migrate to one global brand typically have local brands in different geographies that attract a similar set of customers with a similar set of products at a similar price point. For example, Norwich Union targeted similar customers with similar products in the UK as its Ireland-based sister company Hibernian, and as Aviva operating in twenty-three other

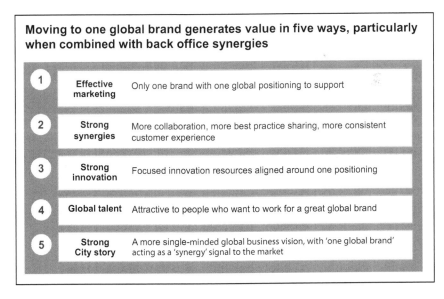

Figure 5.8 Moving to one global brand generates value in five ways, particularly when combined with back office synergies

international markets, making the transition to one global brand possible. Similarly, brands that are bought when people travel (e.g., McDonalds or Mars) have even more incentive to move to one global brand.

So how should companies assess whether moving to one global brand makes good business sense?

At times, there are 'showstoppers' that make it unattractive for a company to migrate to one brand worldwide. For this reason, it's important to first establish whether such a move would add 'real value' to the company by assessing the upsides of such a change – as well as whether there are any 'showstoppers' that might cause value to be lost. To do this, the company should review a number of factors, including:

- Its global brand portfolio – are its brands attracting similar customer segments with similar needs, or using similar products and services?
- Whether there is a high risk of customer defection due to brands having incompatible images; for example, many boys defected when the more male-orientated boy teenage skincare brand Biactol was merged with the more female-oriented teenage skincare brand Clearasil.
- The likely incremental value of moving to one global brand, either through lower costs, such as marketing synergies, or increased revenue from greater best practice sharing or shared innovation.
- The company's ability at this point in time to execute a brand migration well, in terms of being able to invest adequate spend and resources to ensure it's successful.

How does a company migrate to one brand successfully?

Brand migrations tend to be either a huge success or failure – depending on how well they are executed.

In strong cases, brand migrations create growth, especially when companies utilise the high communications spend invested to rebrand the company to simultaneously offer something *new* to the marketplace, as a way to encourage people to reappraise the brand.

At the other end of the spectrum, poor brand migrations tend to haemorrhage sales – mostly due to customer confusion, poor customer service during the migration, a weak product offer versus competitors, or a lack of brand credibility in the new categories that the brand is stretching into.

Successful brand migrations take the time and money to ensure that the parent brand is in no way compromised – ensuring that employees don't lose focus, momentum or motivation during the name change, that customers are not confused or disenfranchised due to the move, and that partners (such as retailers and intermediaries) actively recommend the new brand as much as the old one. To do this, they adhere to six 'brand migration golden rules' (Figure 5.9):

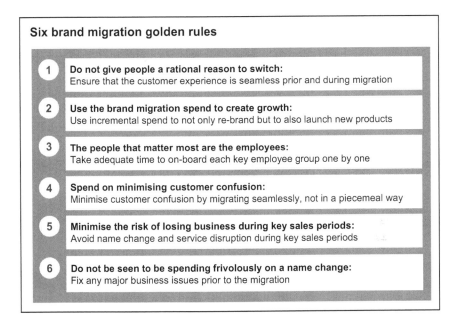

Six brand migration golden rules

1   **Do not give people a rational reason to switch:**
Ensure that the customer experience is seamless prior and during migration

2   **Use the brand migration spend to create growth:**
Use incremental spend to not only re-brand but to also launch new products

3   **The people that matter most are the employees:**
Take adequate time to on-board each key employee group one by one

4   **Spend on minimising customer confusion:**
Minimise customer confusion by migrating seamlessly, not in a piecemeal way

5   **Minimise the risk of losing business during key sales periods:**
Avoid name change and service disruption during key sales periods

6   **Do not be seen to be spending frivolously on a name change:**
Fix any major business issues prior to the migration

Figure 5.9 Six brand migration golden rules

Which brings us to the question, how do companies decide what to migrate to?

Firstly, what should the new brand name be – an existing one, a hybrid of the merged brands, or a completely new one?

When Norwich Union and CGU merged, everything was migrated to the existing Norwich Union brand name, as it had the stronger heritage. When Lloyds and TSB merged, they created a hybrid name – Lloyds TSB – helping to ensure that both customer groups were comfortable with the merger. HSBC, when taking over the Midland Bank, retained the Midland Bank name but replaced its logo with the HSBC lozenge – to signal change but minimise risk – before fully migrating the Midland Bank name to HSBC two years later.

Secondly, what should the global brand positioning be?

Moving to one brand positioning creates the global synergies needed to drive business value – for instance, by creating one global innovation team, encouraging more best practice sharing, using more global marketing that all countries can benefit from, etc. But trying to find a big idea that is generic enough to be able to work across multiple geographies and products – yet also compelling enough to stand out versus local competitors – can be a tough challenge. To resolve this, companies should look externally at up-and-coming global consumer trends, as well as internally, at what makes their brand proposition unique and different from competitors, to find an ownable and distinctive positioning that they can deliver day to day.

Finally, what should the global brand governance model be to create the optimal balance of global, as well as local, decision-making and input?

Some companies, such as HSBC and UBS, take a more centralised brand governance approach, valuing a similar look and feel across markets and more global best practice sharing. Others, such as Aviva and RBS, allow more local control, enabling countries to adapt a global template to the specific needs of their local markets.

In summary

Over the past fifteen years, Boards have successfully reduced company complexity by focusing their scarce resources (both investment capital and people's time) on those brands and products that will deliver the greatest return for the company today, as well as those that are likely to grow and therefore be important for the future.

Consequently, it's important for marketers to engage the Board when choosing which brands and products – and importantly which not – to support.

Savvy marketers should be able to optimise their brand and product portfolio, from both a commercial perspective and a consumer perspective, by being able to answer:

- Which *products* are most important, both now and in the future?
- Which *customer segments* are most likely to buy these products, both today and in the future?
- Which *brands* can best support these products in the most important geographies and attract the most valuable customer segments?

By working in this way, marketers can demonstrate which brands and products to support for growth and maintenance – and which to merge, milk, divest or kill.

Marketers should then optimise each brand's brand architecture – thereby making it easy for consumers to find the right product, as well as enable the brand to stretch across as many adjacent product categories as possible. By doing this, they can increase the effectiveness of each pound spent.

In extreme cases, marketers should also consider the ultimate Board-level branding question – whether to migrate all of the brands within a company to one global brand.

To do this, marketers should assess where future growth is most likely to come from. For instance, does it have a broad brand portfolio with a range of more locally tailored, discrete brands that can be flexed to address local market issues? Can it create more growth by being more locally tailored and relevant? Are there any 'showstoppers' that would make it unattractive to merge the brands? If so, then it probably makes sense to be increasingly locally tailored and thereby to stand out versus the global competitors.

If not, could migrating to one global brand create internal efficiencies and synergies – to a level that will outweigh the short-term brand migration costs? Will employees, customers and partners support the name change? Is the company able to invest adequate resources and spend to ensure its success? If so, then perhaps biting the bullet and moving to one global brand is timely.

Notes

1 Stephen J. Carlotti Jr., Mary Ellen Coe and Jesko Perrey, November 2004, "Making Brand Portfolios Work," *McKinsey Quarterly*.
2 Mark Gottfredson, "The Focused Company," Bain & Company website, June 28, 2012, www.bain.com/Images/BAIN_BRIEF_The_focused_company.pdf.
3 Nirmalya Kumar, "Kill a Brand, Keep a Customer," *Harvard Business Review*, December 2003.
4 Michael Shrage, "Lafley's P&G Brand Cull and the 80/20 Rule," *Harvard Business Review*, August 2014.
5 Nirmalya Kumar, "Kill a Brand, Keep a Customer," *Harvard Business Review*, December 2003; Adam Jones, "Stumbling Blocks on Unilever's Path to Growth," *Financial Times*, August 2004, www.ft.com/cms/s/1/8600c7a6-f464-11d8-9911-00000e2511c8.html?ft_sit e=falcon&desktop=true#axzz4ThfdYyRF; Samuel Solley, "ANALYSIS: The Final Step on the Path to Growth," Campaign Magazine, February 2004, www.campaignlive.co.uk/ article/202955/analysis-final-step-path-growth; "Unilever Unveils Big Hit Innovations, Brand Cull Progress," *AdvertisingAge*, February 2001, http://adage.com/article/news/ unilever-unveils-big-hit-innovations-brand-cull-progress/31965/ Wikipedia, "Unilever," https://en.wikipedia.org/wiki/Unilever.
6 Rebecca Mann, "'Fewer, bigger, better': P&G Prestige Outlines Launch Strategy to Counter the Tough Times Ahead," *The Moodie Report*, December 2008, https://www. moodiedavittreport.com/fewer-bigger-better-pg-prestige-outlines-launch-strategy-to-counter-the-tough-times-ahead-081208/.
7 Serena Ng, "P&G to Shed More Than Half Its Brands," *Wall Street Journal*, August 2014, http://www.wsj.com/articles/procter-gamble-posts-higher-profit-on-cost-cutting-1406892304; Sarah Vizard, "P&G Nears End of Brand Cull, after Beauty Deal with Coty," *Marketing Week*, July 2015, https://www.marketingweek.com/2015/07/09/pg-nears-end-of-brand-cull-after-beauty-deal-with-coty/.
8 Shrage, "Lafley's P&G Brand Cull and the 80/20 Rule."
9 BBC News, "Reckitt Benckiser's Profits Soar," August 2001, http://news.bbc.co.uk/1/hi/ business/1514505.stm; Rosie Murray-West, "Advertising Spend Reaps Results for Reckitt Benckiser," *Telegraph*, November 2000, www.telegraph.co.uk/finance/2741960/Profits-boosted-as-Reckitt-does-the-housework.html; "Reckitt Benckiser Announce 2001 Annual Results," Press Release, February 20, 2002, www.evaluategroup.com/Universal/View. aspx?type=Story&id=80194.
10 Gottfredson, "The Focused Company."
11 Kumar, "Kill a Brand, Keep a Customer."
12 *Business Week*, "Make It Simple," June 1997.

13 P&G, "Company website," March 2016, http://news.pg.com/blog/company-strategy/strategy-simple.

14 Sandra Ng, "P&G Looks to Lift Olay Sales with Fewer Choices on the Shelves," *Wall Street Journal*, December 2015, http://www.wsj.com/articles/p-g-looks-to-lift-olay-sales-with-fewer-choices-on-the-shelf-1451340551.

15 Elaine Watson, "Unilever Slashes 1,200 SKUs in Waste Reduction Drive," *Foodmanufacturer.co.uk*, November 2010, www.foodmanufacture.co.uk/Supply-Chain/Unilever-slashes-1-200-SKUs-in-waste-reduction-drive.

16 Scheherazade Daneshkhu, "Unilever to Prune Back Product Offering," *Financial Times*, December 2013, https://www.ft.com/content/95d480b8-5dd3-11e3-b3e8-00144feabdc0.

17 Mark Gottfredson and Chuck Whitten, "Focused Products," Bain & Company website, August 2012.

18 Zoe Wood and Sarah Butler, "Tesco Cuts Range by 30% to Simplify Shopping," *The Guardian*, January 2015.

19 Mondelez International, "Our Dream, Belief and Values," www.mondelezinternational.com/about-us/our-dream-belief-and-values.

20 Reference, "What Is Cadbury's Mission Statement?" Reference.com, www.reference.com/business-finance/cadbury-s-mission-statement-2d3e7bc774f85629.

21 Millward Brown, "Press release," May 2015, http://www.millwardbrown.com/global-navigation/news/press-releases/full-release/2015/05/26/apple-overtakes-google-for-the-top-spot-in-the-10th-annual-brandz-top-100-most-valuable-global-brands-ranking.

Bibliography

BBC News. "Reckitt Benckiser's Profits Soar." August 2001. http://news.bbc.co.uk/1/hi/business/1514505.stm.

Brown, Millward. "Press Release." May 2015. www.millwardbrown.com/global-navigation/news/press-releases/full-release/2015/05/26/apple-overtakes-google-for-the-top-spot-in-the-10th-annual-brandz-top-100-most-valuable-global-brands-ranking.

Carlotti, Stephen J. Jr., Mary Ellen Coe and Jesko Perrey. "Making Brand Portfolios Work." *McKinsey Quarterly*, November 2004.

Daneshkhu, Scheherazade. "Unilever to Prune Back Product Offering." *Financial Times*, December 2013. www.ft.com/content/95d480b8–5dd3–11e3-b3e8–00144feabdc0.

Gottfredson, Mark. "The Focused Company." Bain & Company website, June 28, 2012.

Gottfredson, Mark and Chuck Whitten. "Focused Products." Bain & Company website, August 2012. www.bain.com/Images/BAIN_BRIEF_The_focused_company.pdf.

Jones, Adam. "Stumbling Blocks on Unilever's Path to Growth." *Financial Times*, August 2004. www.ft.com/cms/s/1/8600c7a6-f464-11d8-9911-00000e2511c8.html?ft_site=falcon&desktop=true#axzz4ThfdYyRF.

Kumar, Nirmalya. "Kill a Brand, Keep a Customer." *Harvard Business Review*, December 2003. "Make It Simple." *Business Week*. June 1997.

Mann, Rebecca. "'Fewer, bigger, better': P&G Prestige Outlines Launch Strategy to Counter the Tough Times Ahead." *The Moodie Report*, December 2008. www.moodiedavittreport.com/fewer-bigger-better-pg-prestige-outlines-launch-strategy-to-counter-the-tough-times-ahead-081208/.

Mondelez International. "Our Dream, Belief and Values." www.mondelezinternational.com/about-us/our-dream-belief-and-values.

Murray-West, Rosie. "Advertising Spend Reaps Results for Reckitt Benckiser." *Telegraph*, November 2000. www.telegraph.co.uk/finance/2741960/Profits-boosted-as-Reckitt-does-the-housework.html.

Ng, Sandra. "P&G Looks to Lift Olay Sales with Fewer Choices on the Shelves." *Wall Street Journal*, December 2015. www.wsj.com/articles/p-g-looks-to-lift-olay-sales-with-fewer-choices-on-the-shelf-1451340551.

Ng, Serena. "P&G to Shed More than Half Its Brands." *Wall Street Journal*, August 2014. www.wsj.com/articles/procter-gamble-posts-higher-profit-on-cost-cutting-1406892304.

P&G. "Company website." March 2016. http://news.pg.com/blog/company-strategy/strategy-simple.

"Reckitt Benckiser Announce 2001 Annual Results." Press Release, February 20, 2002. www.evaluategroup.com/Universal/View.aspx?type=Story&id=80194.

Reference. "What Is Cadbury's Mission Statement?" *Reference.com*. www.reference.com/business-finance/cadbury-s-mission-statement-2d3e7bc774f85629.

Shrage, Michael. "Lafley's P&G Brand Cull and the 80/20 Rule." *Harvard Business Review*, August 2014.

Solley, Samuel. "ANALYSIS: The Final Step on the Path to Growth." *Campaign Magazine*, February 2004. www.campaignlive.co.uk/article/202955/analysis-final-step-path-growth.

"Unilever Unveils Big Hit Innovations, Brand Cull Progress." *Advertising Age*, February 2001. http://adage.com/article/news/unilever-unveils-big-hit-innovations-brand-cull-progress/31965/.

Vizard, Sarah. "P&G Nears End of Brand Cull, after Beauty Deal with Coty." *Marketing Week*, July 2015. www.marketingweek.com/2015/07/09/pg-nears-end-of-brand-cull-after-beauty-deal-with-coty/.

Watson, Elaine. "Unilever Slashes 1,200 SKUs in Waste Reduction Drive." *Foodmanufacturer.co.uk*, November 2010. www.foodmanufacture.co.uk/Supply-Chain/Unilever-slashes-1–200-SKUs-in-waste-reduction-drive.

Wikipedia. "Unilever." https://en.wikipedia.org/wiki/Unilever.

Wood, Zoe and Sarah Butler. "Tesco Cuts Range by 30% to Simplify Shopping." *The Guardian*, January 2015.

Chapter 6

Choosing 'why' to be in business

"There is only one boss. The customer. And he can fire everyone in the company, from the chairman on down simply by spending his money somewhere else."

Sam Walton, founder of Walmart

Getting people's attention can be tough. But getting them to convert their attention into action can be even tougher. In 2015, more than 170,000 brands were advertised in the UK alone, equating to almost five hundred new and different brands advertising each and every single day of the year. We are so inundated by choice that it can take something special for a brand to stand out and be attractive enough to change people's behaviour.[1]

Savvy marketers know that they can't please everyone. Instead, they need to create a strong brand purpose – by deciding what business they're in and what attributes they need to invest in to make the business customer-centric.

To achieve this, marketers should select which customer segments they want to attract, as outlined in Chapter 4. They should then identify what their chosen customer segments are looking for when shopping the category – namely the purchase drivers that influence which brands they choose and stay loyal to – and focus their scarce innovation and advertising resources on delivering these, as part of the everyday customer experience.

Next, they should distil these purchase drivers into a compelling brand essence. In part, this brand essence should be rational – it should demonstrate what is being offered that is *rationally superior* to what's on offer today. But it should also be emotional – it should adopt a brand personality and tone that is *emotionally attractive* to its target audience and distinctive to competitor brands, thereby making it difficult for competitors to copy.

On top of this, marketers need to develop signature products and services that better meet the purchase driver needs of their customer segment. This can include offering superior products, or making the offer more accessible to people, or delivering the offer at a better price, or giving customers a superior service experience. Essentially, the brand should *deliver something tangible that will make people want to switch and stay loyal.*

In this way, Boards can focus their investment on doing fewer, bigger, better initiatives well – rather than behave in a 'mass average' way – and in turn build compelling brands that deliver a truly superior customer experience.

In this chapter, we look at:

A   Why it's important to know what business you're in.
B   Identifying and focusing on the most influential purchase drivers.
C   Distilling these purchase drivers into a compelling brand essence.
D   Developing signature products and services that better meet customers' needs.

A: Why it's important to know what business you're in

Savvy marketers know that having a strong brand purpose is critical.

A strong brand purpose helps companies define what business they're in and what attributes they are investing in to make it customer-centric – namely, which customers they are targeting and what they are offering them to better meet their needs.

Internally, it helps to communicate a clear, consistent strategy of what the brand stands for and where it's going, which helps to galvanise cross-functional teams. Additionally, it helps to convey to employees that they are doing something worthwhile every day, above and beyond making money, cultivating internal belief and pride.

Externally, it helps to ensure that scarce innovation and marketing resources are focused on creating a superior product or service experience that their chosen customer segments will love. If done well, this will encourage customers to switch and stay loyal and in turn deliver strong, sustainable sales growth.

It's important for marketers and Boards to be aligned on what the brand purpose is, and thus on where – and importantly *where not* – they should be investing for growth.

As we saw in Chapter 4 when addressing 'who' to target, the impact that these decisions will have on brand performance will be high. If the team gets it right, sales are likely to be strong. But if the team gets it wrong, sales will suffer. So it's critical that everyone is agreed that this is the right course of action to take.

Secondly, to deliver a superior product and service experience, the recommendations are likely to impact multiple cross-functional teams – for example, which new products and services the innovation team develops, and how the retail and digital teams configure the day-to-day customer experience. Therefore it's important that everyone is aligned on what needs to be done and how to do it.

Many Boards and CEOs have been highly involved in these types of decisions. Let's look at some real-life examples.

Amazon

Amazon's founder, Jeff Bezos, said, "Our vision is to be earth's most customer centric company; to build a place where people can come to find and discover anything they might want to buy online."[2] Bezos wanted to build a "Customer First Culture" – one that understood its customers and their needs better than anyone else, and delivered a product and service experience that they would love. As Bezos said, "We're not competitor obsessed, we're customer obsessed. We start with what the customer needs and we work backwards."

Amazon has delivered this vision by focusing its resources on the things that matter most to its customers – namely, 'great value for money' and 'a highly personalised service'.

It's done this by creating the largest online shop, with low prices on millions of items.

Additionally, in spite of being an online provider, it provides a highly personal customer experience. It enables people to access what they want when they want it, and offers a next day guaranteed delivery service with a 'no questions asked' money-back guarantee. It sends people personalised product recommendations, based on their online search history and previous purchases. And it tries to resolve a customer issue to a satisfactory level regardless of where fault lies.

Bezos claims that this vision has been the guiding force behind many of his leadership decisions. For example, in December 2011, Bezos was 'very proud' that Amazon had successfully delivered 99.9 percent of packages to customers before Christmas. But he then went on to say, "We're not satisfied until it's 100%."

Consequently, it's no wonder that in the UK, Amazon tops the UK Customer Satisfaction Index and continues to grow – delivering strong, sustained, often double-digit sales growth each year.[3]

As Bezos says, "If we can arrange things in such a way that our interests are aligned with our customers, then in the long term that will work out really well for customers and it will work out really well for Amazon."[4]

John Lewis

Retailer John Lewis continues to lead the way in delighting its customers, which in turn has enabled it to grow from strength to strength. John Lewis is consistently rated as one of the top three most-loved UK brands in Nunwood's Customer Experience survey, and in 2015 its UK annual sales reached over £4.5 billion, supported by strong, steady sales growth of almost 10 percent per annum over the last five consecutive years.[5]

So, how has John Lewis achieved this?

Like Amazon, John Lewis has focused its resources on giving customers a superior shopping experience in the two areas that matter most in retail – 'a competitive price' and 'a superior service experience'.

John Lewis customers know that, while John Lewis might not be the cheapest, it is consistently competitive on price, based on its 'Never Knowingly Undersold' price guarantee.

Additionally, all of John Lewis's employees (or 'Partners' as they are called) share a percentage of the annual profits, making it one of the UK's largest employee-owned businesses, and are therefore incentivised to go the extra mile to deliver a superior customer experience every day.

For example, Partners are encouraged to personally resolve any issues that a customer has right then and there, without referring it up to a manager, and are trained to recommend the best product for a customer, even if it delivers less profit for John Lewis. Given that daily they see what delights and frustrates customers, Partners are encouraged to challenge the status quo and submit ideas and complaints to the company's staff council that can be fed up to the Board. When online, customers are able to contact a real person as soon as they want to, with the names and contact details of the relevant customer service managers made easily accessible.

As Steven Lewis, the son of John Lewis, said to John Lewis Partners: "If we offer the best customer experience that we can, it will positively impact our trading and business results, which will then go on to benefit you."[6]

QVC

Another example of a company that has created a customer-centric business, which in turn has resulted in strong business performance, is QVC, a leader in digital commerce and one of the largest mobile commerce multi-category retailers.

In the UK, QVC has a strong customer following, with more than one million unique customers. Ninety-six percent of its revenues come from repeat customers, 93 percent of customers rate it as eight or more out of ten on overall satisfaction, 79 percent claim that they will definitely shop with QVC in the future and 72 percent claim that they will definitely recommend QVC to a friend.[7]

These impressive figures have translated into strong, sustained business growth. In the UK alone, QVC turns over more than £450 million annually – a level that has steadily grown year by year since its launch as "The Shopping Channel" in 1993.[8]

Its phenomenal growth journey stems from a relentless focus on its three core pillars – Quality, Value and Convenience – hence its name QVC.

It offers "quality" brands – many with product exclusives that can't be bought on the high street – that are demonstrated on screen by passionate presenters who build strong empathy with their viewers.

It offers superior "value" across the whole range, including daily limited edition promotions, which go live at midnight and are only available for twenty-four hours, invariably making them the best-selling item of the day.

And it offers superior 'convenience', by enabling customers to shop from their sofa 'just by the click of a button' – supported by an award-winning 24–7 call centre, a next day delivery service and a thirty-day money back guarantee, no questions asked.[9]

QVC is consistently rated as one of the top three most-loved UK brands in Nunwood's Customer Trust and Customer Experience surveys. QVC UK's director of customer services, James Keegan, commented: "Being named in the top three amongst such well-known brands is testament to our ongoing quest to provide unrivalled customer service. Our customers are at the heart of everything we do and so everyone, from our presenters through to our contact centre staff, should be proud to receive this recognition."[10]

M&S Simply Food

A fourth example is M&S Simply Food.

Over the past ten years, the top team at M&S Simply Food has focused on giving their more discerning customers what they're looking for – higher quality food with a steady flow of new, innovative recipes to try. And it's paid off.

M&S Simply Food is ranked the fifth most-liked UK brand in the 2015 UK Customer Satisfaction Index[11] and the tenth most-liked in the 2014 Nunwood Customer Experience Excellence survey.[12] In turn, this has translated into a strong sales performance, with M&S now selling over £5 billion of food products a year – which, unlike M&S's clothing business, has grown steadily and consistently year on year, over the past five years.[13]

As Marc Bolland, M&S's then CEO, said: "Our food business again outperformed the market . . . as our focus on quality and innovation continues to set us apart."[14]

From a quality perspective, M&S Simply Food has built a reputation for ethically sourced and competitively priced restaurant-quality food. Examples include deliciously decadent desserts, such as its gold-covered Billionaire Bullion Bar; a strong focus on provenance, such as its farm-assured, naturally fed, extra-succulent Oakham chickens; and its 'Dine In deals', offering a meal for two for £10 including wine, making them perfect for Valentine's Day or a 'cosy night in' weekend treat.

From an innovation perspective, M&S Simply Food refreshes about a quarter of its entire food range each year. Its teams of chefs, technologists and nutritionists search the world for new exotic and authentic recipes that their customers will want to try. For instance, in 2015, M&S's Belgian Chocolate Jaffa Sphere became its fastest-selling dessert ever with over 170,000 sold in six weeks, resulting in the supplier producing around the clock to try to meet demand.[15]

Additionally, this relentless focus on 'quality' and 'innovation' has made M&S Simply Food a 'go to' food retailer for celebrations, delivering record sales performances over Christmas and Easter periods.

The company's focus on 'higher quality food' was initially brought to life in M&S Simply Food's advertising campaign – 'Not Just Food, Your M&S Food', a campaign that acted as a rallying cry to galvanise staff, customers and shareholders that M&S was run by the public for the public – using mouth-watering language, a seductive voiceover and 'food porn' visuals to summarise the difference in its food quality. For example:

- "This is not just cabbage, this is Lincolnshire red cabbage with apple and cranberries, slow braised in red wine and Tawny port sauce."
- "This is not just a new potato, this is a fresh, tender skinned Jersey Royal new potato."
- "This is not just a chocolate pudding, it's a melt-in-the-middle Belgian chocolate pudding."

More recently, M&S Simply Food has focused on its 'innovation' with its "Adventures in Imagination" campaign, using the same high-quality food visuals to demonstrate its offer of "Over 100 new ideas every month".

As these examples show, companies that have a strong, customer-centric brand purpose tend to build a loyal customer base, which in turn delivers strong business performance. To be customer-centric, businesses need to be clear about what business they're in – namely, which customers they are targeting and which products and services they are investing in, and importantly which they are not investing in, to better meet their customers' needs.

B: Identifying and focusing on the most influential purchase drivers

To deliver a superior product and service experience, companies need to understand what drives the purchase behaviour of their chosen customer segments – specifically, what their target customers are looking for when shopping the category, and thus what they need to see or hear to make them switch and stay loyal to a brand.

Purchase drivers might be product led, such as "Leaves my hair softer and silkier" as leveraged by Pantene, or "Does the job more effectively" as leveraged by Dyson.

They might be service led, such as First Direct's "Goes out of its way to resolve a problem", or Amazon's "Personalised recommendations that people like you love".

They might be convenience-led, such as QVC's "Buy from your sofa at the touch of a button", or Moneysupermarket's "It's easy to find a great deal".

They might be price led, such as "Low fares" as leveraged by RyanAir, or John Lewis's "Never knowingly undersold".

Or they might deliver greater peace of mind, such as QVC's "30 day money back guarantee, no questions asked" or "The expert's choice" as leveraged by Colgate.

To understand what motivates their chosen customer segments, marketers should get out into the real world and talk with customers in person – particularly at that moment when they are deciding which brand to buy and are most open to influence. They should probe to understand what makes a customer choose one brand over another, along with any frustrations customers may have with the category that stop them from buying more.

They should also talk with category experts – such as category practitioners, journalists and retailers – as they are likely to know the underlying reasons why people choose one brand over another, as well as future trends that might change the nature of the market.

Based on this qualitative research, the marketing team can compile an exhaustive list of possible purchase drivers that a brand could focus on – both those that are important to many customer segments, as well as those that are highly relevant to one customer segment and less relevant to others.

Next, the team should use quantitative research to 'prove' which of these purchase drivers are most important to each customer segment – namely which drive a segment's commitment to a brand. Marketers can use one of two quantitative modelling techniques to do this – 'stated needs' or 'derived needs'.

'Stated needs' involves *directly asking* people how important each of the purchase drivers are when choosing which brand to buy – and hence relies on people consciously knowing what makes them choose one brand over another. This technique is proven to overstate the more functional, rational attributes (for example, 'I choose the chocolate bar with the nicest dark chocolate') and understate the more intangible, emotional attributes (for example, 'I choose the most indulgent chocolate bar').

The second option, 'derived needs', *derives* what is most important to people when choosing which brand to buy. It asks people which brands they like most, and then asks them to rate how well two brands (one that they like a lot and one that they like less) perform along each of the purchase drivers. By doing this, marketers can 'derive' which attributes people ascribe to their most-loved brands – and thus which attributes tend to build customer loyalty.

In practice, the 'derived needs' technique is seen to be more reflective of what really drives each segment's behaviour, as it enables some of the more emotional attributes to come into play alongside the rational ones.

At this point, it's important to discriminate between hygiene factors and differentiators.

Hygiene factors are the mandatory attributes that the brand must possess to be considered a credible contender in the category. For example, 'mildness' is a hygiene factor in the baby skincare market. If a baby skincare product is not 'mild', then parents are unlikely to use it on their baby's skin.

Differentiators are those attributes that differentiate a brand versus other competitors within the category – making the brand superior. Without an appealing point of difference versus the category incumbents, there's no reason for people to try your brand and it will almost undoubtedly fail. For example, Dyson's 'cyclone technology' is a compelling differentiator that enables Dyson vacuum cleaners to pick up more dust than its competitors do.

By 'proving' which purchase drivers are most important (including hygiene factors and differentiators), marketers can build the Board's confidence on which customer segments to target and which product and service attributes to invest in – and importantly which not to invest in – for growth. By eliminating non-core activities, the Board is able to free up valuable resources that can be put to better use in building a truly superior customer experience that its target customers will prefer.

To illustrate, let's revisit the wine segmentation example that we saw in Chapter 4.

Two of the four segments, 'Enthusiasts' and 'Aspirers', enjoy drinking and experimenting with wine. 'Enthusiasts' like to do their own research and make their own decisions – and so companies looking to attract them should invest in creating high-end wines with distinctive flavours, as well as in building strong relationships with wine publications, online websites and wine clubs with the aim of being regularly reviewed and recommended. 'Aspirers' are further down the learning curve, and so rely more heavily on advice – and so companies looking to attract them should offer high-end wines to specialist wine stores on the high street, taking the time to educate the in-store wine experts on what's special about their range.

In contrast, 'Conservatives' and 'Delegators' are less involved in the category – and so tend to enjoy a safer, more limited repertoire of wines. 'Conservatives' tend to know what they like and stick to what they know – and so companies looking to attract them should offer a range of classic, well-known wines in grocery retailers, at a good price. 'Delegators' drink wine least frequently and are overwhelmed by the high level of choice – and so companies wishing to attract them should offer a simplified range of classic wines in grocery retailers, and incentivise the in-store experts at the wine counter to recommend their range.

C: Distilling purchase drivers into a compelling brand essence

To stand out in the marketplace, marketers need to distil the purchase drivers into a compelling *brand essence*.

Brand essence is the heart and soul of the brand, representing its fundamental nature or quality. It is used to distil what a brand stands for – thereby setting a future direction for the brand that is clear, own-able and differentiating, and that the whole organisation can adhere to.

A strong brand essence demonstrates what a brand is offering that is rationally superior to what's on offer today – namely, how their products and services are better meeting customer needs. But it also adopts a brand personality and tone that is more *emotionally attractive* to the target audience than competitor brands. In some categories, it can be relatively easy and quick for competitors to copy a leading brand's products and services – but if they try to copy a brand's 'personality' or 'tone', chances are that they will more quickly be exposed as 'me too'.

When creating a brand essence, it is typically seen as a 'single thing' that over time is fixed at the heart of the brand, irrespective of changing market contexts. Consequently, marketers spend considerable time trying to distil a brand's essence down to a particular 'word' or 'set of words' – only for it to become so bland or generic that it's no longer differentiating, or it dates so quickly that it never truly catches on and, in essence (to coin a phrase), the brand essence model stays 'static'.

Chris Barnham, a leading qualitative researcher and semiotician, and I both disagree with this thinking.

As the examples at the beginning of this chapter illustrate, the concept of having 'one static brand essence' is flawed; brands are living, breathing, multifaceted entities. For instance, Amazon offers its customers both "great value for money" and "a highly personalised service". John Lewis offers "a competitive price" and a "superior customer experience". QVC offers "Quality", "Value" and "Convenience". And M&S Simply Food offers "superior quality, farm assured food" and "a constant stream of new food products to try".

Most brands contain many different essences or 'nesses' that may vary by market geography, or over time. For example, Coca-Cola contains 'youthfulness', 'American-ness' and 'fizziness'. Guinness contains 'Irishness', 'timelessness' and 'mellowness'. So, it's logical that brands don't have just one essence, but a combination of 'sub-essences', or 'values', that form a unique structure.

Brands structure these sub-essences or values differently, with some being more associated with the brand and some less so. This explains why two brands can contain similar values but remain entirely different from each other. To illustrate, Volvo and BMW play in a similar segment of the market; for Volvo 'safety' plays a defining role in what the brand is about, with 'safety' being one of its core brand attributes, but for BMW it's secondary, with 'sheer driving pleasure' much more at the forefront. Both brands contain the same sub-essence or value, but in quite different places in their respective 'brand hierarchies', and consequently each brand is known for different things.

By thinking about brands as living, breathing entities, marketers view their brands more realistically. Most brand models are constructed as idealistic summaries of how the brand owners want their brands to be seen by the consumer and, therefore, contain nothing but positive values for a brand. Yet, in the real world, most brands have negative values too – for instance, the flip side of Volvo's 'safe' value could be 'dull' – creating a branding issue, which is not commonly observed in conventional brand models.

While it pays to keep in place a high-level brand essence to act as a guiding principle for the entire employee base, the 'true essence' of a brand should be managed in a more dynamic way, by:

- Identifying the key values or sub-essences each brand contains (namely, the top five or so relevant values that people associate with a brand).
- Understanding which values are associated most with the brand – and which are less so.
- Identifying, in more detail, 'what sort of sub-essence' each value is (for example, exactly what type of 'American-ness' Coca-Cola has) and whether this is a positive or negative influence on the brand.

To illustrate, let's go back a step. Marketers have traditionally used 'brand pyramids' or 'onions' to convey brand essence, placing the *one* phrase that best defines the brand at the top of the pyramid, or in the heart of the onion. As such, the static brand essence model for Olay in the early 1990s may have looked something like Figure 6.1, with the marketing team focused on the 'young looking skin' essence at the top of the pyramid:

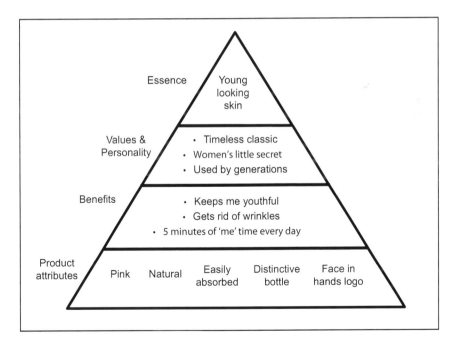

Figure 6.1 Possible Olay static brand essence model, 1990s

In contrast, we believe that the model should convey not just one 'brand essence' phrase, but the top three to five brand values that people associate with the brand. In Olay's case in the early 1990s, these could have included 'young looking skin' – as shown at the top of the static brand essence model – but also other important values such as 'pink, natural fluid' and 'original and classic'. It should then show the hierarchy of these values – depicting those that are most dominant at the top (for example, for Olay: 'young looking skin'), and the others underneath, in order of importance. Additionally, it should describe what sort of value each is – unlike the static brand essence model, both its positives *and* negatives.

In this way, Olay's dynamic brand essence model in the early 1990s could have looked more like Figure 6.2:

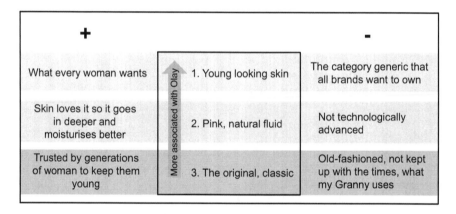

Figure 6.2 Possible Olay dynamic brand essence model, 1990s

For marketers and creative agencies, the 'dynamic brand essence' model *transforms* how brand positionings are brought to life. By comparing brands versus their competitors, it helps identify which 'core' values to lead on, which 'lesser' values to build and which 'negative' values to address.

Using the example of Olay in the mid-1990s, the brand needed to move away from the category generic of 'young looking skin' to 'prove' why Olay was better than competitors. It did this with its groundbreaking "We Can Prove You Can Look Younger" campaign and compelling "See the difference in 14 days" claim, featuring older women who "know about ageing" to make the claims credible. It also needed to address its negative, old-fashioned image by launching new technologically advanced creams, gels and fluids (that weren't 'pink') and communicating why they were scientifically proven to be better. By doing this, Olay reasserted its market leadership position and significantly increased its market share, with the "Proven Effective" campaign being rolled out worldwide – a staggering result at the time.

The dynamic brand essence model also helps agencies manage the increased media and segment fragmentation, by dialling up different values or 'nesses' in different mediums according to which message is most relevant. For example, M&S Simply Food's current television advert "Adventures in Imagination" focuses on 'innovation' (with its one hundred new food products every month), whilst its press adverts focus on 'provenance' (for example, it's link with Fairtrade) and on addressing its 'high price perception' (with its offer to 'Dine in for £10').

Similarly, it helps frontline teams, such as sales and call centre people, to bring the brand to life when talking with customers. By identifying the major brand values that need to be communicated and understanding their importance in the hierarchy, sales people can communicate the key messages in order of importance, as well as address any negatives that are stopping customers from buying the brand today.

Importantly, no matter how much marketers try to control what the brand says, what really matters is what the consumer sees day to day. To quote management consultant Scott Cook: "A brand is no longer what we tell the consumer it is – it is what consumers tell each other it is."[16]

D: Developing signature products and services that better meet customers' needs

In today's consumer-driven market, if companies innovate at the minimum level, the business is likely to decline – as opposed to stand still – as competitors and new entrants innovate around them.

If a company's goal is growth, then the Board must invest in developing and delivering the breakthrough innovation ideas needed to better meeting customer needs, and importantly stay ahead of competitors.

Yet, worryingly, studies show that the percentage of new product innovations that fail falls somewhere between 40 percent and 90 percent, depending on the category. In fact, in the United States, of the thirty thousand packaged goods products launched every year, 70 percent to 90 percent of them do not survive on store shelves beyond a year.[17]

Innovation is a high-stakes game.

To deliver groundbreaking products and services that have a chance of success in today's saturated market, companies *must* break out of the prosaic 'me too' follower thinking and focus resources on developing truly innovative products and services. To quote serial entrepreneur, Mark Cuban: "If you're looking for the next big thing, and you're looking where everyone else is, you're looking in the wrong place."[18]

These innovative products and services need to be relevant and appealing to a high proportion of the brand's target audience, distinctive from the products and services that competitors are offering and credible given the company and brand heritage. Crucially, the business *must* also be able to manufacture and sell the new products and services profitably. As Kevin Stirtz, author of *Marketing for Smart People* says: "Know what your customers want most and what your company does best. Focus on where those two meet."[19]

To deliver this, marketers need to work with their peers, most notably the innovation and finance teams to:

1   Define their innovation objectives.
2   Develop innovative ideas that better meet customer needs, profitably.
3   Select and gain Board agreement to which idea or ideas to launch.

Let's look at each of these in turn.

1. Defining the company's innovation objectives

To develop breakthrough ideas, companies should start by clearly defining their *strategic objectives* – namely, what they want their company to achieve over the next five to ten years, which markets they wish to play in to achieve their goals, and where they are willing to invest for success. This helps to ensure that any innovation-focused work fits with the company's mid- to long-term vision.

Once these are in place, marketers should work with the innovation and finance teams to define the company's *innovation objectives*, for instance:

- What their innovation goals are over the next one-, three-, five- and ten-year periods.
- How this needs to be delivered over the ten-year period to achieve the desired company returns. For example, does the growth need to be front-weighted to the early years? Or can it be balanced across the whole period? Or can it be back-weighted to later years to enable more breakthrough innovations to be developed?
- How much risk they're willing to bear to achieve a higher size of prize taking into account the other company projects that are being undertaken.
- Which categories and brands they wish to focus their innovation resources on.
- Which purchase drivers they want to be superior in, to better meet customers' needs.

As soon as the type and scale of innovation required is agreed, the marketing, innovation and finance teams should jointly define which innovation projects to focus on and assign teams to each. For example, is one of the projects to develop the next-generation hairspray that holds hair without stickiness? Or could it be to extend the brand into the baby category? Or could it be creating a new range of flavour variants to stimulate trial?

Once a project team is assigned to a clearly defined project, it can start innovating with the aim (at this stage) of developing as many innovative ideas as possible to find where the sweet spot lies.

2. Developing innovative ideas that better meet customer needs, profitably

In practice, the most crucial step in developing truly innovative product and service ideas is to understand what your target customer segments either knowingly or unknowingly want, but are not getting today. This enables the team to expose gaps that it can potentially fill – profitably.

The best way to do this is to go out into the real world to talk with people, asking them about what they want and what they are frustrated by.

It's useful to talk with both loyal users about which products they like and why – this helps to work out what to say to non-users to build interest – as well as infrequent users, dissenters and defectors to better understand what's stopping them from using the category or brand regularly.

As well, the team should observe people when buying and using the products day to day. This helps to identify any unmet needs or frustrating aspects of the product or service that people might find hard to remember or articulate when they're not actually using it.

Marketers should also talk with category experts, such as retailers, journalists, academics and category practitioners. These experts are likely to know what customers are looking for and what issues frustrate them – as well as what the big future trends are, and which future technologies might be coming down the pipeline that might radically change the nature of the market.

The more the team talks with people, the more the team should be able to spot market gaps that it can fill and issues that it can address.

As soon as the initial product and service ideas have been developed, they should be shown to customers and experts for their thoughts and feedback – enabling the ideas to be quickly refined and optimised.

Ideally, set up a series of waves of consumer and expert interviews, using each wave as an opportunity to identify new ideas, refine existing ones and assess which have the highest potential. As fresh insights come in, the product or service can be refined and then tested in the next interview wave, thus enabling the team to ensure that any final ideas are as appealing, credible and distinctive as they need to be.

In parallel, the marketing team should assess the company's capability to deliver the product or service profitably. For example, can we manufacture and store the product profitably? Can we distribute and advertise it in a way that will get traction, but at a price and retail margin that still delivers a good profit margin?

At this stage, the team should conduct a rough 'back of the envelope' calculation, to assess what the initiative would need to achieve to yield the required business return – and whether this is feasible. We will look at this in more detail at the end of Chapter 9.

3. Select and gain Board agreement to which ideas to launch

By now, the company should have identified a core group of innovation ideas that it believes are appealing and distinctive to customers and that the company is capable of producing and selling profitably.

Typically, the team's next task is to embark on a more detailed phase of rigorous assessment, which will most likely include:

- Quantitative customer research to validate which ideas are strongest and whether they are appealing, distinctive and credible enough to be launched.
- A more detailed feasibility assessment to validate how the products can be sourced, manufactured, distributed and advertised and, if so, at what cost at each stage.
- A more detailed financial assessment to ensure that the products can be made and sold profitably – and will produce an acceptable return on investment and net present value versus other potential projects that the company could focus on.

During this phase, it's important for teams to not get snared in the 'me too' follower trap.

Truly innovative product and service ideas often require innovative features that are expensive or difficult to add. As the ideas are assessed internally, these unique features can be chipped away – deemed either too costly or too difficult to execute. If the differentiators are diluted to a level where the product is no longer noticeably superior, or the team cannot make compelling superiority claims in the advertising, then the brand will not be as differentiated as it needs to be versus the market incumbents.

The likely result is that what started as a truly innovative product idea ends up, at launch, as very similar to those products that are already in the market today. The brand becomes a 'me too' follower rather than an innovator, lacking the superiority to deliver the financial objectives that were originally set – resulting in the year one launch budget being cut, and the project underperforming its original objectives.

This all-too-frequent scenario highlights why it's critical for marketers to ensure that the final products and services that are launched are *truly superior at addressing the unmet needs* that were identified early on in the project – and that the product claims are robust and distinctive enough to be used in advertising – thus, ensuring that the launch will deliver the necessary sales and profit targets required for launch.

If the product or service offer isn't superior, or expected profits are too low, the team should continue to iterate the product or service solution until it meets both criteria.

If this is not feasible, then – given the high failure rate of new products – the company should reassess whether it is worth launching the product or service at all.

Getting it right isn't easy, highlighting precisely why it's so important that marketers take the time to:

- Develop and launch superior products that really *do* meet customer needs.
- Ensure that they can source, produce, distribute and advertise distinctive products profitably.
- Ensure that the project will deliver an acceptable return on investment and net present value.

Let's put this all of this into context by reviewing a real-life case study

PZ Cussons, a manufacturer of personal healthcare products and consumer goods, saw room in the mother and baby personal care market for a competitor to Johnson & Johnson. It responded by leveraging its global mother and baby experience to build a compelling mother and baby range in the UK.

By conducting a series of in-home and in-store observational visits with pregnant and new mums, as well as one-on-one interviews with mother and baby experts (including midwives, doctors, nurseries, journalists and mother and baby companies in other sectors), PZ Cussons uncovered that many of a new mother's needs were unmet.

There was a lack of products for pregnant and new mums (for example, a soothing bath soak to relax their body in after giving birth, or ways to erase red stretch marks). There was also a lack of products for babies (for example, baby massage oils to aid circulation and digestion) and toddlers (for example, quick and easily applied moisturising sprays, or fun bath products that make bath time more educational and enjoyable).

In addition, PZ Cussons staged four waves of internal workshops and focus groups to hone a distinctive brand positioning and tone that would appeal to mums. On the positive side, the Johnson & Johnson brand personality has a trusted, traditional tone – it is the brand that has been helping mothers for generations with safe baby care solutions. But on the negative side, it is not regarded as particularly 'natural', or as 'in touch' with the chaos of new motherhood – with its advertising conveying a 'perfect new mum world' that few modern mothers relate to.

With this in mind, PZ Cussons developed the compelling Mum & Me mother and baby range comprising innovative, high-performing products designed to address all of the needs of a new mother, from pregnancy to post-birth, and for babies and toddlers. Additionally, it adopted a distinctive brand personality, conveying Mum & Me's sympathetic understanding of how enjoyable yet chaotic being a new mother is – and used natural ingredients (such as camomile, jojoba oil and lavender) to create a more holistic new mum and baby solution.

The range performed strongly in qualitative and quantitative research, leading to its refinement and launch in 2012.

In summary

Savvy marketers know that they can't please everyone. Instead, they need to create a strong brand purpose, by deciding what business they're in and what attributes they are investing in to make it customer-centric.

To achieve this, they should:

- Select which customer segments to target and attract, as outlined in Chapter 4.
- Identify what their chosen customer segments are looking for when shopping the category – namely, the purchase drivers that influence which brands they choose and stay loyal to.
- Focus their scarce innovation and advertising resources on delivering the purchase drivers as part of the everyday customer experience – by selecting which products and services they should invest in (and importantly which not to invest in) to better meet their customers' needs.

Next, they should distil these purchase drivers into a compelling brand essence, one that:

- Demonstrates what is being offered that is rationally superior to what's on offer today.
- Adopts a brand personality and tone that is *emotionally attractive* to its target audience and distinctive to competitor brands, thereby making it difficult for competitors to copy.

Additionally, marketers should develop signature products and services that better meet the purchase driver needs of their chosen customer segments and will encourage people to switch and stay loyal, by:

- Defining the company's innovation objectives.
- Developing innovative products that better meet the needs of their customers, profitably.
- Selecting and gaining Board alignment on which idea or ideas to launch.

In this way, marketers can build Board confidence to focus their investment on doing fewer, bigger, better initiatives well – rather than behave in a 'mass average' way — and in turn build compelling brands that deliver a truly superior customer experience.

Notes

1 Sourced directly from Nielsen Media Research Limited, Ad Dynamix media measurement 2015.
2 Amazon, "Jobs," www.amazon.jobs/en-gb/jobs/364216, accessed October 2016.
3 Institute of Customer Service article, "Customer Service on the Rise as Organisations Respond to Changing Consumer Demands," 20th January 2016, www.instituteofcustomer service.com/media-centre/press-releases/article/customer-satisfaction-on-the-rise-as-organisations-respond-to-changing-consumer-demands; Gideon Spanier, "Amazon UK's Annual Sales Hit £6.3 Billion," *Campaign Live*, February 2016, www.campaignlive.co.uk/article/amazon-uks-annual-sales-hit-63-billion/1381647; Patrick O'Brien, "Amazon UK Sales Growth Slowdown," *Verdictretail.com*, January 2015, www.verdictretail.com/amazon-uk-sales-growth-slowdown/; "Amazon Reveals Last Hurrah under Pooled Tax Structure," *Theweek.co.uk*, June 2015, www.theweek.co.uk/64138/amazon-reveals-last-hurrah-under-pooled-tax-structure.
4 Amazon, www.amazon.co.uk/forum/amazon?cdForum=Fx20NG9OQFCP0QF&cdPage= 11&cdThread=Tx3TROA9NWXUJ6, accessed October 2016; Tricia Morris, "What Makes Amazon Customer Service So Satisfying," *Parature*, December 2013, www.parature.com/amazon-customer-experience/; Kevin Baldacci, "Seven Customer Service Lessons from Amazon CEO Jeff Bezos," *salesforce.com*, June 2013, www.salesforce.com/blog/2013/06/jeff-bezos-lessons.html.
5 Nunwood UK Customer Experience Excellence Centre, 2015, "2015 UK Analysis," www.nunwood.com/customer-experience-excellence-centre-2015-uk-analysis/; John Lewis Annual Reports, 2012 to 2015, www.johnlewispartnership.co.uk/financials/financial-reports/annual-reports.html; Chloe Rigby, "John Lewis Sees Fast Growth via Mobile and Online," *Internet Retailing*, March 2016, http://internetretailing.net/2016/03/john-lewis-sees-fast-growth-online-and-via-mobile-but-waitrose-ecommerce-sales-are-down/.
6 Maya Fowell, "What Can Retailers Learn from John Lewis's Winning Approach to Customer Experience," *www.cxnetwork.com*, October 2015, www.cxnetwork.com/cx-employee-engagement/articles/what-can-retailers-learn-from-john-lewis-winning-a.
7 QVC UK, "Welcome to QVC UK," April 2012, www.qvcuk.com/UK/images/vr_pdfs/QVC_Corp_Brochure_JUN2012.pdf.
8 Rebecca Gonsalves, "QVC: How the American Home-Shopping Channel Became One of the Biggest Players in British Beauty," *The Independent*, November 2015, www.independent.co.uk/life-style/fashion/qvc-how-the-american-home-shopping-channel-became-one-of-the-biggest-players-in-british-beauty-a6731806.html; Liberty Interactive Corporation Report, February 2015, http://ir.libertyinteractive.com/releasedetail.cfm?ReleaseID=898376; Andrew Cave, "QVC Has Come a Long Way from Selling VW Beetle Clocks for £16.50," *The Telegraph*, August 2013.
9 Anna-Marie Solowij, "QVCool?" *The Daily Mail*, July 2013; QVC UK, "Why Shop with Us?" April 2016, www.qvcuk.com/WhyShopWithUs.content.html.
10 Nunwood, "2015 UK Analysis," www.nunwood.com/customer-experience-excellence-centre-2015-uk-analysis/; "Portfolio," www.nunwood.com/?portfolio=uk-2014-top-20-3-qvc
11 TLF Research, "UK Customer Satisfaction Index Survey," January 2015, www.tlfresearch.co.uk/downloads/UKCSI_Exec_Summary_Jan15.pdf.
12 Nunwood, "2015 UK Analysis," www.nunwood.com/customer-experience-excellence-centre-2015-uk-analysis/.
13 M&S's Company Accounts, 2011 to 2015.
14 FG Insight, November 2015, https://www.fginsight.com/news/marks-and-spencer-sees-strong-food-growth-despite-profit-fall-7551.

15 M&S's Annual Report, 2015.
16 Cited in Eric Savitz, "Listening to Social Media Cues Doesn't Mean Ceding Control," *Forbes*, August 2012, www.forbes.com/sites/ciocentral/2012/08/04/listening-to-social-media-cues-doesnt-mean-ceding-control/#344e032331f5.
17 John T. Gourville, "Eager Sellers and Stony Buyers: Understanding the Psychology of New Product Adoption," *Harvard Business Review*, June 2006.
18 Deanna Lazzaroni, "75 Quotes to Inspire Marketing Greatness," *LinkedIn*, June 2014, https://business.linkedin.com/marketing-solutions/blog/7/75-quotes-to-inspire-marketing-greatness, accessed October 2016.
19 Ekaterina Walter, "40 Eye-Opening Customer Service Quotes," *Forbes*, March 2014, www.forbes.com/sites/ekaterinawalter/2014/03/04/40-eye-opening-customer-service-quotes/#3ed21cb14dc8, accessed October 2016.

Bibliography

Amazon. "Forum." Accessed October 2016. www.amazon.co.uk/forum/amazon?cdForum=Fx20NG9OQFCP0QF&cdPage=11&cdThread=Tx3TROA9NWXUJ6.

Amazon. "Jobs." Accessed October 2016. www.amazon.jobs/en-gb/jobs/364216.

"Amazon Reveals Last Hurrah under Pooled Tax Structure." *Theweek.co.uk*, June 2015. theweek.co.uk/64138/amazon-reveals-last-hurrah-under-pooled-tax-structure.

Baldacci, Kevin. "Seven Customer Service Lessons from Amazon CEO Jeff Bezos." *salesforce.com*, June 2013. www.salesforce.com/blog/2013/06/jeff-bezos-lessons.html.

Cave, Andrew. "QVC Has Come a Long Way from Selling VW Beetle Clocks for £16.50." *The Telegraph*, August 2013.

FG Insight. November 2015. www.fginsight.com/news/marks-and-spencer-sees-strong-food-growth-despite-profit-fall-7551.

Fowell, Maya. "What Can Retailers Learn From John Lewis's Winning Approach to Customer Experience?" *www.cxnetwork.com*, October 2015. www.cxnetwork.com/cx-employee-engagement/articles/what-can-retailers-learn-from-john-lewis-winning-a.

Gonsalves, Rebecca. "QVC: How the American Home-Shopping Channel Became One of the Biggest Players in British Beauty." *The Independent*, November 2015. www.independent.co.uk/life-style/fashion/qvc-how-the-american-home-shopping-channel-became-one-of-the-biggest-players-in-british-beauty-a6731806.html.

Gourville, John T. "Eager Sellers and Stony Buyers: Understanding the Psychology of New Product Adoption." *Harvard Business Review*, June 2006.

Institute of Customer Service article. "Customer Service on the Rise as Organisations Respond to Changing Consumer Demands." 20th January 2016. www.instituteofcustomerservice.com/media-centre/press-releases/article/customer-satisfaction-on-the-rise-as-organisations-respond-to-changing-consumer-demands.

Lazzaroni, Deanna. "75 Quotes to Inspire Marketing Greatness." *LinkedIn*, June 2014. Accessed October 2016. https://business.linkedin.com/marketing-solutions/blog/7/75-quotes-to-inspire-marketing-greatness.

John Lewis Annual Reports, 2012 to 2015. www.johnlewispartnership.co.uk/financials/financial-reports/annual-reports.html.

Liberty Interactive Corporation Report. February 2015. http://ir.libertyinteractive.com/releasedetail.cfm?ReleaseID=898376.

Morris, Tricia. "What Makes Amazon Customer Service So Satisfying." *Parature*, December 2013. www.parature.com/amazon-customer-experience/.

M&S's Annual Report. 2016. http://annualreport.marksandspencer.com/.

M&S's Company Accounts. 2011 to 2015. http://annualreport2011.marksandspencer.com; http://annualreport2012.marksandspencer.com; http://annualreport2013.marksandspencer. com; http://annualreport2014.marksandspencer.com; http://annualreport2015.marksand spencer.com.

Nielsen Media Research Limited. Ad Dynamix media measurement 2015.

Nunwood UK Customer Experience Excellence Centre. "2015 UK Analysis." www.nunwood. com/customer-experience-excellence-centre-2015-uk-analysis/.

Nunwood UK Customer Experience Excellence Centre. "Portfolio." 2015. http://www.nunwood. com/?portfolio=uk-2014-top-20-3-qvc.

O'Brien, Patrick. "Amazon UK Sales Growth Slowdown." *Verdictretail.com*, January 2015. www. verdictretail.com/amazon-uk-sales-growth-slowdown/.

QVC UK. "Welcome to QVC UK." April 2012. www.qvcuk.com/UK/images/vr_pdfs/ QVC_Corp_Brochure_JUN2012.pdf.

QVC UK. "Why Shop With Us?" April 2016. www.qvcuk.com/WhyShopWithUs.content.html.

Rigby, Chloe. "John Lewis Sees Fast Growth via Mobile and Online." *Internet Retailing*, March 2016. http://internetretailing.net/2016/03/john-lewis-sees-fast-growth-online-and-via-mobile-but-waitrose-ecommerce-sales-are-down/.

Savitz, Eric. "Listening to Social Media Cues Doesn't Mean Ceding Control." *Forbes*, August 2012. www.forbes.com/sites/ciocentral/2012/08/04/listening-to-social-media-cues-doesnt-mean-ceding-control/#344e032331f5.

Solowij, Anna-Marie. "QVCool?" *The Daily Mail*, July 2013.

Spanier, Gideon. "Amazon UK's Annual Sales Hit £6.3 Billion." *Campaign Live*, February 2016. www.campaignlive.co.uk/article/amazon-uks-annual-sales-hit-63-billion/1381647.

TLF Research. "UK Customer Satisfaction Index Survey." January 2015. http://www.tlfresearch. co.uk/downloads/UKCSI_Exec_Summary_Jan15.pdf.

Walter, Ekaterina. "40 Eye-Opening Customer Services Quotes." *Forbes*, March 2014. Accessed October 2016. www.forbes.com/sites/ekaterinawalter/2014/03/04/40-eye-opening-customer-service-quotes/#3ed21cb14dc8.

Chapter 7

Choosing 'where' to market

"If you want to catch fish, fish where the fish are."

Anonymous

When it comes to 'where' to market a brand, it's important to sell through sales channels that make the brand both visible and accessible to people in a way that is easy to engage with and purchase. Otherwise, it's likely to get lost in today's market clutter.

Yet, to develop marketing strategies that drive shareholder value and thus engage the Board, marketers need to find cost-efficient and effective ways to manage and grow their brands.

The growth in new technology has reduced barriers to entry. Rather than having to go through more expensive traditional distribution channels, today's companies can sell through new, more cost-efficient channels.

Entrepreneurs, more than anyone, have taken advantage of this, by unearthing innovative, more cost-efficient distribution channels through which to sell their products and services. In doing so, they have been able to prove the concept to their investors before investing at scale. This, in turn, has fundamentally altered the dynamics of some categories, changing the way people purchase and, in some cases, making traditional brands obsolete.

Choosing which channels to market through, however, is only part of the picture – success also hinges on optimising a brand's performance within that channel.

To do this, companies need to understand the customer's mindset throughout the shopping experience – for example, when will they be most open to the brand, what if anything can be done to make the brand stand out, and what can be said to them at that moment to convince them to buy.

Additionally, it involves identifying and unblocking any existing barriers to purchase – for example, issues that might stop customers considering a brand (such as a lack of positive PR), or enquiring about it (such as a confusing website) or buying it (such as a poor in-store service experience). Companies can successfully pinpoint precisely where in the purchase funnel their brand is losing customers and *why*, providing invaluable insights on which go-to-market issues to prioritise and fix.

In this chapter, we focus on three marketing and sales strategies that marketers have successfully used when engaging the Board on where and how to go to market, namely:

A   Finding effective and cost-efficient sales channels.
B   Optimising channel performance.
C   Identifying and unblocking purchase funnel bottlenecks.

A: Finding effective and cost-efficient sales channels

It's important for marketers to ensure that their products and services are easy to find and purchase, while also leveraging cost-efficient distribution channels that will deliver the greatest return.

Advancements in new technology have reduced some of the barriers to entry that brands previously had to overcome, enabling entrepreneurs to find new, more cost-efficient channels that they can use either alongside or in place of traditional distribution channels.

To demonstrate, let's look at a number of new brands – many now deeply embedded in our daily lives – that changed their category dynamics forever, by respectively:

- Setting up their own one-stop stores instead of using traditional retailers.
- Selling directly through virtual channels, such as the telephone and online.
- Selling directly to people in their homes.
- Selling through non-traditional channels, such as on street corners or on shopping channels.

Setting up their own one-stop stores

Some brands have changed the category dynamics by selling everything their customer needs in one place. For example, Pets At Home transformed the world of pet care by opening up easy-to-access, out-of-town stores, providing pet owners with everything they need to care for their pets, as well as a destination to take their children to on a wet weekend afternoon.

As a one-stop pet shop, it helps customers select and care for a pet, by offering a comprehensive range of pet care products, from pet food and treats to accessories and veterinary care, supplemented by pet care advice.

By bringing together everything under one roof, Pets At Home has gone from strength to strength with phenomenal sales growth since its launch in 1991, resulting in an estimated turnover of over £600 million annually across more than 350 stores. Additionally, it has built a successful own-brand business that accounts for a healthy share of the cat and dog food markets.[1]

Similarly, when Confetti launched in 1999, it revolutionised the wedding industry by creating an online portal for brides-to-be – a one-stop shop providing them with everything they needed to plan their wedding. The company sold wedding products (such as party favours and invitations), helped brides-to-be research and find suppliers (such as cake makers, wedding venues and photographers), and offered advice on topics ranging from speech writing to table decoration. Within its first year, despite being third to market with only £500,000 to spend, it encouraged 93 percent of its target audience to sign up, making it the UK's number one online wedding portal. Additionally, it created the UK's largest wedding database – larger than those owned by big, established brands such as John Lewis, Moss Bros and Debenhams. On the back of this success, Confetti built a retail presence, locating stores in major towns across the UK. These quickly became destination stores, with brides-to-be travelling upwards of one hundred miles with family and friends to see demonstrations on how to lay the perfect wedding reception table or to be coached on how to write a great wedding speech.

One of the latest retail channels worth mentioning is the rise of the pop-up store, which accounts for over £2 billion of sales in the UK.[2] Pop-ups provide both budding entrepreneurs and established brands an opportunity to test the viability of a new concept and optimise it, before investing further. Similarly, they are a cost-efficient way for entrepreneurs to publicise a new brand and win more customers for just a few weeks of the year – and for larger brands such as Levi-Strauss and AT&T to target niche younger audiences. They also have the added benefit of encouraging people to buy today for 'fear of missing out' – in essence, "while it's there, enjoy it, once it's gone, it's gone".

Pop-up stores come in a variety of formats. There's the traditional bricks and mortar store, typically used by brands such as Carluccio's to sell Christmas food products and gifts in the run-up to Christmas, or entrepreneurs who rent a pop-up outlet for a month to boost brand awareness and sales.

Then there's the 'store within a store' format. For example, Samsung set up Samsung Open Houses in three Best Buy stores, Liberty's set up luxury designer stores in five Nordstrom stores, and J. Crew launched a 24-hour pop-up store within one of its New York outlets, showcasing three finalists of The Council of Fashion Designers awards.

There are stand-alone kiosks, such as Adidas and Nike pop-up kiosks in football grounds and at sporting events, or Pimm's pop-up bars during Wimbledon fortnight.

And there's even motorised vehicles, made famous by Kogi BBQ – a truck in Los Angeles that was launched in 2008 to sell a new type of upscale cuisine, combining Korean barbecue with Mexican tacos. Using Twitter, Kogi constantly updated customers on its changing location, creating a groundswell of plugged-in urbanites tracking Kogi's whereabouts. Within months, Kogi was attracting hundreds of customers at several stops every day – with *Newsweek* calling it "America's first viral eatery". This spawned what is estimated to be at least an $800 million annual industry.[3]

Selling directly through virtual channels

Other brands have changed their category dynamics by selling directly to customers through virtual channels, such as over the telephone and online. Well-known examples include Amazon and LOVEFiLM, who succeeded in revolutionising the book and DVD markets respectively by enabling people to browse, order online and have the product delivered to their door or, as in LOVEFiLM's case, streamed immediately to a computer or TV.

In spite of being online brands, both Amazon and LOVEFiLM built a highly personalised service. They offered their users book, product and film recommendations based on their users' online search and purchase history – and they guaranteed a next day or even same day delivery, significantly reducing the time that a customer has to wait after clicking the 'confirm order' button.

Within ten years, LOVEFiLM emerged as the third biggest paid-for entertainment subscription service in the UK, after Sky and Virgin, with sales of almost £125 million and more than two million customers.[4]

Today, Amazon no longer just sells books. Its mission to be "Earth's most customer-centric company, where customers can find and discover anything they might want to buy online ... at the lowest possible prices" has propelled it into the top ten Fortune 500 companies and made it arguably the earth's biggest store.[5]

In contrast, the Blockbuster name is really all that exists of the once-mighty video rental store chain, which a mere decade ago boasted a market value of $5 billion, with nine thousand stores staffed by sixty thousand film buffs and wannabe filmmakers.[6]

First Direct, a telephone- and Internet-based retail bank, is known for its superior telephone and online customer experience. Its brand mission is to achieve "pioneering amazing service".[7] To achieve this, all new call centre recruits undergo a full-time training induction period of eight weeks, where they are taught technology skills, as well as trained on attitudes and approach. By the end of this period, they are able to handle 80 percent of customer requests right then and there. Also, one of First Direct's brand values is Kaizen (a Japanese philosophy meaning 'Continuous Improvement' or 'Change for the Best'), in which everyone within the organisation is encouraged to constantly challenge the status quo, with the aim of continually identifying new and better ways to attract and serve customers. Today, First Direct's reputation in the market continues to be unassailable – it is the UK's most recommended bank, with First Direct customers more likely to recommend their bank than customers of any other major GB bank or building society.[8]

Similarly, in 2012, the investment management company, Nutmeg, launched an online business that helps people invest more intelligently – by challenging the industry norms to give them a better deal. It has achieved this by "taking the best elements of a high-end investing service, and stripping out the complexity and cost by providing the service online". This enables Nutmeg to charge lower fees than traditional investment companies, resulting in higher investment returns. For example, it claims that an investment in a Nutmeg Stocks and Shares ISA over twenty years could generate a 25 percent higher return than the same investment in a high street Cash ISA.[9]

Selling directly to people in their homes

Other brands have changed their category dynamics by hosting parties in the relaxed setting of someone's home – creating the at-home personal shopping experience. Brands like Ann Summers, Body Shop and Stella & Dot have successfully generated significant sales or, in Stella & Dot's case, built a revolutionary business, by selling products to their customers in the comfort of their home, where they can host friends for an evening of personalised shopping over a glass of wine or two. Not only that, all three brands offer enterprising women a chance to run their own party plan business.

For example, mention Ann Summers and one thinks immediately of lingerie, party wear and sex toys. Add to this, party hosts who boast that they can offer you "the most fun you can have in your own living room" and you've got a thriving business. Alongside its 144 stores that create a strong national presence, Ann Summers also has 7,000 party organisers who host more than 3,500 exclusively women-only parties every week in the informal setting of people's homes. At these private parties, guests are invited to "try before they buy" the range of Ann Summer's lingerie, play with sex toys without the embarrassment of being in a public place, and join in party games to win prizes.

Ann Summer's party plan concept was launched in 1981 when Jacqueline Gold, the current chief executive officer, was a guest at a Pippa Dee party (the clothes version of a Tupperware party) hosted in a council flat in South East London. Observing that the women were having fun, bonding and shopping at the same time, Gold wondered whether Ann Summer's products could be sold in this way. She held some test evenings, which were an instant hit with the female guests, resulting in significant product sales.

When Gold proposed her idea of launching a formal party business to the company's then all-male Board, one Board member famously said that the idea wasn't going to work because "women aren't interested in sex." But how wrong he was. The Board invested £40,000 and the company now reports a turnover of over £100 million.[10]

Similarly, the Body Shop maintains a solid presence of more than two hundred and fifty retail stores in the UK, bolstered by a team of more than four thousand consultants who sell Body Shop products in the privacy of people's homes. Typically, anyone who wants to host an at-home party organises, in conjunction with the Body Shop, the date, theme and guest list. Then, on the day, a Body Shop professional consultant arrives with armfuls of make-up and skincare products – along with a wealth of beauty tricks and tips to share with the guests for an evening of pampering and indulgence.[11]

Stella & Dot, considered to be 'the 21st-century answer to Avon', is a thriving business that has primarily been built through the hosting of at-home jewellery parties. The company mission is "to give every woman the means to style their own life", by both selling stylish jewellery and accessories that are affordable, as well as offering people (often stay-at-home mums) a fun, flexible and rewarding way to work from home as a Stella & Dot stylist. For a small fee, 'stylists' buy a starter kit that provides samples, tools, training and back office customer service, enabling them to start their own business and host their own jewellery and accessory 'trunk shows'. In just ten years, Stella & Dot has achieved a global turnover of over £125 million supported by more than ten thousand stylists, including in the UK where, in its first three years, it has achieved a turnover of over £7 million supported by more than one thousand stylists.[12]

Selling through non-traditional channels

Traditional brands have achieved incremental sales by selling their products through non-traditional channels and retailers, alongside mainstream ones.

For example, within retail, Toys "R" Us sells nappies at breakeven prices or at a loss to attract young parents to the store – and, in doing so, enables nappy manufacturers to drive incremental sales through non-traditional retail outlets. Once in-store, the young parents can't resist picking up a small toy or two for their children.

Similarly, air fresheners and odour eliminators, such as P&G's AmbiPur, were extended beyond the home into car perfumes. To significantly increase its sales, AmbiPur distributed these car fresheners in petrol stations, siting them next to car accessories as an impulse purchase.

Others have changed their category dynamics by selling in non-traditional ways, such as through TV channels like QVC or on the street.

Many beauty brands have had huge success on the QVC channel, a channel that is typically watched by the over-forty age group looking for a great deal or something innovative to try. Take, for example, Liz Earle, a brand that launched its first product on QVC in 1996 (by Liz Earle herself). This brand set a precedent – in less than thirty minutes it had completely sold out of its cleanse, tone and moisturise essentials and Eyebright Soothing Eye Lotion. Liz Earle now employs more than five hundred employees with a turnover of almost £50 million.[13]

Similarly, beauty brand Elemis credits QVC with its launch success, shifting an astounding eighty-five thousand products in one day via the QVC channel, giving the brand a huge awareness and trial boost.[14]

Meanwhile, Leslie Blodgett primarily used non-traditional channels to build beauty brand Bare Escentuals from a small, relatively unknown brand that in 1994 was close to bankruptcy, into a successful business with over £375 million in annual turnover. Leslie Blodgett, herself, regularly appeared on the QVC channel to demonstrate how to apply mineral make-up. She also used a fleet of pink 'Quickie vans' to tour the United States "giving people a flawless makeover in under five minutes". In tandem, she recruited a select group of volunteer brand ambassadors, 'Leslie's Angels', who were given the chance to test products while still in the development stage as well as sample free kits and products before they were launched. All they had to do in return was offer free make-up advice to friends, family and colleagues.[15]

Weighing up the options

As we can see, the growth in new technology has opened up many new cost-efficient and effective channels. These have proved a highly succcesful and cost-efficient way to engage with and sell to people, and can thereby help to increase a brand's return on investment.

Additionally, a strong multi-channel strategy, leveraging both traditional and new channels, has enabled many companies to engage customers more successfully. When done well, it can help to deliver a seamless customer experience whenever the customer interacts with the brand, attract new customers who prefer to use non-traditional channels, and increase profitability by lowering the cost to serve.

But for those selling through traditional channels, it may not be a simple decision to add non-traditional distribution channels. Marketers need to balance the desire to create new business with the need to maintain the core business.

For example, marketers need to ensure that the new channels bring in new business – by better engaging existing customers or bringing in new customers – rather than cannibalise existing business.

Similarly, marketers need to ensure that any additional sales costs – such as the additional cost of building an online store, setting up a next day delivery service, providing 24–7 telephone support and of ongoing software maintenance – don't eat up valuable profits.

Conversely, if your target audience is increasingly shopping online, you may have to offer an online channel – even if it results in lower profitability. If you don't, you may risk losing customers and ultimately sales, to a level that is unsustainable.

Pulling it all together, to develop a strong, profitable multi-channel strategy, marketers need to assess:

- Which distribution channels are necessary to engage with and sell to customers today.

- Which distribution channels will be vital to business success in the future, based on market and technology trends.
- Which distribution channels will have the greatest fit with the brand's positioning and pricing strategy.
- The additional revenues each channel is likely to add to the business, excluding any cannibalisation from one channel to another.
- The additional costs of introducing each channel, including pre-sale, during sale and post-sales costs.

B: Optimising channel performance

Choosing which channels to market through is only part of the picture – success also hinges on optimising your brand's performance within that channel. This entails understanding your customer's mindset throughout the shopping experience – for example, when will they be most open to your brand, what if anything can be done to make your brand stand out, and what can you say to them at that moment to convince them to buy.

As a manufacturer, optimising channel performance will most likely involve convincing the retailer to position your brand on-shelf in the optimal position, as well as providing them with in-store brochures, samples, promotions and expert advice that will give your brand the edge. When positioning their brand in-store, marketers should consider:

- Where in the store their brand should be stocked.
- Where on the aisle their brand should be stocked.
- What, if anything, can be done to make their brand stand out.

Where in the store to stock your brand

Categories and brands perform best when they are adjacent to other relevant categories. Consequently, *category adjacencies* can be vital in driving sales, particularly if a category is an 'impulse purchase' (such as chocolate) or 'emerging' (such as air and fabric fresheners).

For example, most shoppers are unlikely to walk to an impulse category such as chocolate, preferring to avoid the temptation of buying something fattening. Yet if that category is stocked next to a high traffic category (such as tea and coffee), many more shoppers are likely to pick up a chocolate bar or two as they pass. Similarly, sales of salty snacks or crisps increase when they are located next to alcohol, sales of crisps and fizzy drinks increase when located next to children's toys, sales of batteries increase when located next to goods that require batteries (such as alarm clocks or torches) and sales of specialist laundry detergents (such as soap powder for delicates) increase when located alongside clothing, for example, within fashion accessories.

Because these secondary purchases tend to be more impulsive, these products tend to be sold at full price, thereby maximising return.

Beacon brands also play a significant role in driving sales. These are well-known brands with strong colour ways that people typically recognise at a subliminal level as they walk around the store – brands like Coca-Cola with its distinctive red, or the Gillette Fusion range in bright orange, or Pampers with its distinctive green.

Beacon brands are used to catch the shopper's eye and draw them into an aisle. For instance, an aisle that features a well-recognised and well-liked beacon brand at the end of it (such as a Coca-Cola promotion on a gondola end) will entice more shoppers to walk down that aisle and, in turn, buy the brands that are stocked on that aisle.

Manufacturers of brands stocked at the checkout pay a premium for the privilege. Once the shopper has reached the checkout their shop is effectively over, so anything they buy at this point is an additional purchase that they would otherwise not have made, creating incremental sales for the manufacturer. Checkouts are a perfect place for increasing sales of impulse purchases such as chocolate and razor blades, which people are often happy to stock up on, as and when they spot them.

Where on the aisle to stock your brand

Brands sell most when positioned at just below eye level on the shelf – between waist and shoulder height, or at an angle within the range of fifteen to thirty degrees downward from eye level. Sales can increase by as much as 50 percent when a brand is moved from the bottom shelf to eye level, making it in both the retailers' and the consumers' interests to place top-performing brands in prime shelf locations. Similarly, children's brands often site their products at a child's eye level, to attract their attention.

Likewise, brands sell most when placed three to four feet (or 1 to 1.2 metres) along the aisle. This is because when shoppers enter a new aisle, they typically walk faster – both to get their bearings as well as to ensure that they aren't in anyone's way – and products placed within those first few feet of the aisle can be missed. Once they have their bearings, shoppers tend to slow down, taking time to peruse what's on offer – hence three to four feet into the aisle is the ideal location for product placement. Then, as shoppers continue to walk down the aisle they get bored and speed up, making it much more difficult for those products placed further down the aisle to attract attention.

Shoppers assess how a brand is positioned, based on which of its competitor brands it is sitting next to. For example, if a new brand wants to be seen as 'premium', it should be sited alongside the premium beacon brand. If it wants to be seen as the 'best value' brand, it should sit between the other value brands with the premium brand sited in the next tier up. This helps shoppers quickly perceive how the brand compares with its peers.

What, if anything, can be done to make your brand stand out

The right sensory experiences – such as colours, sounds, smells and textures – can boost sales.

Products that are shelved in a more visually impactful way (for example, using wood panelling for wine, lighting for cosmetics or multiple brand facings in confectionery) tend to attract the shopper's eye and sell more – despite often having less on-shelf product facings.

Fragrance can also influence sales. Fresh, mouth-watering smells (such as freshly baked bread and chocolate) both slow people down and stimulate feelings of hunger, encouraging them to buy more, or enticing them to gravitate to the bakery or patisserie to check out what's on offer. In 2014 and 2015, ethical retailer Lush Cosmetics was named the best high street brand two years in a row according to *Which?*'s annual retailer survey – this is believed to be in part due to the retailer's heavy reliance on the power of scent marketing, with consumers being hit by fun and fruity fragrances as they enter the store.[16]

Music has been proven to significantly impact sales performance. Slow music can entice people to buy more – it relaxes and slows people down so that they spend more time browsing the various brands on offer. Equally, it can influence which products they select. A study conducted by Adrian North and his colleagues at the University of Leicester showed that on days when French music was played in-store, 77 percent of the wine sold was French, and on days when German music was played in-store, 73 percent of the wine sold was German. This equates to shoppers being three or four times more likely to select a wine from a country that matched the music that was being played. Interestingly, when asked if the music had affected their wine choice, 86 percent of shoppers said that it hadn't.[17]

Videos can be highly effective at bringing a brand's positioning and personality to life. For example, Silver Jeans uses video walls and Indie music in its new 'loft' concept store in the United States to "celebrate its independent and free brand values" and its integral link to denim culture.

In essence, marketers should spend time optimising their brand's performance within each channel by understanding their shopper's mindset throughout the shopping experience – considering, for example, who the shopper is (they may not be the end user), when will they be most open to your brand, what if anything can be done to make your brand stand out, and what you can say to them at that moment to convince them to buy. This doesn't need to be an expensive exercise – accompanying people when they shop or watching people when they are in-store can lead to rich insights. By doing this, marketers can better engage their customers as well as convince them to buy, and in turn boost the return on their sales and marketing investment.

C: Identifying and unblocking purchase funnel bottlenecks

When choosing which brand to buy, people often consciously or subconsciously start with a number of brand options before whittling them down and making a final decision. Marketers can plot this decision-making process along a 'purchase funnel'. Pinpointing precisely where in the purchase funnel the brand is losing customers and *why* – namely, the purchase funnel bottlenecks – will provide valuable insight into the reasons people are choosing competitor brands over your brand, and, most importantly, identify the issues that you need to fix to help your brand attract and retain more customers.

Many marketers have successfully identified where their brand is losing customers and why, and have used this analysis to build Board confidence on which purchase funnel bottlenecks to focus on and unblock. This is because this type of analysis, when done well, is:

- *Clear*, in terms of the analysis and recommendations.
- *Succinct*, with the analysis and 'so whats' summarised on one page.
- *Robust*, based on real-life customer research.
- *Jargon-free*, using customer rather than marketing language.
- *Intuitive*, in terms of which go-to-market issues to fix.

Let's look at how this works in practice.

Customers drop out of purchase funnels for a variety of reasons. For example, some brands lose customers due to service issues in the call centre; it could be something as simple as follow-up letters not being sent out, or the wrong brochures being included with the letter, or being kept hanging on the telephone for an unacceptably long time, or the telephone options being ambiguous or difficult to navigate. Others may lose customers because of problems with the website. Perhaps it's difficult to find the right telephone contact number or to identify which product is most appropriate for what the customer needs. For other brands, it could be that a valued product feature is missing – maybe the product does not come with a one-year warranty or perhaps the broadband package does not include unlimited access. Other brands may be struggling to convert people as a result of strong claims made in a competitor's advertising campaign. Or it could be that competitors are undercutting your brand on price – with your customers being offered an incredibly competitive new joiner deal when they call into a competitor's call centre.

Purchase funnel analysis not only exposes the bottlenecks – it can also size each blockage, as well as identify the underlying issues that are causing the greatest loss of customers and sales.

Typically, this involves asking recent category buyers (for example, those who have bought in the last six months) about their last purchase. For example, asking people who have recently bought a car which brands they were aware of, which they considered, which they actually enquired about, which they purchased and whether they have gone on to buy any additional products from this brand.

Then, for each stage, buyers are asked why they behaved as they did. For example, 'you said you considered buying a BMW but didn't enquire about them, why?' Or, 'you enquired about the Audi A4 but didn't buy one, why?' This provides detailed information on where people are dropping out of the purchase funnel and why – enabling the company to identify which are the critical issues that need to be fixed.

To illustrate, in a financial services case, purchase funnel analysis reviewed the percentage of people who were aware of a brand, the percentage who considered it, the percentage who enquired about it, the percentage who actually purchased it and then the percentage of those who went on to buy additional products. This quantitative analysis identified that, in absolute terms, the client was losing most customers (61 percent) between the awareness and consideration stage (Figure 7.1).

It's fair to say that as a low-interest, highly competitive category, most financial services brands are *not* considered, due to the vast choice of brand options and the little time that people are willing to spend researching this category. This means that for a more accurate picture, it's important to evaluate where in the purchase funnel the brand is losing more customers *in comparison to its core competitors*. This particular example revealed that the brand, relative to its key competitors, was performing less well at converting strong consideration into actual enquiries (11 percent points worse) and purchase

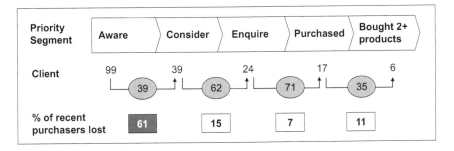

Figure 7.1 Purchase funnel analyses – absolute scores

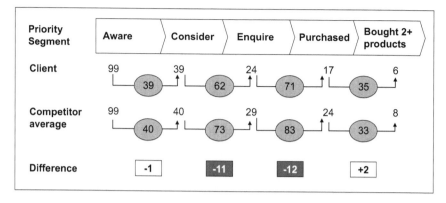

Figure 7.2 Purchase funnel analyses – relative scores

(12 percent points worse). Therefore, these were the primary blockages that the brand needed to focus on and fix (Figure 7.2).

Let's look at how the company resolved these issues.

Consumer research identified that some people who were aware of the brand didn't shortlist it, as it was perceived as being poorer value than the competitors' brands (mentioned by 36 percent of people). Some people considering the brand failed to go on to enquire about it because of an over-complicated website (mentioned by 27 percent of people), difficulty finding the right contact details (17 percent), a competitor's call centre team actively denigrating our brand's product features (15 percent) and problems getting through to the call centre (14 percent). Similarly, some people who enquired about the brand didn't go on to buy it due to finding a better offer (mentioned by 27 percent of people), negative PR from industry experts (16 percent) and an overly complex switching process (14 percent).

By sizing each of these issues and assessing how easy it was to fix each one (both from a time and cost perspective) the Board was able to prioritise which to fix – giving precedence to those that were both sizeable and easy to fix and deprioritising those that were small or difficult to fix (Figure 7.3). In this way, it could focus its scarce resources on fixing those issues that were causing the company to lose most customers.

In this particular piece of work, the CEO was personally engaged and made it a company priority to rectify the difficult-to-navigate website and weak call centre performance. Concentrating on these key factors enabled the Board to deliver quick wins as well as steady, sustainable growth. In fact, this piece of work was so successful that it was repeated annually to track brand performance and maintain the growth momentum.

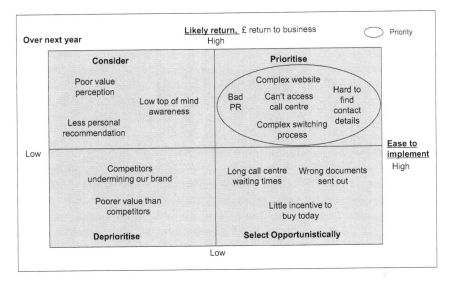

Figure 7.3 Issue prioritisation – by likely size and ease of implementation

In summary

When it comes to 'where' to market your brand, it's important to make it accessible to people in a way that they can easily engage with and purchase. Otherwise, it's likely to get lost in today's market clutter.

Yet it's also important for marketers to leverage cost-efficient distribution channels that will deliver the greatest return.

Therefore, to maximise their brand's performance and thereby help drive shareholder return, marketers should consider using new, more cost-efficient channels to reach their customers – either alongside, or in place of, traditional distribution channels. For example:

- Setting up their own one-stop stores.
- Selling through virtual channels, such as the telephone and online.
- Selling directly to people in their homes.
- Selling through non-traditional channels, such as on street corners or on TV shopping channels.

Choosing which channels to market through, however, is only part of the picture – success also hinges on optimising a brand's performance within that channel. Marketers should understand their customer's mindset throughout the whole shopping experience – for example, when customers will be most open to their brand. They should then use this information to assess where in store and on the aisle to stock their brand, and what if anything can be done to make their brand stand out, to convince customers to buy it.

Additionally, when in-market, marketers should identify *where* in the purchase funnel their brand is losing customers and *why*, and get Board buy-in to unblock these purchase funnel bottlenecks. For example, are there issues that are stopping customers from considering your brand, or enquiring about it or buying it?

By doing this, marketers can help build Board confidence on where to focus their scarce resources to attract and retain more customers, and thereby deliver greater investment returns.

Notes

1 James Titcomb, "Pets At Home Unveils Plans for £1.5bn Float," *The Telegraph*, February 2014, www.telegraph.co.uk/finance/newsbysector/retailandconsumer/10648100/Pets-At-Home-unveils-plans-for-1.5bn-float.html; Wikipedia, "Pets at Home," https://en.wikipedia.org/wiki/Pets_at_Home.

2 Sophie Christie, "We Made £2,000 in a Month by Selling Our Clothes in a Pop-up Store," *The Telegraph*, November 2014, www.telegraph.co.uk/finance/personalfinance/11180264/We-made-2000-in-a-month-by-selling-our-clothes-in-a-pop-up-store.html.

3 David Brindley, *The National Geographic*, July 2015, http://ngm.nationalgeographic.com/2015/07/food-trucks/brindley-text.

4 Sarah Bridge, "Amazon's Online Rental Subsidiary LoveFilm Slumped Into Loss Last Year after Mounting Costs Offset Sharp Rise in Sales," *Financial Mail*, September 2013, www.thisismoney.co.uk/money/markets/article-2428018/Amazons-online-film-DVD-subsidiary-LoveFilm-loss-costs-soar.html.

5 Amazon.com, "Amazon Jobs," www.amazon.jobs/en-gb/working/working-amazon, accessed October 2016; Stephen Gandel, "These Are the Top 10 Most Valuable Companies in the Fortune 500," *Fortune.com*, February 2016, http://fortune.com/2016/02/04/most-valuable-companies-fortune-500-apple/; Robin Lewis, "Amazon . . . From Earth's Biggest Bookstore to the Biggest Store on Earth," *The Robin Report*, January 2012, www.therobinreport.com/amazon-from-earths-biggest-bookstore-to-the-biggest-store-on-earth/.

6 Ethan Alter, "Life after Blockbuster: Catching Up with the Owner of Some of the Last Remaining Blockbuster Video Stores," September 2014, www.yahoo.com/movies/life-after-blockbuster-catching-up-with-the-owner-of-97752912042.html.

7 Best Companies, "First Direct," www.b.co.uk/Company/Profile/96594.

8 First Direct, "GfK NOP FRS Data, 6 Months Ending May 2015," http://www1.firstdirect.com/1/2/; Alex Garrett, Roopalee Dave, Hugh Wilson and Moira Clark, "First Direct Comes of Age," Cranfield University School of Management, November 2007.

9 Nutmeg, April 2016, www.nutmeg.com.

10 Emma Sinclair, "How Ann Summers' Jacqueline Gold Continues to Pleasure the Nation," *The Telegraph*, April 2013, www.telegraph.co.uk/women/womens-business/10025319/How-Ann-Summers-Jacqueline-Gold-continues-to-pleasure-the-nation.html; Ann Summers, April 2016, www.annsummers.com/party-plan-be-an-ambassador.html; Will Smale, "How Jacqueline Gold Made Ann Summers a Respectable Brand," October 2015, *BBC News*, www.bbc.com/news/business-34475607.

11 The Bodyshop, April 2016, www.thebodyshop.com/en-gb/store-finder; www.thebodyshop.com/en-gb/landing-at-home.

12 Rebecca Gonsalves, "Stella & Dot, a Stellar Idea," *The Independent*, June 2013, www.independent.co.uk/life-style/fashion/features/stella-dot-a-stellar-idea-8680472.html; Julia Llewellyn Smith, "Meet the Woman Transforming Lives – One Necklace at a Time,"

The Telegraph, July 2015, www.telegraph.co.uk/women/womens-business/11741646/stella-and-dot-direct-selling-jewellery-business.html; Stella & Dot, April 2016, www.stelladot.co.uk/stylists; Vikram Alexai Kansara, "Jessica Herrin of Stella & Dot on Remaking Direct Sales for the Digital Age," *Business of Fashion*, October 2013, www.businessoffashion.com/articles/founder-stories/jessica-herrin-stella-dot-sequoia-capital.

13 Liz Earle, "Liz Earle's Caroline Archer Talks 18 Years at QVC," March 2014, http://blogs.qvcuk.com/liz-earles-caroline-archer-talks-18-years-at-qvc/; Natalie Whittle, "Nordic Walking with the FT: Liz Earle," *The Financial Times*, August 2012, www.ft.com/content/a6359830-dc32–11e1–86f8–00144feab49a.

14 Phong Luu, "Quality, Value – But Can QVC Ever be Cool?', *The Daily Telegraph*, March 2013, http://fashion.telegraph.co.uk/news-features/TMG9925156/QVC-Quality-Value-but-can-QVC-ever-be-Cool.html.

15 Bare Escentuals, "bareMinerals," www.bareescentuals.com, accessed April 2016; Liz Welch, "How I Did It – Leslie Blodgett of Bare Escentuals," *inc.com*, July 2010, www.inc.com/magazine/20100701/how-i-did-it-leslie-blodgett-of-bare-escentuals.html; Cindi Lieve, "Bare Escentuals Executive Chairman Leslie Blodgett on Building a Beauty Empire *Her Way*," *Glamour.com*, April 2015, www.glamour.com/story/bare-escentuals-executive-chairman-leslie-blodgett-career-advice; Wikinvest, "Bare Escentuals," April 2016, http://www.wikinvest.com/stock/Bare_Escentuals_(BARE).

16 *Which?*, http://www.which.co.uk/.

17 Tom Stafford and Matt Webb, *Mind Hacks* (Sebastopol, CA: O'Reilly Media Inc., 2005).

Bibliography

Alter, Ethan. "Life after Blockbuster: Catching Up with the Owner of Some of the Last Remaining Blockbuster Video Stores." September 2014. www.yahoo.com/movies/life-after-blockbuster-catching-up-with-the-owner-of-97752912042.html.

Amazon. "Amazon Jobs." Accessed October 2016. www.amazon.jobs/en-gb/working/working-amazon.

Ann Summers. April 2016. www.annsummers.com/party-plan-be-an-ambassador.html.

Bare Escentuals. "bareMinerals." April 2016. https://www.bareescentuals.com.

Best Companies. "First Direct." www.b.co.uk/Company/Profile/96594.

The Bodyshop. April 2016. www.thebodyshop.com/en-gb/store-finder; www.thebodyshop.com/en-gb/landing-at-home.

Bridge, Sarah. "Amazon's Online Rental Subsidiary LoveFilm Slumped Into Loss Last Year after Mounting Costs Offset Sharp Rise in Sales." *Financial Mail*, September 2013. www.thisismoney.co.uk/money/markets/article-2428018/Amazons-online-film-DVD-subsidiary-LoveFilm-loss-costs-soar.html.

Brindley, David. *The National Geographic*, July 2015. http://ngm.nationalgeographic.com/2015/07/food-trucks/brindley-text.

Christie, Sophie. "We Made £2,000 in a Month by Selling Our Clothes in a Pop-up Store." *The Telegraph*, November 2014. www.telegraph.co.uk/finance/personalfinance/11180264/We-made-2000-in-a-month-by-selling-our-clothes-in-a-pop-up-store.html.

Earle, Liz. "Liz Earle's Caroline Archer Talks 18 Years at QVC." March 2014. http://blogs.qvcuk.com/liz-earles-caroline-archer-talks-18-years-at-qvc/.

First Direct. "GfK NOP FRS Data, 6 Months Ending May 2015." http://www1.firstdirect.com/1/2/.

Gandel, Stephen. "These Are the Top 10 Most Valuable Companies in the Fortune 500." *Fortune.com*, February 2016. http://fortune.com/2016/02/04/most-valuable-companies-fortune-500-apple/.

Garrett, Alex, Roopalee Dave, Hugh Wilson and Moira Clark. "First Direct Comes of Age." Cranfield University School of Management, November 2007.

Gonsalves, Rebecca. "Stella & Dot, a Stellar Idea." *The Independent*, June 2013. www.indepen dent.co.uk/life-style/fashion/features/stella-dot-a-stellar-idea-8680472.html.

Kansara, Vikram Alexai. "Jessica Herrin of Stella & Dot on Remaking Direct Sales for the Digital Age." *Business of Fashion*, October 2013. www.businessoffashion.com/articles/founder-stories/jessica-herrin-stella-dot-sequoia-capital.

Lewis, Robin. "Amazon . . . From Earth's Biggest Bookstore To the Biggest Store on Earth." *The Robin Report*, January 2012. www.therobinreport.com/amazon-from-earths-biggest-bookstore-to-the-biggest-store-on-earth/.

Lieve, Cindi. "Bare Escentuals Executive Chairman Leslie Blodgett on Building a Beauty Empire Her Way." *Glamour.com*, April 2015. www.glamour.com/story/bare-escentuals-executive-chairman-leslie-blodgett-career-advice.

Luu, Phong. "Quality, Value – But Can QVC Ever be Cool?" *The Daily Telegraph*, March 2013. http://fashion.telegraph.co.uk/news-features/TMG9925156/QVC-Quality-Value-but-can-QVC-ever-be-Cool.html.

Nutmeg. April 2016. www.nutmeg.com.

Sinclair, Emma. "How Ann Summers' Jacqueline Gold Continues to Pleasure the Nation." *The Telegraph*, April 2013. http://www.telegraph.co.uk/women/womens-business/10025319/How-Ann-Summers-Jacqueline-Gold-continues-to-pleasure-the-nation.html

Smale, Will. "How Jacqueline Gold Made Ann Summers a Respectable Brand." October 2015, *BBC News*. www.bbc.com/news/business-34475607.

Smith, Julia Llewellyn. "Meet the Woman Transforming Lives – One Necklace at a Time." *The Telegraph*, July 2015. www.telegraph.co.uk/women/womens-business/11741646/stella-and-dot-direct-selling-jewellery-business.html.

Stafford, Tom and Matt Webb. *Mind Hacks*. Sebastopol, CA: O'Reilly Media Inc., 2005.

Stella & Dot. April 2016. www.stelladot.co.uk/stylists.

Titcomb, James. "Pets At Home Unveils Plans for £1.5bn Float." *The Telegraph*, February 2014. www.telegraph.co.uk/finance/newsbysector/retailandconsumer/10648100/Pets-At-Home-unveils-plans-for-1.5bn-float.html.

Welch, Liz. "How I Did It – Leslie Blodgett of Bare Escentuals." *inc.com*, July 2010. www.inc.com/magazine/20100701/how-i-did-it-leslie-blodgett-of-bare-escentuals.html.

Which?. http://www.which.co.uk/.

Whittle, Natalie. "Nordic Walking with the FT: Liz Earle." *The Financial Times*, August 2012. www.ft.com/content/a6359830-dc32–11e1–86f8–00144feab49a.

Wikinvest. "Bare Escentuals." April 2016. www.wikinvest.com/stock/Bare_Escentuals_(BARE).

Wikipedia. "Pets at Home." https://en.wikipedia.org/wiki/Pets_at_Home.

Chapter 8

Choosing 'when' to engage people

"Words calculated to catch everyone may catch no one."

Adlai E. Stevenson Junior, American politician

As we saw in Chapter 7, to develop robust marketing strategies that drive shareholder value and engage the Board, marketers need to find ways to manage and grow their brands as cost-efficiently and effectively as possible.

When choosing "when" to talk with people, marketers should optimise their marketing investment returns by focusing their spend on those *high-impact touch points and messages* that have the greatest influence on people.

Entrepreneurs probably understand the value of focusing on high-impact touch points better than anyone.

Typically entrepreneurs start a company with limited money – be it their own or that of an equity partner – as well as limited time to prove the success of the concept. So, they often start small – looking for touch points that will deliver a bigger bang for their buck and give them the initial foothold that they need.

They also tend to highly value every customer that comes to them, particularly at the outset. Entrepreneurs instinctively grasp that if the customer feels well looked after throughout the customer journey, they are much more likely to purchase more products, as well as recommend the company to their peers, family and friends.

If marketers behave with an entrepreneurial attitude – that is, if they spend the advertising budget as if it were *their own hard-earned money* and make it go further by pinpointing and leveraging those touch points and messages that are *most effective and cost-efficient at changing customer behaviour* – they can demonstrate to the Board that they are handling the company's money responsibly. This in turn helps the Board to invest with confidence to create a truly differentiated and compelling brand experience.

In this chapter, we look at two communication strategies that help optimise investment return and therefore interest the Board:

A   Making a communications budget work harder by leveraging highly influential, low cost touch points and giving people a reason to act now.

B   Turning a new customer relationship into a deep customer relationship in the first 180 days.

A: Leveraging highly influential, low cost touch points and giving people a reason to act now

Customer touch points are those moments during the purchase journey when a customer, or potential customer, comes into contact with a brand – be it before, during, or post purchase.

For example, pre-purchase, customers might be influenced by television adverts, posters, banner adverts, the brand's website, PR, packaging, or what their friends and family say.

During the purchase experience, they may be influenced by the call centre experience, the information on the website, sales brochures and literature or how easy they've heard it is to switch.

Post-purchase, they may be influenced by the level of technical support they receive (for example, when getting set up or when something goes wrong), the day-to-day online experience, the on-going service experience, or the renewals process.

As I have experienced when working with entrepreneurial companies, not all touch points are equal. Some influence customers more than others, and some are much more cost-efficient than others. Many large brands focus the majority of their spend on mainstream communication touch points, such as television, press, sponsorship, promotions. Yet, over recent years, the number of channels has multiplied exponentially – primarily driven by the onset of digital technology – with an abundance of other touch points that are not only more influential, but also less costly. For instance, some, such as landing pages, call centre scripts or on-shelf packaging cost little (or even nothing).

Let's look at some of these examples in practice.

Examples of companies that have built their business using low-cost touch points

When launching a new brand, many entrepreneurs are forced to start modestly, looking for more creative ways to communicate with their customers and thereby build their brand cost-efficiently.

Confetti

One example of this is confetti.co.uk. In 1999, David Lethbridge and Andrew Doe started Confetti.co.uk – an online wedding site for brides-to-be. It was initially funded by venture capitalists with a phase one investment of £1.75 million, with which to prove the financial viability of their business model. However, this £1.75 million was to cover all aspects of the start-up – i.e., not only the advertising but also the offices, the employment of staff, the development of the website etc. – and even if stretched to its limit, would last no longer than six months. Hence, the Confetti team had six months and £500K of advertising spend to prove Confetti's long-term financial viability to venture capitalists, in the hope of convincing them to invest more money.

Based on the team's knowledge of brides-to-be, Lethbridge and Doe wanted Confetti to be the "virtual" equivalent of the "traditional bride's mother". So they positioned Confetti as the website that "takes the stress out of organising a wedding" – with a tone that was the antithesis of stress by being light-hearted, modern and fun.

They focused much of their advertising spend on 'drive time' media, given that many urban brides-to-be travel to work each day. These included press ads in the *Metro* and *Evening Standard*, with a minimalist layout and a strong purple colour way to generate cut-through – as well as 'drive time' radio ads, featuring the popular and humorous TV presenter Graham Norton as Confetti's spokesperson.

Focus groups identified that brides-to-be scour celebrity-wedding articles in *Hello* and *OK* magazines for wedding ideas. Armed with this insight, Confetti approached *Hello* magazine and for a mere £10,000 negotiated ten one-page wedding advertorials, each to be placed directly after a celebrity engagement or wedding article, congratulating the couple with a bespoke personalised message. The personal nature of these advertorials (both message and placement) made them disproportionately impactful and memorable to the target audience.

Confetti also approached well-known brands in other categories that might benefit from talking with brides-to-be – brands such as Max Factor ('big day' make-overs), British Airways (honeymoons), Liberty's (wedding lists) and Moss Bros (wedding attire). With no money changing hands, Confetti offered to promote these brands to its database of 'brides to be', on the basis that these big brands promoted Confetti to their customers. For example, Max Factor advertised its endorsement of Confetti on all of its promotional displays in Boots, and British Airways advertised Confetti in its customer holiday destination brochure, next to the articles on honeymoons.

Finally, Confetti offered people who registered on its website the opportunity to enter into a monthly £10,000 prize draw to help pay for their wedding – an attractive offer given that at this time the average cost of a wedding was £12,500.

In spite of its low level of advertising spend, research confirmed that Confetti's target audience was responding to the adverts. By March 2000, Confetti's brand and advertising awareness among its core target audience had reached 46 percent and 35 percent respectively. When Confetti customers were asked why they had come to the site, a staggering two-thirds claimed to have done so because of the advertising and over half claimed that they registered because of the chance of winning the £10,000 monthly prize draw.

This resulted in 93 percent of Confetti's target audience registering in six months – exceeding Confetti's first year goal by 8 percent – making it the UK's number one online wedding portal (in spite of being third to market) and the UK's largest wedding database.[1]

Ella's Kitchen

Another example is Ella's Kitchen. Paul Lindley started Ella's Kitchen, an organic baby food company, in 2006 when his two-year-old daughter, Ella, stopped eating certain foods for no apparent reason – a scenario that many parents experience. He launched Ella's Kitchen as a one-man band, working out of his children's playroom. Within six years, it had become one of the UK's fastest-growing businesses with global sales of £60 million and a 14 percent share of the baby food market – and was ranked in the *Sunday Times* Top Fast Track 100 List for four consecutive years, between 2009 and 2012. So how did Lindley achieve this?

Initially Lindley spent his first two years – and £25,000 of savings – fine-tuning his idea, including utilising the support of the University of Reading's Department of Food and Nutritional Sciences to ensure that the products were as healthy and nutritionally balanced as possible. The result was a range of "good baby food that stimulates all of their senses", using tasty, 100% organic ingredients in fun-to-play-with squishy, colourful packs.

To gain distribution, Lindley then bombarded the supermarkets with more than five hundred phone calls and five hundred e-mails but to little avail. With his savings running low, he approached Nickelodeon with a revenue share deal. In exchange for giving Ella's Kitchen free advertising space and co-funding some adverts, Lindley gave Nickelodeon a cut of the firm's profits. From Nickelodeon's point of view this was attractive, as it helped to address some of the criticism that the children's television channel was receiving at the time concerning the nutritional quality of children's foods that featured on the channel.

Next, he approached Sainsbury's and the offer of a free advertising campaign helped secure distribution in 350 Sainsbury's stores for twelve weeks, giving Lindley enough time to prove the value of the brand to the Sainsbury's buying team. The pilot worked and the business has grown extensively ever since.[2]

Vitabiotics

In 1971, Dr. Kartar Lalvani founded Vitabiotics – a nutraceutical company specialising in vitamin and mineral based products for different areas of health – such as pregnancy, skin, hair and nails. Although it started small, by 2016 it operated in over one hundred countries yielding a turnover of close to £100 million. Let's look at what propelled Dr. Lalvani's success.

Throughout the 1990s and 2000s, the Vitabiotics business grew significantly in the UK, supported by a small annual spend of circa £3 million. Vitabiotics focused its small advertising spend on targeting a tight audience of urban professionals and mothers, by leveraging cost efficient urban press and posters, particularly on buses, tube trains and in tube stations.

To make its small communications budget work harder, it used hard hitting efficacy claims. It leveraged category leadership accolades (such as "The UK's number one vitamins company"), research claims (such as "90% of women reported a significant benefit"), expert endorsements (such as "Bupa Approved"), business awards (such as "Boots Award for Number One Overall Supplier of the Year") and testimonials from leading sports people (such as the cricketer, James Anderson). Additionally, Vitabiotics consistently communicated these claims, awards, endorsements and testimonials across everything it did – including 'free' touch points such as its packaging, in-store leaflets, promotional materials and website.

Tej Lalvani, the founder's son, who is now chief operating officer, puts the company's success down to owning the research and marketing expertise. "More care goes into elements like the packaging if we own the process ourselves."[3]

Bought By Many

Bought By Many is a tech-savvy, 'new generation' business that uses crowdsourcing to harness the collective buying power of the Internet to negotiate better specialist insurance deals for relatively small groups of people with common needs.

Launched by Stephen Mendel and Guy Farley in 2012, it uses group buying to help online communities buy insurance with lower premiums and on better terms than would otherwise be available to them as individuals.

This business model has proved especially helpful to those people with specialist insurance needs – for example, people with pre-existing medical conditions (such as diabetes) who want to travel, owners of exotic pets, and fanatical amateur cyclists who own expensive bicycles and bicycling kit.

When starting out, the Bought By Many team reviewed 104 million Internet searches that people had made about insurance to identify which niche insurance opportunities to focus on. By doing this, they were able to size each of the insurance opportunities, as well as assess the size of the gap between what people wanted and what mainstream insurance companies were offering. One of the opportunities that emerged was a travel insurance package for people with Crohn's Disease – a sizeable population with a strong need for help.

Then, instead of using traditional advertising vehicles such as television and press, Bought By Many utilised 'community word of mouth' to drive awareness and trial. This was supplemented by adverts on social media platforms (such as Facebook, LinkedIn and Twitter) to gain awareness among niche interest groups and make it easy for users to invite their friends. This enabled the company to quickly and cost-efficiently gain traction among relevant niche customer groups.

Bought By Many also asked people which types of specialist insurance they would like Bought By Many to offer, enabling them to generate and assess the potential for new insurance opportunities. For example, dog breed enthusiasts asked Bought By Many to offer insurance for specialist dog breeds, such as Sprokers (a Springer Spaniel and Cocker Spaniel cross) and Cockapoos (a Cocker Spaniel and Poodle cross) – which, given the size of the opportunity, Bought By Many duly did.[4]

These are all examples of great entrepreneurial launches leveraging influential and cost efficient touch points. So, do more mainstream, established brands do the same?

Mainstream brands have also successfully leveraged influential and cost efficient touch points

Take, for instance, teenagers. One of the reasons teenagers read teen magazines is to get top tips on how to manage the wealth of new teen issues that they are facing – making teenage magazines highly influential. Clearasil approached *Sugar* magazine with the challenge of "encouraging teenage girls to wash their face with Clearasil twice a day to keep their spots away". In response, *Sugar* magazine jointly ran an advertorial with Clearasil at the end of Spring, encouraging girls to get their skin in great shape for summer, in line with that year's 'no make-up' fashion trend. As a result, one £10,000 Clearasil advertorial in *Sugar* magazine generated as much sales uplift as a monthly TV burst (costing £350,000 at that time) due to its high impact and relevance in a highly trusted and influential magazine.

Another example is an insurance company, which ran a carefully orchestrated city advertising campaign. Each week, it aired a television advert in a different city letting people know that throughout the week it would be calling residents in that city to try to beat their current insurance quote. Interestingly, when the sales team called households to see if they could better their current insurance deal, around half of the residents contacted were happy to engage in the conversation, a staggeringly high number given the small level of investment.

Or take my favourite example, Walkers Crisps. Aisle-cruising is one of the most critical times for fast-moving consumer goods brands to engage with shoppers, given they are about to decide which products to buy. But it is also an incredibly cost-efficient way to capture attention, as bringing the brand positioning to life on packaging can incur little or no incremental cost. At the time, Walkers Crisps was running a TV campaign featuring the footballer Gary Lineker as their celebrity spokesman, along with other well-liked footballers, such as Michael Owen. Walkers cleverly saw an opportunity to remind people of its distinctive brand advertising when in-store by naming the crisp flavours after its on-TV sporting celebrities – Salt & Vinegar became 'Salt & Lineker', Cheese & Onion became 'Cheese & Owen', Smokey Bacon *almost* became 'Smokey Beckham' (but David Beckham objected). More recently Ready Salted became a 'Vardy Salted' Limited Edition, in recognition of James Vardy's contribution to Leicester City's 2016 Premier League title win. By doing this, shoppers not only noticed the brand when walking down the aisle but also were reminded of the distinctive TV campaign. Recalling the warmth and cheekiness of the adverts, they were more drawn to choosing Walkers crisps over other crisp brands.

Driving trial by giving people reasons to act now

Getting people's attention can be tough. But getting them to convert their attention into action can be even tougher. In 2015, more than 170,000 brands were advertised in the UK alone, equating to almost five hundred new and different brands advertising each and every single day of the year. We are so inundated by choice that we may want to purchase something but don't get around to it.[5]

Even if people notice and fancy trying your brand, it doesn't mean that they'll actually buy it. How frequently have you heard yourself say "Yes, that sounds like a great idea – I'll definitely try it – but not today, I've got too much on" – and then it gets forgotten?

Engaging consumers is more than just creating attractive products and services that people want to buy and coming up with advertising campaigns that build brand awareness, consideration and a strong brand image. It's also about giving people a convincing reason to act today.

Let's consider the first time I changed bank accounts. I was frustrated with my bank's poor service, and so decided to enquire about switching my account to another bank. As with all complicated, low-interest purchases, I wanted to make the switch, but couldn't be bothered – 'perhaps I'll do it tomorrow'. But, as always, tomorrow never came, and I put up with my existing banking relationship. Nine months later, the competitor bank I was interested in wrote to me asking why I hadn't switched, and offered me £25 if I switched within the next month. I was tempted, but not tempted enough, and so did nothing. A month later, the bank wrote to me offering me £50 to switch. I thought about it, but again did nothing – £50 wasn't doing it for me. A month later, it offered me £100 and I bit – it had found my price and I was happy to switch.

So how can companies encourage people to act now?

There are a number of ways to persuade people to act now.

Many companies do this by offering superior products and services

Some launch noticeably superior products and service – for example, Dyson redesigns mainstream electrical products, such as vacuum cleaners, fans and hand dryers, to create ones that are clearly superior to others on the market, thus making them worth switching to. Hair care brand, Pantene, launched the noticeably superior two in one shampoo for softer, shinier, healthier looking hair, using door-to-door sampling to demonstrate how much better Pantene was compared to competitors.

Other companies create interest by 'seeding and weeding' – constantly weeding out poorly performing products to make way for innovative ones that people will want to try. For example, Pret A Manger frequently introduces new sandwich formats, such as the 'no bread sandwich', and Max Factor regularly launches new beauty products, such as the latest and greatest mascara for even better coverage, or lipstick to reflect this year's fashion trends.

Other companies create interest by offering limited editions that are available for a limited time only. For example, Mars, Walkers Crisps and McDonalds are masters of limited editions, offering products such as Mars Dark, Walkers 'Pulled Pork in a Sticky BBQ Sauce' Crisps and McDonalds' Chicken & Chutney Indian Burger for a matter of weeks. These encourage people to try them while they can, within the window that they are available.

Other companies use pricing and promotions

Airlines have tended to run annual low-price flight promotions, for instance, British Airway's Great Escape sale, where BA gives away a suite of cheap flights on a first-come, first-served basis. Similarly, Ryan Air's flash sale has given away £1 flight tickets, also on a first-come, first-served basis.

Asda has historically offered WIGIG (When It's Gone It's Gone) promotions, constantly rotating its half-price product range (including TVs, DVDs, home ware and bicycles) to maintain interest.

A U.S. clothing retailer identified that people who tried on clothes in-store were more likely to buy them, prompting them to offer customers who tried on clothes a $10 voucher to spend on any item of clothing over $50.

Brewer's Fayre, the family restaurant chain, successfully drove trial of its new restaurants by dropping coupons to mothers with children in key catchment areas at the start of the summer holidays, offering 'two children's meals for the price of one' for the limited holiday period.

*Other companies talk to customers when they are most
likely to be open to purchasing a new product*

Bounty offers pregnant and new mums a range of free Bounty packs, each tailored to the key stages of the 'pregnant and new mum' journey – including a Pregnancy Information Pack, a Mum-to-be Pack, a Newborn Pack and a Growing Family Pack. These are full of practical advice on what changes to expect and how to deal with them, as well as a host of 'try before you buy' samples and money-off coupons on products that they will most likely have never thought of buying before – such as baby skincare products, baby wipes, non-biological washing powders and fabric conditioners – providing women with some of the support and advice needed to navigate this new life stage.

Wesleyan, a life & pensions provider, builds a relationship with future doctors when they are still at university, by offering them the medical insurance product required to practice medicine in the UK. Because doctors tend to have a fairly standard career and salary path, Wesleyan knows exactly when to offer them additional financial services products and services that they might find relevant and helpful.

So, in summary, many large brands focus the majority of their spend on mainstream communication touch points, such as TV, press, sponsorship, promotions. Yet there's an abundance of other touch points that are not only more influential, but also less costly. Marketers should aim to get more 'bang for their buck' by thinking of their advertising spend as their own money – thus encouraging them to:

- Understand where people go for ideas and advice and thereby identify which are the most influential and cost efficient touch points.
- Give people reasons to act now rather than procrastinate.

B: Turning new customer relationships into deep customer relationships in the first 180 days

In service-orientated businesses, a customer's first 180 days are key to building customer loyalty and thereby future business success. Yet many companies don't invest in engaging with their customers at this most influential time.

With this in mind, we come to a second customer strategy that is important to Boards: how to create deeper customer relationships within the first 180 days to help turn new customer relationships into valuable ones.

Typically, the first 180 days set the standard for what the customer relationship will be like. If the joining experience is positive, the customer is more likely to purchase incremental products. On average, 77 percent of cross sales are established in the first 180 days of the relationship, with customers more likely to buy other products if the first purchase has been easy.[6]

Similarly, customers are five times more likely to engage with the brand in the first ninety to one hundred days – resulting in a high level of referrals as people reinforce their purchase decision by telling their peers, friends and family.[7]

In contrast, if the joining experience is poor, the company has failed at the first hurdle, missing the opportunity to demonstrate what it can do and disappointing clients from day one. At best, this can result in passive customers who don't leave but also don't engage with the company and, at worst, high customer churn due to customers perceiving the company to be indifferent to their needs. An annual retail banking study showed that customers are up to three times more likely to churn during the first ninety days of opening a new account.[8] Additionally, it may cause reputational damage when new customers tell their friends, families, peers and possibly even a wider audience via social media, not to engage with this company – on average this is likely to be nine to fifteen people.[9]

What do new customers want?

New customers want to feel that they have made a good decision in deciding which brand to buy. If the experience has been positive, they are likely to do more business with the brand, as well as refer it to others.

If not, customers might regret buying it, refuse to give the company more business, leave at the first opportunity and even discourage others from joining.

When dealing with a service-orientated brand, new customers want to feel that it was 'easy to do business' – that the joining process was smooth, seamless, painless and effortless, and that going forward, the company will continue to be as easy to do business with. If it was difficult to make the switch, customers may be reluctant to engage in any future business with the company.

Customers want to feel that intelligent advice and help is on hand when they need it. Joining a new company can be time-consuming in terms of administration and set-up. If the new customer feels that they are spending more time than expected to get set up, with no easy way to access help from the company, they may regret making the leap. Similarly, if the new customer feels that the level of personalised service and advice that they were expecting doesn't exist, they may be tempted to look elsewhere.

Crucially, customers want to feel valued – they want to feel that the company is as excited about them joining, as they are excited to join. Once on board, companies should regard this as a start of the customer relationship (rather than the end of the sale) valuing the customer as a new member of the 'club'. There's nothing worse than a company wooing a new customer and lavishing time, attention and care upon them, only for the customer to be 'dropped' once they've joined as the company moves on to its next recruit.

At the end of the day, new joiners don't want to think that they've got it wrong – they want to believe that they've made a good decision. Initially they tend to cut new companies quite a bit of slack – but only up to a point. By and large, if they believe that the company is easy to do business with and is 'there' for them, they will be delighted that they've made the switch and will be looking for opportunities to do more business with the company, while willingly recommending it to their friends, family and peers.

Why do so many companies get it wrong?

There are a number of internal issues that can cause companies to get customer on-boarding wrong.

A common one is a lack of consistency – often an indication of there being no standardised process in place. For example, it can be unclear what each new joiner should receive as standard, such as a day two welcome call or a new joiner welcome letter or an invite to a welcome event. If left to the discretion of each client relationship manager, the new joiner experience can vary greatly – with some new customers being contacted regularly and invited to a number of events, and others being ignored.

Another common issue is a lack of ownership – either for the new joiner experience as a whole, or for a significant part of it. A lack of ownership can result in no one ensuring that the new joiner experience is working seamlessly, as well as no one being responsible for monitoring or fixing on-going issues, or looking for new ways to improve it. For instance, if a customer has a specific issue, then who is taking ownership for fixing it?

At the other end of the spectrum, if there are too many 'owners' there can be 'competing agendas', resulting in a lack of clear direction on what the new joiner experience should look like.

A third issue can be a lack of joined up processes creating a lack of visibility on where a new joiner is along their on-boarding process. Customers expect issues to happen – in themselves, these issues don't matter as much – but what *does* matter is how quickly, efficiently and proactively they're fixed.

Similarly, customers often don't mind waiting as long as they know that people are on top of the issues. But if the application process takes longer than expected and the company representative that they talk with can't tell them what to expect, the company can appear, at best, not to value the new joiner's business or, at worst, incompetent.

How can companies create a great first impression?

There are three distinct ways that a service-orientated brand can create a great first impression with its customers:

- Being fast and efficient, showing just how speedy and responsive the organisation can be, and how it won't waste customers' valuable time.
- Creating a more personalised relationship with their customers by tailoring the brand to the customer's specific needs as well as educating people on what they can do to personalise the brand experience.

- Giving customers a sense that 'they've arrived', by demonstrating that the company is as excited about the customer joining them, as the customer is about joining.

To deliver this, it's important that companies empower front and back office teams to identify and solve customer issues as quickly as possible as well as challenge on-going processes that are sub-optimal. If they don't feel empowered to challenge the status quo, then little will change day to day.

This service experience must then be backed up with streamlined processes that are simple yet consistent, so that everyone in the front and back office teams can understand them, remember them, adhere to them, and know who to go to if an issue arises. Additionally there should be a seamless IT system that speeds up the time it takes to complete the new joiner process.

Examples of companies that encapsulate all three of these attributes

Some service-orientated brands have designed their new joiner process to encapsulate all three of these attributes. These brands create a great first impression that has encouraged new joiners to not only stay but also deepen their relationship with the brand.

First Direct

A renowned brand in this space is First Direct. First Direct has created a more engaging and personalised customer experience, in spite of being an online rather than a retail banking brand.

As we saw in Chapter 7, First Direct's brand mission is to achieve "pioneering amazing service".[10] To achieve this, all new call centre recruits undergo a full-time training induction period of eight weeks before they are let loose on real live customers, and everyone within the organisation is encouraged to continuously challenge the status quo to deliver a better customer experience.

These factors have helped to create a more seamless and personalised new joiner experience.

For example, during the application process, applicants are sent text and e-mail updates notifying them when each stage of the joining process has completed, thereby reassuring customers that their application is on track. Once the applicant has been accepted, the welcome team calls each new joiner in their first week to help sort out any issues either straightaway on the phone or as a follow-up. Each customer issue is treated as a specific case with a case owner assigned to it, to ensure it's handled promptly and to the customer's satisfaction. An EasySwitch team handles direct debits, standing orders and salary transfers – with new customers given the expected transfer dates, all new accounts monitored for eight weeks to ensure that the transfers go through smoothly, and customers automatically paid £20 if a mistake is made by First Direct.

In the first month, customers are not targeted with marketing for any additional products. Instead the team helps customers make the most out of First Direct by ensuring that their Internet banking services are fully up and running. Additionally, at the end of their first quarter, all new joiners are sent a questionnaire asking them about their first impressions of First Direct, both positive and negative, with the aim of continuously ensuring that they are delivering the brand mission of "pioneering amazing service".[11]

Metro Bank

Metro Bank also delivers a superior customer experience. It takes pride in being the most warm, friendly and attractive bank on the high street, encouraging people to "Love your bank at last." Branches are open seven days a week, and from 8 a.m. to 8 p.m. on a weekday, enabling people to visit their bank at a time that suits them. A door greeter welcomes its customers when they arrive – offering dog bowls and treats for those with pets, baby-changing facilities for parents and free-to-use magic money changing machines (from coins to notes). Customer-facing employees don't take their lunch breaks when customers do, with extra employees on duty at peak times. A new joiner can open an account then and there within fifteen minutes, provided they have one form of identification, rather than the standard two – with cards and cheque books issued immediately. Metro Bank's employees don't have sales targets – instead they are incentivised to enhance the customer experience. They are trained to say 'yes' as much as possible, and can only say 'no' once they have asked a colleague for a second opinion. As Metro's chief executive, Craig Donaldson, says, "Customer service is the differentiator for us. If you make the customer happy and give them a good experience, they're much more likely to stick around."[12]

Ten Group

In the concierge sector, Ten Group's new joiner experience showcases its superior service from day one. For instance, when meeting with a new client, a Lifestyle Manager asks to visit them at home to get a feel of who they are. During this initial meeting, the Lifestyle Manager asks at least ten open-ended questions to find out how Ten Group can be of help to them and records any specific 'passions' (from Chelsea Football Club to Beyonce). Straight after the interview, Ten Group demonstrates how quick and responsive it is, by sorting two 'quick wins' that same day.

Then, in the first three months, a senior Ten Group manager calls the client to ensure that the chemistry fit with their Lifestyle Manager is working well and, if not, reassigns another Lifestyle Manager, no questions asked.

Within the first month, Ten Group looks for at least one unexpected win based on the passions that were mentioned in the first interview, for example,

"We're able to get tickets to the Chelsea versus Manchester United game, would you like us to buy some for you?" As well, it contacts new joiners to check how the joining process has gone and address any issues, paying particular attention to those clients who only contact Ten Group occasionally, and thus may not be happy.[13]

Apple

Apple's customer service is renowned, not only for new joiners but also for existing customers whenever they come into an Apple store.

Most of us know that when entering the store, the customer is approached and asked what kind of help they need and directed to the right person. When choosing what to buy, the sales person advises the customer on what might be the optimal option for them, even if it's less expensive than alternatives, as well as any add-ons that might be worth considering. When paying, the cash register comes to the customer for them to sign electronically, speeding up the process. While the payment is going through, the merchandise is carried to the desk so it's ready to go, with people on hand to transport the merchandise to the customer's car if needed.

The sales person offers to activate the products then and there (or overnight if the job is more complicated). They then show the customer how to navigate the new product and offer to book them in for training classes at the store.

All devices are beautifully packaged in protective boxes – opening it is an initiation into Apple's finely attuned aesthetic world. An elegant Quick Start Guide greets you – containing easy-to-follow instructions on what the different buttons do and top tips illustrated by clear, hand drawn arrows – and the product itself is cradled in well-crafted internal packaging. No bubble wrap, polystyrene chunks, jiffy bags or cheap cable ties in sight.

Once home, the customer can access a toll-free number for help with the support person staying on the line until they are satisfied that everything is working. Finally, a questionnaire is sent to the customer by e-mail asking for feedback on the quality of the service.

Fedex

When a friend of mine joined Fedex, she experienced a highly personalised joining service. The day after joining, a Fedex representative called her to ask how she envisaged using Fedex – for example, for international or domestic delivery, and likely frequency and speed of service required.

The following day a representative called her to ask when she expected to use Fedex for the first time and for what purpose, and talked her through how to make that happen.

When she experienced problems sending a package online, a Fedex representative called her to say that they had noticed her struggling and offered to help in any way they could. At the end of the first month, she was assigned a named Fedex account manager to help with any queries she might have. Each call was warm and friendly (not sales-y), and informed (e.g., 'last time we talked you said . . ., is that still true?' or 'I saw you were trying to do X online, can I help you do that?').

Additionally, the Fedex tracking system enabled her to track where her package was in the delivery process, reassuring her that it would be delivered on time.

Examples of companies that encapsulate one of the three attributes

Some brands have been highly effective at demonstrating one of the three 'on-boarding' attributes when on-boarding new customers.

For example, some companies are effective at on-boarding new customers quickly and efficiently

At Vodafone, an agent will help customers get their Sure Signal product up and running over the phone, using the customer's postcode to get the product reconfigured.

After completing a new mortgage application, customers of Commonwealth Bank of Australia are speeded through a rapid "straight-through" decision process, supported by e-alerts that keep them updated on their application status. They can use the bank's mobile payments capability to transfer funds to the vendor on the go, and they can use an online drop box storage facility to store all relevant papers in one place.

Scottish Power claims to try to resolve any customer issue immediately, the first time that the customer contacts them. If this is not possible, then the customer will be given a unique reference number and assigned a dedicated complaint handler to fix the issue as quickly as possible.

Some brands are effective at building deeper relationships with their customers

LOVEFiLM, recognised that when new customers join they typically have a designated night-in in mind, typically the next day or the one after. To accommodate this, the new joiner delivery run was reconfigured to be just before the last post deadline on the 'joining day', enabling new joiners to receive their first DVD the very next morning, which was a big customer 'wow' at the time. Similarly, LOVEFiLM worked out that people are more loyal if they select which films they want to see in their first week of joining. So, from day one, LOVEFiLM encouraged people to pick films from its most popular and best rated film lists on their 'Joiner Starting Up Page'. LOVEFiLM then used people's click-through behaviour to segment new joiners into the film genres they are most likely to enjoy – for example, are they most likely to enjoy watching horror movies, romcoms or foreign films – and added 'films that people like you also enjoy' onto its 'Joiner Starting Up Page'.

Online betting sites recognise the importance of getting new joiners started, and that people are more likely to make bets if they use a range of betting vehicles. So, they telephone new joiners who have registered online but not yet made a bet, to ask what sport they like, suggest different ways to bet on their favourite sport, guide them through how to make that first bet, and give them an incentive to do so – such as a £50 welcome bonus.[14]

Amazon and Linked In recognise that the more personalised a brand is, the more a customer will keep coming back. In response, Amazon reviews people's click-through behaviour to identify other products that they might like to buy, and then sends tailored recommendations to them by e-mail. Linked In encourages people to fill in their profile, enabling others to find and connect with (as well as headhunt) them – and fosters a culture of people inviting friends and colleagues to join. In doing so, it makes it a 'must-stay' place to connect with 'people you know', with a 'fear of missing out' if you don't.

Dyson proactively helps its customers look after their product throughout its life cycle, making it last for as long as possible. The company gives new customers a handbook advising them on how to care for their product and what to do if there's an issue. If that doesn't fix it, the customer can call a Dyson engineer, someone who knows the machine inside out, who will talk them through the repair over the phone, with the aim of fixing it together. And if that doesn't work, then a Dyson engineer can come to their home to fix it, within seventy-two hours, for a fixed fee.

Zopa, the online community lending company, realised that people are more comfortable lending to others in their own community. So it hosts local community parties, local messaging boards and an annual birthday party that any lender or borrower can attend, thereby helping to make its customers feel valued members of the Zopa community.

Some brands have been highly effective at making their customers feel valued

In the luxury industry, many high-end brands are great at giving customers a sense that 'they've arrived' – demonstrating that they are as excited about the customer joining the brand as the customer is about joining.

Top-end brands like Christies invite clients to exclusive wine tastings – giving clients the opportunity to meet artists, or collectors a chance to meet other collectors, as well as take a bottle of their favourite wine home. As part of its end-to-end upmarket service, the auction house takes valuable clients to art shows, both at home and abroad, exposing them to new ideas on what to buy. Christies has even been known to put on a private viewing for a client by request and, in rare cases, bring artwork to a client's house pre-auction to view in situ.

When Mandarin Oriental chauffeurs collect guests at the airport, they let the hotel reception desk know that they're on their way so that the staff can greet the guest by name when they arrive. Similarly, highly valued guests are invited to exclusive events with one of Mandarin Oriental's celebrity fans who endorse the brand in its advertising. For example, thirty guests might enjoy a private concert with Helen Grimmau prior to the opening of the Group's new hotel in Paris. Or guests might be invited to their fiftieth anniversary party with the entertainment provided by Karen Mok and Bryan Ferry.

Porsche customers are invited to the Porsche factory to pick up their new car, tour the production plant and Porsche museum, and drive several Porsches on their private test track, before enjoying getting to know their new car on the long drive home.

In Australia, Lexus drivers were invited to a sponsored Lexus event at the Sydney Opera House and were exclusively allowed to use the reserved car parking spaces closest to the door. Mercedes owners had a long walk past a lot of Lexus cars, when making their way to the Sydney Opera House entrance.

The American Express Centurion (or Black) Card is the ultimate status symbol. People can't apply for one – they are personally invited by American Express to join – with the card arriving unexpectedly in the mail, presented in a svelte, padded and scented box. American Express is secretive about the card's benefits, but they are rumoured to include automatic airline and hotel upgrades, 'rare experiences' such as access to a coveted ticket to New York's Fashion Week or a Private Box at the Superbowl, and the ability to rent high-end cars. But the real benefits stem from the personal services offered by each customer's personal concierge, who can help with anything from travel or special occasion planning, birthday reminders and gift selection, or locating hard to find items. As James Bush, senior Vice President of Consumer Marketing at American Express describes: "We created the Centurion Card in response to customer research that identified a small but affluent group of card members, for whom individual attention and access to previously unavailable elite travel benefits was of great interest."[15]

In summary

To develop robust marketing strategies that drive shareholder value and engage the Board, marketers need to find ways to manage and grow their brands as cost-efficiently and effectively as possible.

To achieve this, marketers should look for ways to make their marketing budgets work harder, by thinking of their advertising spend as their own money. They should:

- Identify and focus on those high impact touch points and communication activities that are most influential and cost-efficient.

- Drive trial by giving people reasons to act now – by offering them superior products and services as well as great deals, and talking with them when they are most open to influence.

Additionally, in service-orientated businesses, it's important that companies turn new customer relationships into deep customer relationships, thereby driving cross-sell and referral. They should do this by investing in creating a smooth on-boarding experience and making new joiners feel welcome and valued in their first 180 days.

In essence, brands can achieve this during the customer on-boarding process by:

- Being fast and efficient, showing just how speedy and responsive the organisation can be, and how it won't waste customers' valuable time.
- Creating deeper customer relationships by personalising the brand to the customer's specific needs as well as educating people on what they can do to personalise the brand experience.
- Giving customers a sense that they've arrived, demonstrating that the company is as excited about the customer joining them, as the customer is about joining.

Notes

1 Ruth Saunders, "Confetti IPA Paper," *Advertising Works 11*, compiled by the Institute of Practitioners in Advertising and edited by Tim Broadbent (Henley: World Advertising Research Center, 2000).
2 Ella's Kitchen, April 2016, www.ellaskitchen.co.uk; Nathalie Brandweiner, "Food for Thought: The Story Behind the Success of Ella's Kitchen," *Businesszone*, December 2011, www.businesszone.co.uk/do/customers/food-for-thought-the-story-behind-the-success-of-ellas-kitchen; Will Smale, "The Man Who Built the UK's Largest Baby Food Firm," *BBC News*, December 2014, www.bbc.co.uk/news/business-30411724.
3 Jonathan Moules, "How to Avoid Being a One Hit Wonder," *The Financial Times*, June 2010, www.ft.com/content/62bdc9fc-6feb-11df-8fcf-00144feabdc0; DueDil, "Vitabiotics Limited," *The Financial Times*, April 2016, www.duedil.com/company/01012146/vitabiotics-limited.
4 Steven Mendel and Sam Gilbert, "About Us," *Bought By Many*, https://boughtbymany.com/about/.
5 Source directly from Nielsen Media Research Limited, Ad Dynamix media measurement 2015.
6 McKinsey & Company's Financial Services Practice, "Back to the Future: Rediscovering Relationship Banking," *McKinsey Quarterly*, November 2010.
7 Paula Tompkins, "42 Experts Reveal Their Top Tips and Strategies on How Organizations Can Improve Customer Retention," January 2016, www.ngdata.com/how-to-improve-customer-retention/.
8 Grant Turner, "J.D. Power & Associates Annual Retail Banking Survey Research," January 2014, www.onovativebanking.com/why-your-customers-first-90-days-are-critical-to-your-banks-growth.html.
9 Colin Shaw, "15 Statistics that Should Change the Business World – But Haven't," *LinkedIn*, June 2013, www.linkedin.com/pulse/20130604134550–284615–15-statistics-that-should-change-the-business-world-but-haven-t.

10 Best Companies, "First Direct," www.b.co.uk/Company/Profile/96594.
11 Alex Garrett, Roopalee Dave, Hugh Wilson and Moira Clark, "First Direct Comes of Age," Cranfield University School of Management, November 2007; Christopher Ratcliff, "How First Direct Handles Social Customer Service," *econsultancy.com*, September 2014, https://econsultancy.com/blog/65508-how-first-direct-handles-social-customer-service/; Paul Say, Marketing Director of First Direct, 2009–2011; First Direct call centre (0345 6100100).
12 Elliott Holley, "Metro Bank All about Customer Care," *www.bankingtech.com*, November 2013, www.bankingtech.com/184801/metro-bank-all-about-customer-care-says-donaldson/; Peter Crush, "How HR Is Helping Metro Bank to Buck the Banking Trend," *Personnel Today*, May 2013, www.personneltoday.com/hr/how-hr-is-helping-metro-bank-to-buck-the-banking-trend/; Thomas Krommenacker and Ben Robinson, "Case Study – Metro Bank – Breaking the Mould but Breaking the Malaise?," Temenos, Geneva, 2010, www.temenos.com/globalassets/mi/cs/cs-metro-breaking-the-mould.pdf.
13 Alex Cheatle, *Ten Group*, www.tengroup.com.
14 Lewis Holland and Antoine Bonello, "Improving Outbound Calling Conversion Rates," *www.isixsigma.com*, April 2016, www.isixsigma.com/methodology/dmaic-methodology/improving-outbound-calling-conversion-rates/.
15 "How to Get the American Express Black Card," *www.pursuitist.com*, April 2016, http://pursuitist.com/how-to-get-the-american-express-black-card/; Credit Card Insider, "The American Express Centurion Black Card," April 2016, www.creditcardinsider.com/blog/the-american-express-centurion-black-card/.

Bibliography

Best Companies. "First Direct." www.b.co.uk/Company/Profile/96594.
Brandweiner, Nathalie. "Food for Thought: The Story Behind the Success of Ella's Kitchen." *Businesszone*, December 2011. www.businesszone.co.uk/do/customers/food-for-thought-the-story-behind-the-success-of-ellas-kitchen.
Cheatle, Alex. *Ten Group*. www.tengroup.com.
Credit Card Insider. "The American Express Centurion Black Card." April 2016. www.creditcardinsider.com/blog/the-american-express-centurion-black-card/.
Crush, Peter. "How HR Is Helping Metro Bank to Buck the Banking Trend." *Personnel Today*, May 2013. www.personneltoday.com/hr/how-hr-is-helping-metro-bank-to-buck-the-banking-trend/.
DueDil. "Vitabiotics Limited." *The Financial Times*, April 2016. www.duedil.com/company/01012146/vitabiotics-limited.
Ella's Kitchen. April 2016. www.ellaskitchen.co.uk.
First Direct call centre (0345 6100100).
Garrett, Alex, Roopalee Dave, Hugh Wilson and Moira Clark. "First Direct Comes of Age." Cranfield University School of Management, November 2007.
Holland, Lewis and Antoine Bonello, "Improving Outbound Calling Conversion Rates." *www.isixsigma.com*, April 2016. www.isixsigma.com/methodology/dmaic-methodology/improving-outbound-calling-conversion-rates/.
Holley, Elliott. "Metro Bank All about Customer Care." *www.bankingtech.com*, November 2013. www.bankingtech.com/184801/metro-bank-all-about-customer-care-says-donaldson/.
"How to Get the American Express Black Card." *www.pursuitist.com*, April 2016. pursuitist.com/how-to-get-the-american-express-black-card/.
Krommenacker, Thomas and Ben Robinson. "Case Study – Metro Bank – Breaking the Mould but Breaking the Malaise?" Temenos, Geneva, 2010. www.temenos.com/globalassets/mi/cs/cs-metro-breaking-the-mould.pdf.

McKinsey & Company's Financial Services Practice. "Back to the Future: Rediscovering Relationship Banking." *McKinsey Quarterly*, November 2010.

Mendel, Steven and Sam Gilbert. "About Us." *Bought By Many*. https://boughtbymany.com/about/.

Moules, Jonathan. "How to Avoid Being a One Hit Wonder." *The Financial Times*, June 2010 www.ft.com/content/62bdc9fc-6feb-11df-8fcf-00144feabdc0.

Nielsen Media Research Limited. Ad Dynamix media measurement 2015.

Ratcliff, Christopher. "How First Direct Handles Social Customer Service." *econsultancy.com*, September 2014. https://econsultancy.com/blog/65508-how-first-direct-handles-social-customer-service/.

Saunders, Ruth. "Confetti IPA Paper." *Advertising Works 11*. Compiled by the Institute of Practitioners in Advertising and edited by Tim Broadbent. Henley: World Advertising Research Center, 2000.

Shaw, Colin. "15 Statistics that Should Change the Business World – But Haven't." *LinkedIn*, June 2013. www.linkedin.com/pulse/20130604134550–284615–15-statistics-that-should-change-the-business-world-but-haven-t.

Smale, Will. "The Man Who Built the UK's Largest Baby Food Firm." *BBC News*, December 2014. www.bbc.co.uk/news/business-30411724.

Tompkins, Paula. "42 Experts Reveal Their Top Tips and Strategies on How Organizations Can Improve Customer Retention." January 2016. www.ngdata.com/how-to-improve-customer-retention/.

Turner, Grant. "J.D. Power & Associates Annual Retail Banking Survey Research." January 2014. www.onovativebanking.com/why-your-customers-first-90-days-are-critical-to-your-banks-growth.html.

Part three

Getting the Board on-board

Summary

As we've seen in Parts one and two, it's tougher than ever before for companies to grow and survive.

The lower barriers to entry have made it easier for new, more risk-taking competitors to launch innovative products and services that better meet customer needs. If a company invests at the minimum level, the business is likely to decline as competitors outpace them and erode their market share.

Instead, if a company wants to grow, the Board must invest for growth. They need to innovate, while simultaneously protecting their core business – with marketing's ability to create customer-led growth clearly pivotal to delivering this.

To achieve this growth, marketers need to demonstrate to the Board why their projects are worth investing in, over and above other projects.

Yet it's no secret that marketing punches below its weight in the boardroom – with the Board perceiving marketers as not being as commercially credible as their peers – resulting in much-needed breakthrough ideas not getting approved, with Board members exposing cracks in the investment strategy and marketing teams being forced to go back to the drawing board.

So how can marketers be commercially impactful in the boardroom?

Making the most of Part three

In Part three, we look at how marketers can get the Board on-board, by winning over Board members' minds, hearts and confidence.

Marketers need to win over Board members' minds by making a rational Board recommendation and business case that the Board can buy into – using clear, succinct, rational storylines that outline the business opportunity, why the Board should engage and what they want the Board to agree to.

In practice, however, a logical, well-articulated Board recommendation may not be enough – marketers may also need to win over Board members' hearts, by connecting with the Board members at a personal level – clearly demonstrating how valuable the project is, both for the company and for each of them as part of the senior management team, and how important it is for them to be part of the solution.

Additionally, once in-market, it can be important to win over the Board's confidence – by demonstrating how the team is managing the company's money in a financially responsible way, to ensure that the project delivers the promised targets.

In Part three, we look at each of these in turn.

In Chapter 9, we focus on how to win over Board members' minds, by creating a strong Board recommendation that comprises:

- A succinct one-page storyline outlining the business opportunity, why this is important and what we want agreement to.
- A bespoke, compelling Board presentation deck.
- A robust business case that succinctly shows how the recommended marketing strategies will build shareholder value.

In Chapter 10, we assess how to win over Board members' hearts by:

- Involving senior managers in the problem solving from day one.
- Assessing how to handle challenging Board-level conversations.
- Presenting with the end in mind on the day itself.

Then, in Chapter 11, we review how to win the Board's confidence and thereby keep the Board on-board once in-market by:

- Embracing failure as much as success.
- Investing in pre-agreed tranches and monitoring performance from day one.
- Recognising that the launch is only the beginning, and identifying and addressing any emerging issues early on.
- Optimising in-market performance through 'test & learn'.

But first, let's meet the team

When engaging the Board, it's imperative to get into each of the Board members' mindsets – with the aim of talking their language and anticipating any issues that are likely to arise.

So, before we get into Part three, let's take a look at who each of the chief marketing officer's boardroom peers are and what interests them day to day.

A board of directors is a body of appointed members who are tasked with jointly overseeing the day-to-day affairs of a company, on behalf of the shareholders. The Board is directly accountable to its shareholders – using annual general meetings (AGMs) to outline how well the company is performing and why, and what the future company goals and strategies are.

The Board typically consists of the C-Suite, or C-level executives.

Heading the C-suite is the chief executive officer – or CEO – charged with maximising the company's value and delivering the promised shareholder targets. CEOs take the tough decisions on where to invest for growth, drive the necessary internal change required to deliver this and motivate employees to deliver – and will want to be absolutely certain that any decisions that are made are likely to work and, if not, are course corrected quickly.

The chief operating officer – or COO – is often the second in command, responsible for overseeing the day-to-day company operations and ensuring that the company is able to manufacture, store, distribute and sell its products and services profitably. They are tasked with looking for ways to support the products and services that are the mainstay of today's business, as well as supporting the new products and services that are necessary for future success – and will be concerned that any new product or service launch doesn't create an unacceptably high level of distraction.

The chief financial officer – or CFO – is charged with managing a company's finances and associated risks. Their priority is to ensure that any profit targets that have been promised to the shareholders are delivered, as well as to protect the company's vital assets. Thus they are interested in how much a new project will deliver in the short and long term, what the associated costs are over time, what the likely risk of the project not delivering is, and what is being done during the launch phase to mitigate the risk.

The chief information officer (CIO), or chief data officer (CDO), is responsible for the investment in and smooth running of the company's information technology, including protection and development of its customer data and management of its computer systems. They will be concerned that new technology is developed in line with the business needs, and that customer data is accessed and used appropriately.

Increasingly, there may also be a chief customer officer (CCO) or chief brand officer (CBO). The chief customer officer is responsible for creating and delivering a seamless customer experience, with the aim of maximising customer acquisition, retention and profitability. The chief brand officer's role is to create and deliver a consistent and compelling brand image and experience across all touch points. These two Board members are likely to be supportive allies of the CMO, as they will want to – and can help to – build a consistent and compelling customer and brand experience across all touch points, including those that are outside of marketing's remit, for example, in-store, online and in call centres.

Alongside the C-suite, you might meet:

- The human resources director, responsible for recruiting, managing and training the company's personnel or workforce. They will want the company to have a clear vision and strong brand purpose that will inspire employees to do a great job, day to day.
- The director of investor relations and communications, responsible for developing, sustaining and deepening the company's relationships with

its investors. They will also want the company to have a clear vision and strong brand purpose that engages shareholders to invest.

- The group company secretary, responsible for ensuring that the company is compliant with statutory and regulatory requirements and that the decisions of the board of directors are implemented.
- Non-executive directors – or 'outsiders' who work for the company on a part-time basis, and are tasked with providing an independent, outside-in, critical view on the direction that the company is taking. Their general counsel, based on years of management experience in other companies, is used to challenge the existing internal wisdom, with the aim of optimising the company's future performance.
- The chairperson, who independently manages and provides leadership to the board of directors, ensuring that the highest levels of corporate governance are maintained, and chairing any general meetings such as the AGM, thereby acting as the bridge between the Board and the shareholders.

So now that we've met the characters, let's look at how to win over their minds, hearts and confidence.

Chapter 9

Winning the Board members' minds

"Less is more."

Robert Browning

To get the Board on-board, marketers need to succinctly show how their marketing strategies will build shareholder value by creating clear, compelling business cases that the Board will buy into.

Additionally, they need to develop tight Board presentations that bring the recommendations to life. In essence, this means getting inside the mindset of the Board and viewing the business recommendations from the Board's commercial perspective.

As discussed in Chapter 1, the Board's primary objective is to protect and manage the company successfully, so Board members naturally have a mind-set that is more:

- Analytical, focused on growing shareholder value through profitable growth.
- Risk-aware, centred on optimising the performance of new initiatives, while at the same time minimising the risk of them not delivering.
- Short- to mid-term focused, looking for ways to grow the business in a steady, sustainable way.

In contrast, marketers are focused on building strong brands, and so naturally have a mindset that is more:

- Creative, honing strong brand propositions and generating breakthrough innovation and distinctive marketing campaigns.
- Risk-taking, with the bigger the innovation or creative leap, the bigger the rewards but also the bigger the risk.
- Mid- to long-term focused, taking the time to build and deliver truly breakthrough ideas that will lead to step-change growth.

Therefore, to win the Board over, it's essential that marketers align their thinking and language with that of the Board by being:

- Financially rigorous, demonstrating how the investment will generate healthy returns.
- Financially responsible, showing what they are doing to manage the risk of failure.
- Short-term as well as long-term focused, showing how they will deliver quick wins alongside big breakthroughs.

Additionally, Board members are invariably time-starved. So, it's imperative that marketers create succinct Board recommendations that are:

- *Commercial*, in how they will drive business growth.
- *Credible*, in how they will deliver a sustainable return.
- *Concise*, in their presentation writing and delivery.
- *Clear-cut*, in their proposed requests and next steps.

In this chapter, we look at how to *win the minds* of the Board members, by creating a strong Board recommendation that includes:

A   A succinct one-page Executive Summary (or storyline) outlining the business opportunity, why this is important and what we want agreement to.
B   A bespoke, compelling Board presentation deck.
C   A robust business case that succinctly shows how the recommended marketing strategies will build shareholder value.

Then, in the next chapter, we look at how to *win the hearts* of the Board members by engaging them throughout the problem-solving process.

A: Building a succinct storyline

The importance of being hypothesis driven

At the start of a project, the marketing team should draft an Executive Summary storyline hypothesis that they can test from the outset, as pioneered by Barbara Minto in her book *The Pyramid Principle*.[1] Typically, this is a one-page summary that outlines:

- The business opportunity and how the recommendations will help build business success.
- The proposed strategies to achieve this and why these are right, including the facts that prove the case.

- The agreements that the marketing team want approved, including the key asks and tangible next steps.

Succinct Executive Summary storylines help marketing teams to work more efficiently.

Starting out with the answer in mind compels teams to focus on 'proving or disproving the answer' rather than 'boiling the ocean', enabling them to come up with an answer more quickly. Without it, the team risks wasting time carrying out analyses on irrelevant issues without getting closer to the answer, or fails to get sufficient depth on the issues that really count.

They also help marketing teams to convey their recommendations more effectively.

In the boardroom, Board members can quickly lose patience when it seems to takes ages for the presenter to get to the 'punch line'. Likewise, they often feel frustrated when 'sold to' – rather than 'included' in the problem solving. A succinct, one-page storyline hypothesis can help to the marketing team to:

- Quickly crystallise what they want senior management agreement to and why – which helps identify the facts and data that the presentation needs to include.
- Engage senior management and cross-functional teams at an early stage to get their thoughts and input – thus increasing the likelihood of the recommendations being approved. We will talk more about this in Chapter 10.
- Quickly enable the Board to understand the recommendations and key asks – and why they need to engage.

In practice, this means:

- Using intuition to draft 'an answer' to the project up front that is both tangible and actionable.
- Creating a one-page storyline summary of what the recommendation, rationale and 'so whats' might be. This should typically be written in a top-down way, with the recommendation made clearly up front so that the audience can quickly grasp what is being recommended and why. And it should be structured with a small number of headlines outlining the key messages, each supported by a small number of bullet points that contain the facts that prove the case.
- Syndicating this 'answer' as early as possible among senior management and cross-functional stakeholders in early stage 'listening and problem solving' rather than 'selling' meetings. This enables the team to get input on what the right answer is, identify any concerns or 'show stoppers' and access any support data that will help make the case. Sharing the one-page storyline hypothesis is an ideal way to do this as it's

succinct, enabling time-starved senior managers to engage and input efficiently.

- Using new information to adapt, refine or even rewrite the storyline until it holds true.

Constructing a compelling executive summary storyline

A storyline must have *strong strategic impact* to engage senior management. At the end of the day, it won't matter how much analysis you have done or how accurate your report is – if it doesn't engage senior management or compel them to make a significant strategic decision, then the project will fail.

There are various ways to construct hypothesis storylines.

One is the classic Situation-Complication-Resolution storyline structure:

- *What's the Situation we are in?*
- *What's the Complication we need to resolve?*
- *What's the Resolution to this?*

Another is the Recommendation-Implications-Agreements structure:

- *Recommendation and rationale*
- *Implications of this*
- *What we need your Agreement to now*

To illustrate, let's see these in action.

An example of a situation-complication-resolution storyline

In this situation, the client was questioning whether their new joiner on-boarding experience was good enough – and, if not, how to fix it.

- **Situation: Great client on-boarding is imperative to building deep client relationships.**

  - Clients are more likely to do more business with a company, as well as refer it to others, if it's easy to join and they feel they're getting a personalised service and are valued.
  - If not, then the company has failed at the first hurdle, not only missing the opportunity to demonstrate what it can do, but also disappointing clients from day one.

- **Complication: Our joining experience today is not fit for purpose.**

  - For most it's slow, taking at least ten weeks to open a new account rather than the ten working days people expect.

- For many, there's no follow-up – therefore it is ineffective at building deeper client relationships.
- For a minority, the joining experience is poor, with multiple information requests and errors wasting a lot of customers' valuable time.

- **Resolution: To create a joining experience that sets the right standard, there are two imperatives.**

  - To stop disappointing customers, we need to streamline the new joiner on-boarding process by (i) streamlining application forms and information requests, (ii) capturing and sharing information electronically and (iii) streamlining and empowering the back office.
  - To build deeper relationships, the sales team needs to follow up all new joiners in a systematic way, by (i) helping them get up and running in their first week, (ii) inviting them to a welcome event in their first month and (iii) calling them at the end of the third month to ensure that they are happy.

An example of a recommendation-implications-agreements structure

In this situation, the client wanted to convince the Board to migrate a number of product brands into one strong brand.

- **Recommendation: We should simplify our brand portfolio to one brand 'X'.**

  - By focusing all spend on building one strong brand only, return on investment will increase by 10 percent to 20 percent.
  - It will increase product cross-sell by an estimated 50 percent.
  - 'X' is our strongest brand across all of our categories.

- **Implications: Building one strong brand has three internal implications.**

  - We need to better communicate what brand 'X' stands for in a way that's relevant across all categories.
  - We need to build strong product sub-brands to demonstrate all of the categories that brand 'X' is playing in.
  - The organisation will need to behave in a more joined up way.

- **Agreements: To achieve this, we wish to start migrating now with the aim of full migration by the end of next year.**

  - This year, we wish to develop the brand positioning, product sub-brands and internal culture.

- Next year, we will start the brand migration with the aim of completing it by year-end.
- We estimate that this will cost an incremental £2 million.

Both structures are valid, as are other storyline structures. Which to use depends on which best tells the story you wish to tell. A good way to assess this is to work backwards by asking the following questions:

- What do you want from your audience? For example, investment money to target a new customer segment, launch a new product or service, or launch a new brand – or permission to reallocate marketing spend into new channels?
- What will persuade them? For example, research data, a business case showing expected return on investment or competitor case studies.
- Why should they engage? What's in it for the business as a whole? And what's in it for each of the Board members?

By answering these questions, your optimal storyline structure should emerge. Whichever structure is used, a strong storyline should always be:

- *Relevant* – clear why the audience should read it.
- *Succinct* – so that the reader quickly knows what you are asking for and why.
- *Compelling* – contain clear, fact-based rationale.
- *Actionable* – with clear 'so whats' as to what it means for the business and what you want your audience to agree to today.

Optimising the executive summary storyline

As shown in the above two examples, and championed in Barbara Minto's book *The Pyramid Principle*, the Executive Summary storyline should fit on one page and contain:

- A small number of headlines (ideally three) that make a clear recommendation and summarise the groups of bullet points underneath them.
- Underneath each headline, a small number of bullet points that include the facts that support the headline and are grouped 'at the same logic level' and 'in logical order'.[2]

Additionally, it should contain a clear, succinct, top-down recommendation and rationale as to why the recommendation is right, the 'so whats' on what that means for the business, and a summary of what you want senior management to agree to today.

Using this format of headlines and bullet points, supported with a clear, succinct rationale, helps senior management to more quickly grasp what you're recommending and why, and thus whether they need to engage further – thereby enabling them to focus their scarce time on where it's most needed.

Let's look at these techniques in turn.

Headlines and bullet points

Firstly, headlines help to succinctly clarify what the key story is – as well as keep the team 'on point'.

At the next level down, using bullet points underneath the headlines helps justify the headline.

Critically, these bullet points should be grouped at the same level – for example, they can be all brands, or all drivers of growth, or all root causes, or all different elements of the marketing mix.

They should be logically ordered – for example, in chronological order (such as first, second, third), or structural order (such as 'volume' multiplied by 'price' equals 'value'), or in order of importance.

They should be 'mutually exclusive' (with each bullet point distinct from each other) and 'collectively exhaustive' (working as a group to cover all possible aspects).

And each bullet point should add a distinct, compelling fact that supports the headline – if not, then it shouldn't be included.

To illustrate, consider this example. Here are six statements about our brand and the market it is playing in:

1   In consumer testing, our upgraded product is significantly preferred to the market leader.
2   Over the last six months, our brand has lost market share to local competitors.
3   The market leader 'Y' has gained market share by upgrading their product with a noticeably superior product at a parity price point.
4   Our product upgrade could be launched profitably at a parity price point to the market leader.
5   Own Label has gained market share by running deep price promotions, making their products 33 percent cheaper than our brand, on average.
6   With £1 million of investment, our upgraded product could be launched in six months' time.

This is an unstructured list of issues with *no clear message*.

By using headlines and bullet points, these observations can be structured into a more cohesive argument with clear 'so whats'. For example:

- **Our brand is being squeezed by both the premium and value ends of the market.**

  - Over the last six months, our brand has lost market share to local competitors.

- The market leader 'Y' has gained market share by upgrading their product with a noticeably superior product at a parity price point.
- Own Label has gained market share by running deep price promotions, making their products 33 percent cheaper than our brand, on average.

- **To compete, we should invest £1 million to speed up the launch of our product upgrade, with the aim of bringing it to market in six months' time.**

  - In consumer testing, our upgraded product is significantly preferred to the market leader.
  - Our product upgrade could be launched profitably at a parity price point to the market leader.
  - With £1 million of investment, our upgraded product could be launched in six months' time.

  In summary: We can start to turn around our brand's sales and share decline within six months, if we invest £1 million to speed up the launch of our superior product upgrade.

Creating a clear, succinct, top-down recommendation and rationale

Secondly, it is usually easier and quicker for senior management to understand what you're asking for if you cut to the chase, by writing the argument in a top-down way, bringing out the 'so what' in the headline.

Take the sentence:

> "It takes a month for the customer data team to give marketing a customer data cut for its CRM activity."

What am I trying to say? That's quicker than expected? That's unacceptably slow? The customer data team is under-resourced? The customer data team doesn't care about marketing?

Add the sentence:

> "The digital team is poor at converting advertising activity into online sales."

What am I now trying to say? The digital team doesn't understand the role and importance of advertising? It isn't focused on the right objectives? It doesn't contain the right skill sets? The customer data and digital teams don't care about marketing?

Then add the sentence:

> "The marketing team briefs the customer data and digital teams late in the creative development process."

Now what am I trying to say? Marketing lacks project management skills? It has poor relationships with other functional teams? It is overly focused on television adverts, at the expense of online advertising and CRM?

What I was trying to say was . . .

"To optimise the performance of our communications spend, the Board needs to incentivise the digital, customer data and marketing teams to work better together, as a seamless, joined-up team.

- It takes a month for the customer data team to give marketing a customer data cut for its CRM activity.
- The digital team is poor at converting advertising activity into online sales.
- The marketing team briefs the customer data and digital teams late in the creative development process."

So why didn't I just say that?

B: Creating a compelling presentation deck

Building a succinct storyboard that tells the story

Once the first draft storyline is ready, the marketing team should then turn it into a presentation deck.

As mentioned earlier, Board members typically become frustrated if presentation decks don't tell a clear story. This can happen if a team doesn't have a clear story to guide the presentation structure or if it has cut and pasted existing charts into the deck, instead of creating a bespoke presentation deck. If the team does not have a clear story and a bespoke deck that is crafted to tell that story, the Board presentation will suffer.

To build a bespoke presentation deck, the marketing team should first draft a dummy storyboard that supports the one-page storyline. Ideally, this should be done as soon as the first draft storyline is available.

This, in practice, means creating a storyboard where each bullet point in the storyline becomes the headline of a page or chart. Its structure should mirror the storyline structure – with the chart headers alone recreating the storyline. This enables senior managers to easily find and reference a specific section for more detail.

If the storyboard structure is not telling the story clearly, the team should iterate its sequence and substance until it does.

Each page should contain the facts and data that 'prove' the bullet point. If facts and data are not yet available, the relevant pages should be left blank, making it clear which data points still need to be sourced. Any additional and relevant back-up charts or data can then be included in an appendix, as needed.

By creating a storyboard early on, the team can:

- Identify how many pages need to be prepared to support the recommendation and the one point that each page needs to make to build the case.
- Gauge early on whether the storyline is really working, by testing whether the presentation deck is selling the story clearly and whether the team has all of the necessary facts to make the case. Remember, if the presentation deck is not flowing, the sequence and the substance of the storyline should be iterated until it does.
- Spot data gaps, enabling the team to identify where to focus its time to prove the case and what data it needs to collect to support each point – as well as assign who is on point to populate each chart and how they are going to do this.

Typically, this will result in a dummy presentation deck of about ten to fifteen pages in length – which, similar to the storyline, includes:

- The business opportunity and how the recommendations will help build business success.
- The proposed strategies to achieve this and why they are right – including the facts that prove the case.
- The agreements that the team wants approved, including the key asks and tangible next steps.

Critically, Board members need to feel that they've been listened to throughout the preliminary meetings. Therefore, it's essential that the presentation deck addresses head-on any concerns that have been raised by senior management – by overtly stating and proactively resolving them in the deck, or by addressing them covertly using their language, or by overtly stating why they haven't been addressed.

Let's put this into practice by taking the example storyline outlined earlier in this chapter for 'migrating to one brand':

- **Recommendation: We should simplify our brand portfolio to one brand 'X'.**

  - By focusing all spend on building one strong brand only, return on investment will increase by 10 percent to 20 percent.
  - It will increase product cross-sell by an estimated 50 percent.
  - 'X' is our strongest brand across all of our categories.

- **Implications: Building one strong brand has three internal implications.**

  - We need to better communicate what brand 'X' stands for in a way that's relevant across all categories.

- We need to build strong product sub-brands to demonstrate all of the categories that brand 'X' is playing in.
- The organisation will need to behave in a more joined up way.

- **Agreements: To achieve this, we wish to start migrating now with the aim of full migration by the end of next year.**

  - This year, we wish to develop the brand positioning, product sub-brands and internal culture.
  - Next year, we will start the brand migration with the aim of completing it by year-end.
  - We estimate that this will cost an incremental £2 million.

To turn this storyline into a storyboard, we need to map each bullet point so that it becomes the headline of at least one supporting chart or page, each of which contains the supporting facts and data needed to make a compelling business case (Figures 9.1, 9.2 and 9.3).

To test the storyboard, write each of the separate charts on individual pages and lay them out on a table or on the floor – then rearrange their order until they create a compelling, cohesive, logical argument with an easy-to-follow storyline.

Once completed, a good way to ensure that the storyboard structure is working is to cut and paste all of the storyboard headlines back into the one-page Executive Summary storyline, to check that the high-level story is still tight.

Migrating to One Brand Board Recommendation Date	**Today's Objectives** Get agreement to ▸ Migrating to one brand ▸ Internal changes required ▸ Proposed timeline and cost	**Storyline** • We should simplify our brand portfolio to one brand 'X' • X • X • X • Building one strong brand has three internal implications • We wish to start migrating now with the aim of full migration by the end of next year
We should simplify our brand portfolio to one brand • Show need to be in all categories and geographies • Show cost of maintaining each individual brand • Show why it's impossible to keep maintaining this many	**By focusing all spend on building one strong brand only, ROI will increase by 10–20%** • Show where cost synergies can be realised • Show why if this was reinvested behind one brand how ROI would increase by 10–20%	**It will increase product cross-sell by 50%** • Show lack of cross-sell today • Show increased willingness to purchase once they know the product is made by 'X' • Show why this will lead to 50% cross-sell

Figure 9.1 Building a compelling storyboard

'X' is our strongest brand across all categories and so is the one to focus on	Storyline	We need to better communicate what 'X' stands for in a way that's relevant across all categories

• Show purchase funnel and brand image data by brand
 	
• Show high favourability to 'X' among customers of our other brands
	• We should simplify our brand portfolio to one brand
	  • X
	  • X
	  • X
	• Building one strong brand has three internal implications
	• We wish to start migrating now with the aim of full migration by the end of next year
		• Show today's positioning and why it's not relevant in some categories
		
		• Show possible positionings that 'X' could move to

We need to build strong product sub-brands to demonstrate all of the categories 'X' is playing in	The organisation will need to behave in a more joined up way	Storyline

• Show lack of consistency in product sub-brands today
 	
• Show benefits of having consistent set of product sub-brands (e.g., case studies)
	• Show how organisation operates today
	
	• Show what will need to change to make it more joined up
		• We should simplify our brand portfolio to one brand
		  • X
		  • X
		  • X
		• Building one strong brand has three internal implications
		• We wish to start migrating now with the aim of full migration by the end of next year

Figure 9.2 Building a compelling storyboard

This year, we will develop the brand positioning, product sub-brands and internal culture	Next year, we will start the brand migration with the aim of completing it by year-end	We estimate that this will cost an incremental £2m
Show this year's work plan	Show next year's work plan	• Show costs • Show spend plan (i.e., when the money's needed) • Show stage gates to go through to get next tranche of money
In summary.... • What we want your agreement to today	In summary.... • Next steps, including what you will see next and when	

Figure 9.3 Building a compelling storyboard

Creating compelling charts to support the storyline

Once the storyboard structure has been developed, the marketing team should present the facts, figures, market data and consumer research in a clear, compelling format. Board members can quickly get frustrated when marketing teams make strong assertions with few or weak facts and data to support their case.

A strong recommendation *must* be backed up by robust data and facts, so that each assertion is supported objectively and independently. This way, it makes it difficult for senior managers to disagree – and significantly helps convey that marketing knows, and is managing, the potential risks.

In practice, this means:

- Finding the data and facts that 'prove' or 'disprove' the hypotheses on each chart and modifying the storyline accordingly.
- Creating charts that evidence each bullet point with 'facts' that help back up the assertion – these 'facts' can be business financials, in-market data and testing, quantitative and qualitative research, customer quotes or external case studies.
- Building a convincing business case that demonstrates the business payback of the investment – as well as the risks to the business if the project fails.
- Addressing any concerns that people have raised head-on, to ensure the recommendation is approved.

Relevant facts can come from a variety of sources.

They can be *quantitative* in nature, such as commercial data that show sales and profit trends, both overall and versus competitors. Or in-market data such as distribution, pricing and advertising spend levels. Or in-market testing such as test market results, concept testing, product testing, packaging testing, advertising testing. Or brand health metrics such as purchase funnel or brand image data.

Or they can be more *qualitative* in nature, such as consumer focus group or in-depth interview quotes. Or customer quotes, sourced online, via customer complaints or at trade shows. Or external quotes, from journalists, partners or employees.

Or they can be more *tangential* in nature, such as other company case studies, be they of competitors within the industry or relevant case studies from other industries.

Any fact that is charted should justify the point being made in the headline – which in turn should be one of the bullet points in the storyline. By doing this, it makes it difficult for senior managers to challenge the assertion or dispute the 'so what'. If it doesn't justify the headline, the team needs to question whether this data is relevant and whether there is better data available to make the point.

Additionally, the chart should contain the data source (including the relevant timeline that the data covers), what the data is (e.g., percent of profit) and any relevant clarification footnotes outlining how the data was collected or calculated.

Figure 9.4 shows a good example of quantitative data being used to make the case.

Similarly, qualitative data can be presented in a more robust way, using devices such as Harvey Balls or Moons, as Figure 9.5 shows.

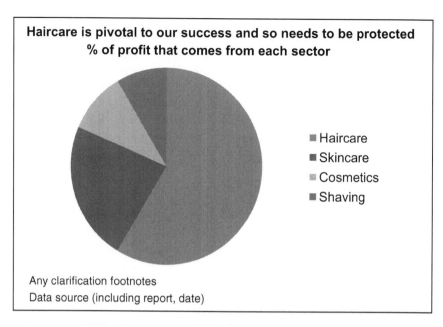

Haircare is pivotal to our success and so needs to be protected
% of profit that comes from each sector

- Haircare
- Skincare
- Cosmetics
- Shaving

Any clarification footnotes
Data source (including report, date)

Figure 9.4 Presenting quantitative data to support the case

Which concept do we progress with?	Concept 1 – Simplicity	Concept 2 – Personalised	Concept 3 – Convenient
Appealing	◑	◕	◔
Relevant	◕	◕	◔
Credible	◑	◑	◑
Differentiated	◔	◕	◔
Can be delivered profitably	◑	◑	◑
Average	◑	◕	◔

'Personalisation' is the strongest concept and thus should be progressed

Source: Concept qualitative research, 2016   Key ● Very High ◑ Medium ○ Very Low

Figure 9.5 Presenting qualitative data to support the case

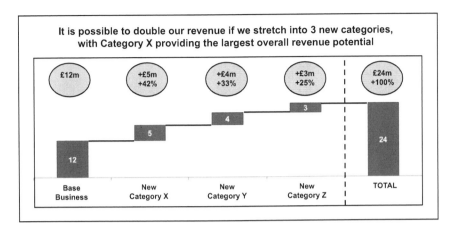

Figure 9.6 Using visualisation to more quickly tell the story

Importantly, visualisation can be more powerful than bullet point lists at quickly telling the story, as the waterfall chart in Figure 9.6 shows.

C: Building a robust business case

In many Board recommendations, it's important to include a robust business case.

The business case sets out the robust data and facts to support the recommendation – in essence, it contains the maths, stats and business financials that, if done well, make it difficult for the Board to reject the case. Essentially, the business case can make or break a business proposal. In the words of Dan Zarella, author and social media scientist, "Marketing without data is like driving with your eyes closed."[3]

The business case should be written in the language of the Board – the language of numbers. Board members analyse company performance, past growth, forecasted growth, return and risk. It's a language they understand and one that the modern marketer needs to communicate in if they are going to win over the Board.

Ideally, the business case should show a size of prize that is large enough to excite the top team, as well as worth the risk.

At the same time, however, it's important to talk to senior management as commercial business people, 'telling senior management like it is' rather than 'selling the ad-man dream'. Doing this requires showing 'truths' rather than 'carefully selected statistics' and 'telling the whole story' rather than 'tempting sound bites'. In essence, the Board will expect you to evaluate the business case as if it were your own money. If you wouldn't invest your own hard cash in this project, nor invest in a staged way that minimises business risk, why should you expect the Board to invest?

When building a robust business case, senior management will typically want to see five components:

1   What the project will most likely deliver, and why.
2   What the project will cost.
3   Over what time frame.
4   Fact-based proof on why we can expect the project to be successful.
5   The risk of the project not delivering.

1: What the project will deliver, and why

At the outset of any project, it's important for marketers to be clear on what the project will most likely deliver and *how* they believe the proposed investment will deliver it – by creating a 'back of the envelope' business model assessment.

While not robust, this enables the team to quickly assess whether the project is a 'go-er' in any shape or form – namely, if the investment level required has any hope of delivering the business uplift the company will be looking for. Additionally, it helps assess what the initiative would need to achieve to deliver the required short- and longer-term business goals – and whether this is feasible.

To do this, the team should answer a number of questions.

Firstly, what is the business problem that the team is trying to solve? For example, are we trying to increase sales, or strengthen the health of our brands? Do we need to see an immediate uplift in sales, or are longer-term business or brand uplifts more important?

Secondly, what is the business model that is being adopted to deliver the increased business growth? For example, will the growth come from recruiting new customers, or from cross-selling more products to existing customers? Will it come from encouraging existing customers to stay with the brand for longer, or from introducing customers to other brands? Will it come from the core, more established products within the range, or from the launch of new products? In essence, this means distilling what the initiative is, including which customers and products to focus on – and how it will change customer behaviour, including whom it will attract, which behaviours it will change and how this will translate into more revenue.

Thirdly, what are the short- and longer-term metrics (or key performance indicators or KPIs) that we are focusing on – and how much do they need to increase by to deliver a healthy return? For instance, if the project 'lives or dies' based on its ability to bring in new customers, how many new customers does it need to bring in to deliver a profitable return that's acceptable to the Board? Or, if project success is linked to greater cross-sell, how many additional products does it need to sell to existing customers – and which types of products are these? Essentially, the team needs to assess:

- For each customer who changes their behaviour, how much incremental revenue and profit will be generated?
- Given the size of the project goals and the proposed investment levels, how many people would need to change their behaviour to achieve the increased revenue and profit objectives?
- Is this achievable, given the size of the target audience, the strength of the brand today versus competitors, the strength of the proposition being launched, and the likelihood of there being cross-brand or cross-product cannibalisation?

While this analysis may not be 100 percent accurate, it gives the team a greater understanding of which customer and brand metrics are important for success and how much customer and brand behavioural change is required to hit the project targets – and hence the likelihood of the project succeeding. For instance, if competitor brands are typically spending £15 million annually on advertising and the slice of the market that you can play in is £20 million with low growth, the project is probably not worth progressing to the next stage. Similarly, if you need every customer to double the number of chocolate bars that they eat in a week to break even, then this probably isn't realistic.

Additionally, it helps ensure that the company investment stays focused on those areas that are likely to deliver the greatest return – for example, on innovating the products and communicating with the customers that will be most crucial to future business success.

When presenting 'what the project is expected to deliver', the marketing team should move beyond the world of brands, customers and marketing and show how the investment will deliver business growth – by linking brand and customer metrics to the bottom line. For example, there may be a clear correlation between brand awareness and short- and longer-term sales. However, simply communicating that this investment will build brand awareness by 20 percent may cause some Board members to think 'so what?'

If, however, the team communicates that the investment will build brand awareness by 20 percent, which in turn is forecasted to build revenue by 8 percent, then the Board is likely to be a lot more receptive. This is typically shown as the estimated sales uplift in both percentage and absolute form, as well as the uplift in company contribution once external costs (such as listing fees or production fees) are removed.

Ideally, estimates should be based around a more conservative scenario, either as the one option that is presented or as the lower end of the estimated range, so that senior management are reassured that a weaker scenario is still palatable. This conservative scenario should not contain 'soft factors' or 'factors that are outside of the company's control', enabling the top team to have confidence that this scenario is truly achievable.

In reality, those in senior management are often more comfortable with multiple scenarios, enabling them to assess their appetite for 'lower risk / lower investment' options versus 'higher risk / higher investment' ones. This also helps to involve them in the debate, ensuring that they don't feel forced into a corner when presented with the recommendation.

When presenting 'how the proposed investment will work', marketers can bring this to life by mapping the expected customer journey – demonstrating the in-market activities that will be invested in, how these are expected to change customer behaviour, and where the resultant business uplifts are likely to come from. Lifting the business case out of the world of marketing – and its associated jargon – and putting it into the real world of consumers tends to make it easier for the Board to understand what is being proposed, and how this will build incremental sales and profitability.

2: What the project will cost

When presenting to the Board what the project will cost, it is important to show the real incremental cost of the proposed activity, including all incremental external costs (such as trade fees, and cost of advertising and promotional support) and internal costs (such as product costs, cost of cannibalised business and cost of any new technology or production equipment needed).

Resulting contribution is then typically shown after all incremental (or variable) internal and external costs are taken into account, both as a percentage and absolute uplift.

To demonstrate the possible business uplift, a typical business case should include a miniature profit and loss statement, outlining metrics such as:

- Revenue growth over time.
- Spend over time.
- Profit and profit margin over time, including both the absolute level of profit the project will make each year, as well as profit as a percentage of total revenue.
- EBITDA – or earnings before interest, tax, depreciation and amortisation – a simple way to show the operational profitability of a project and to get from profit to cash.
- Capex – or the capital expenditure required to deliver the project – which is then amortised or depreciated over the life of the assets in question.
- Operating cash flow – calculated as EBITDA minus Capex – which is the cash that's generated by the project once capital expenditure is accounted for.

Then, to evaluate the expected project performance, it should also include measures that track possible business return, for example:

- Return on investment (ROI) – the percent return that the investment will deliver – this is a less transparent measure than the internal rate of return

(IRR) as people assume different measures for the 'I' (investment) metric within ROI, making it a less accurate cross-project comparison.

- Internal rate of return (IRR) – the percent uplift generated by an investment over a period of time, for example, if after five years I generate £130 from a £100 investment, then my five-year IRR is 30 percent.
- Net present value (NPV) – a time series of incoming and outgoing cash flows – that calculates what a project is worth over time, taking inflation and returns into account; this must be positive and solid versus the other projects on the table.
- Terminal value (TV) – what the project will deliver in perpetuity (assuming it doesn't end), discounted back into today's present value.

The finance team would typically expect to see one-year, five-year and ten-year views of the business case, to assess both short-term issues and longer-term gain, as well as ensure a balanced investment portfolio across the company. A three-year payback is usually seen as good, a one-year payback exceptional, and a five-year payback questionable.

Similarly, long lags between spend and return are seen as concerning (often triggering questions like, why can't the team show a quicker return at this early development stage?) as well as risky (what happens if the market moves?)

Understandably, projects with long return lags are typically challenged.

3: Over what time frame

Senior management typically expects to see the expected business case timeline, including the required upfront cost and expected business uplift at each stage. More specifically:

- How much upfront cost there will be before any business uplift is seen.
- What the peak funding cash level or highest capital expenditure needed is at any point in the project and when this occurs – for example, how far under water do we go before we start to recoup some of our expenditure?
- When the project will break even – or how long before a month's costs are covered by the same month's business uplift?
- How long it will take before the project pays back – or how long before the overall business uplift is greater than all costs spent to date?

The finance team will typically use this data in a number of ways, including:

- How this project's return on investment compares with other projects the company is considering.
- How risky this project is versus other projects in the company portfolio, to ensure that the company is investing in a balanced portfolio of projects, with some that are more risky and others that are less so.

- How to balance the loss making in early years versus other projects, to ensure that the company as a whole doesn't risk too much capital investment.

4: Fact-based proof on why we can expect the project to be successful

Once the project appears to have legs, it's important to build a business case based on as solid assumptions as is feasibly possible. This helps to make a compelling case that the Board will find hard to disagree with, as well as conveys that marketing knows all of the potential risks and is managing them.

The marketing team should include relevant 'facts' that support the assertion and make a more robust case. For example, these could include in-market data such as test market results or competitor performance. Or research data – both quantitative and qualitative research that tests the potential of the launch proposition. Or relevant external case studies, where other brands in similar circumstances, either within or outside of the category, have executed a similar proposition. Or relevant quotes from customers, journalists, partners or category experts.

When using in-market results or case studies as proof of evidence, these should show:

- What the team did, including key activities and investment levels.
- What was achieved in-market, and over what time frame.
- What worked, namely, which activities drove the uplift.
- Why this case is relevant to what we want to do.

When using market research as proof of evidence, the research should show:

- The key measures that were achieved in testing.
- What other projects with scores like these have achieved once in-market.
- What it took for these other projects to be successful.

5: The risk of the project not delivering

In practice, Boards tend to invest in a balanced risk profile, with some projects that are more risky and others that are less so.

Asking Boards to invest in riskier projects is, in itself, not a problem. It's acceptable for some projects to be riskier than others, provided the Board is comfortable with the higher level of risk.

Yet, marketers often shy away from talking explicitly to the Board about risk, perhaps because they find it difficult to assess how risky the project is, or maybe because they are concerned that if the higher-risk project doesn't deliver, then their neck will be on the line.

To mitigate this, marketers should help the Board get comfortable with a project's level of risk. This typically includes outlining:

- The project's expected target.
- The likelihood of the project over- or under-delivering the expected target.
- A view of what the worst-case scenario might look like – specifically, *the greatest business risk*.
- A set of stage gates outlining the capital expenditure needed at each stage and the performance metrics that the project will need to achieve before the next tranche of funds is released.
- A summary of the most likely risks and what the team is doing to mitigate them.

Each element should include fact-based proof and supporting rationale wherever possible.

By being clear from the outset about the level of risk involved, the Board is more likely to stay on-board if the investment takes a while to deliver what was promised.

In summary

To get the Board on-board, marketers need to succinctly show how their marketing strategies will build shareholder value – by creating clear, compelling business cases that the Board will buy into, as well as tight Board presentations that bring the recommendations to life.

To do this, they need to get inside the mindset of the Board, viewing the business recommendation from the Board member's commercial perspective and talking their language.

Because Board members are invariably time-starved, marketers should create a tight one-page Executive Summary storyline that is:

- *Commercial*, making it clear why senior managers should engage (i.e., what's in it for them).
- *Credible*, using facts to demonstrate why this is the right thing to do.
- *Concise*, cutting to the chase and only including what's really important.
- *Clear-cut*, clearly conveying the key messages you want to land, and the key asks and next steps.

The purpose and narrative of the Executive Summary storyline should be clear, outlining:

- The business opportunity and how the recommendations will help build business success.

- The proposed strategies to achieve this and why they are right.
- What we want agreement to, including the key asks and tangible next steps.

The marketing team should then create a bespoke Board presentation deck that clearly and succinctly conveys the Board recommendation and is supported with the necessary facts and data to build Board confidence.

The Board presentation deck should:

- Be ten to fifteen pages in length, focused on what the Board needs to hear and the facts and arguments that will convince them, with any relevant back up in the appendix.
- Mirror the Executive Summary storyline, with:

  - The deck structure in the same logical order as the storyline structure, to enable managers to easily reference a specific section for more detail.
  - Each bullet point in the storyline having at least one page that supports it, demonstrating why it's factually true and relevant.
  - Each page conveying a single message and containing the facts that 'prove' the headline, using data sources that people will believe in, and bringing the data to life visually on the page.
  - Any senior management concerns addressed head-on, either by stating their issues and proactively resolving them in the deck, or by covertly addressing their issues in the deck using their language.
  - A page at the end summarising 'what we want your agreement to today' and 'next steps'.

When requesting investment, marketers should present a compelling and robust business case – enabling the Board to assess the project's likely size of prize and level of risk versus other company projects that the company may wish to invest in. The business case should include:

- What the project will most likely deliver.
- What the project will cost.
- Over what time frame.
- Fact-based proof on why we can expect the project to be successful.
- The risk of the project not delivering.

Having looked at how to win over the minds of the Board members, the next chapter addresses how to win over their hearts, showing them how important the project is for the company – and for each of them as part of the team – by engaging them throughout the problem-solving process.

Notes

1 Barbara Minto, *The Pyramid Principle* (New York: Minto International Inc., 1978; London, UK: Pitman Publishing, 1991).
2 Minto, *The Pyramid Principle*.
3 Dan Zarrella, "Why All Marketers Should Embrace Data," *Forbes*, May 2013, www.forbes.com/sites/danschawbel/2013/05/08/dan-zarrella-why-all-marketers-should-embrace-data/#70ba22d61f65.

Bibliography

Minto, Barbara. *The Pyramid Principle*. New York: Minto International Inc. 1978; London: Pitman Publishing, 1991.
Zarrella, Dan. "Why All Marketers Should Embrace Data." *Forbes*, May 2013. www.forbes.com/sites/danschawbel/2013/05/08/dan-zarrella-why-all-marketers-should-embrace-data/#70ba22d61f65.

Chapter 10

Winning the Board members' hearts

> "When dealing with people, let us remember we are not dealing with creatures of logic. We are dealing with creatures of emotion, creatures bristling with prejudices and motivated by pride and vanity."
>
> Dale Carnegie, *How to Win Friends and Influence People*

As we saw in the previous chapter, to win over senior managers' minds, marketers need to succinctly show how their marketing strategies will build shareholder value – by creating clear, compelling business cases that the Board will buy into, as well as tight Board presentations that bring the recommendations to life.

To do this, they need to get inside the mindset of the Board, viewing the business recommendation from the Board members' commercial perspective, and talking their language.

Yet, to get full buy-in, marketers also need to win over senior managers' hearts – showing them how important the project is for the company, and for each of them as part of the team.

To do this, marketers should engage senior managers throughout the problem-solving process. In this chapter, we look at how to do this by:

A   Involving senior managers in the problem solving from day one.
B   Handling challenging Board-level conversations effectively.
C   Presenting with the end in mind on the day itself.

A: Involving senior managers in the problem solving from day one

Syndicating the storyline early on

Ideally, the team's goal is to secure senior-level agreement to the recommendation *prior* to the Board meeting, so that getting it signed off in the Board meeting itself is more of a formality that takes minutes rather than hours. This means adopting a collaborative and inclusive approach from day one.

Many marketing teams only engage Board members late in the day. They hold off talking with Board members until they know what their recommendations are and what they want agreement to. And, in their drive to get their business strategies approved, they present their recommendations and rationale using 'selling statements' to make their case. In response, Board members tell me that they often feel 'sold to' rather than 'included in the problem solving'. In reality, Board members *prefer* to be engaged early on in the 'team debate' and have much to offer throughout the problem-solving process.

In Chapter 9, we looked at how to create an Executive Summary storyline hypothesis, such as the one shown in Figure 10.1.

To engage senior managers, syndicate the one-page storyline hypothesis with middle and senior managers, cross-functional stakeholders and experts as early as possible in the project.

At this stage, the goal is not to 'sell' but to:

- Involve relevant stakeholders in the problem solving, using them to help to create robust recommendations based on their experience and intuition.
- Access data or facts that can help support the recommendation and business case.
- Identify and address concerns or 'showstoppers' by understanding what senior managers would need to see or hear to overcome them – and debunking any myths that they might mistakenly have.

Starting with middle managers and cross-functional stakeholders, set up half-hour or hour-long one-on-one discussions in which to ask for feedback,

---

EXAMPLE STORYLINE

Situation: Great client on-boarding is imperative to building deep client relationships
- Clients are more likely to do more business with a company, as well as refer it to others, if it's easy to join and they feel they're getting a personalised service, and are valued.
- If not, then the company has failed at the first hurdle, not only missing the opportunity to demonstrate what it can do, but also disappointing clients from day one.

Complication: Our joining experience today is not fit for purpose
- For most it's slow, taking at least ten weeks to open a new account rather than the ten working days people expect.
- For many, there's no follow up - therefore it is ineffective at building deeper client relationships.
- For a minority, the joining experience is poor, with multiple information requests and errors wasting a lot of customers' valuable time.

Resolution: To create a joining experience that sets the right standard, there are two imperatives
- To stop disappointing customers, we need to streamline the new joiner on-boarding process by (i) streamlining application forms and information requests, (ii) capturing and sharing information electronically and (iii) streamlining and empowering the back office.
- To build deeper relationships, the sales team needs to follow up all new joiners in a systematic way, by (i) helping them get up and running in their first week, (ii) inviting them to a welcome event in their first month and (iii) calling them at the end of the third month to ensure that they are happy.

Figure 10.1 Creating a compelling Board storyline

input, intuition and supporting data that will help to build your hypothesis. Refine the storyline as you go, so that by the time that it's taken to senior management, it already has broad cross-functional buy-in.

Next, syndicate the one-page storyline hypothesis with senior managers for their early thoughts and input, in similar half-hour or hour-long one-on-one discussions.

Limiting it to one page in length ensures that it's succinct, allowing time-starved senior managers to engage and input efficiently, and making it easy to adapt as new information and challenges come to light.

Sharing it early on gives the team additional time to collect new data or facts needed to address and rectify senior management concerns that arise – and to course correct the storyline, increasing the team's chances of securing senior management buy-in *before* the Board recommendation meeting itself.

When talking with senior managers in these preliminary sessions, ask questions (rather than make 'selling' statements) to tease out their points of view and suggested ways forward.

Take notes throughout the meeting. This shows that you are listening and value their input and captures their language, which can be helpful when writing the final deck. It also provides you with a solid reference point when comparing the differing views of the various senior manager stakeholders.

Invariably, you will find that some people prefer to read the storyline hypothesis before the meeting, while others prefer to review it in person with you. As well, people have different presentation styles, so it is not uncommon to get conflicting 'style advice'. Where possible, take on-board their advice and write the storyline replicating their style and language so that they will recognise it.

At the end of the meeting, ask whether they would like to be involved in the problem solving going forward and, if so, how much. For example, would they like another one-on-one meeting to review the revised storyline prior to the final Board presentation, once the team has captured and incorporated all senior-level feedback – or are they comfortable enough to not be included in the next round of one-on-one discussions?

Proactively addressing any concerns head-on

During these preliminary meetings with senior managers, it's important to identify the concerns or 'showstoppers' that will prevent the project from being approved. These need to be addressed in the final presentation deck.

Overcoming 'showstoppers' entails sizing the issues, finding creative ways to mitigate them, debunking myths and altering the recommendation and plan as needed. This can be done by analysing data, interviewing key internal or external people to gather more data, conducting bespoke research and/or showing relevant case studies from in or outside of the industry.

As mentioned in the previous chapter, Board members can become frustrated if they feel that they've not been listened to. To counter this, the final presentation deck should address concerns that have been raised by senior management head-on, by overtly stating and proactively resolving them in the deck, or by overtly stating why they haven't been addressed. To help create buy-in, write these concerns and the storyline in language that mirrors theirs so that they'll recognise it consciously or subconsciously.

The ideal outcome is when the Board agrees to the recommendation ahead of the Board meeting itself, as a result of these one-on-one sessions. This way, on the day, all Board members will be supportive of both the recommendation and proposed next steps, and won't speak out or raise reservations or concerns that might stop it being approved. While this is not always possible, I have seen more and more marketers achieve this outcome when using this process.

For this reason, the marketing team should continue to syndicate the adapted storyline among relevant senior managers right up until the Board meeting for ongoing input and thoughts – particularly among those who have reservations or concerns.

Doing so helps the marketing team to:

- Focus on collecting the data and facts needed to best make the case.
- Refine the recommendation until it is communicated clearly and makes 'commercial sense'.
- Proactively address senior management concerns that might prevent the proposal getting through, prior to the Board presentation itself.

B: Handling challenging conversations

Talking with senior managers who have reservations or concerns often gives rise to a more challenging type of senior-level conversation – even more so if their concerns are emotional in nature.

Some marketers find these more challenging conversations easier to handle than others do. These marketers tend to naturally assess whether the concerns are more rational or emotional in origin and, on the back of this, consider whether to 'rationalise', 'negotiate', 'escalate' or 'retreat'.

Let's look at each of these in turn and how they come into play.

Step 1: Rationalise

Most business decisions are made rationally – especially those regarded as good for both the business and the team. In this situation, marketers need to take a rational approach when talking with senior managers, and **rationalise** the benefits of the business proposal using a logical, compelling recommendation that is well supported by a robust business case.

Often a single meeting to review a succinctly written and compelling story-line and presentation deck is enough to get feedback and buy-in.

If, at the end, the senior manager still has concerns, marketers need to collect the necessary data and facts to rectify these issues and meet with the senior manager again to share the new information, discuss key agreements and next steps, and ask for agreement to proceed to the next stage.

Step 2: Negotiate

Sometimes business decisions can be more emotional in nature, often when they involve personal risk, such as 'It might negatively impact my team's sales or profit performance', or 'It may result in me losing some of my power base', or 'It might force me to do something that my peers or boss would disapprove of'.

Take, for instance, a project that I worked on involving the migration of the local brand name to a global brand name. Understandably, local marketers were apprehensive that being taken over by a global marketing team would mean losing their local power base as well as their local brand name. During a brand migration workshop set up to discuss this, the situation became so fraught that the local marketing director exclaimed, "Stop, you're killing my baby."

A similar reaction occurred when a Board was assessing whether to invest in building a strong global brand – a strategy that is likely to pay off in the long term, but rarely pays out in the first year or so. In these circumstances, senior managers can be nervous about agreeing to the recommendation, based on their fears that if they approve it, the short-term performance of their team will suffer, which may reflect badly on them.

A third example involved the company being asked to move from a local to a global brand positioning. This can evoke strong emotions, particularly when the global brand positioning is likely to be less popular in the local market. Senior marketers are caught between conflicting business objectives – the desire of the global marketing team to move to globally aligned brand positionings versus the desire of the local general manager to optimise sales and profit performance in their own country. In this situation, the local marketers can quite understandably be concerned that if they acquiesce to the global team's request, then their local boss will disapprove.

When emotional concerns exist, a logical, compelling recommendation and a robust business case is unlikely to be enough. In these cases, you need to **negotiate**.

Marketers need to take the time to listen to, understand and respect the concerns of those senior managers who will be affected. By bringing the underlying emotional issues to light, the team can be sympathetic to and address them overtly, increasing its chances of quickly finding a win-win solution that is mutually acceptable.

If there are signs of emotional resistance, the marketer should conduct a fact-finding (rather than 'selling') meeting with the respective senior manager early on, to assess whether these issues are potential road blocks, identify the likely causes and determine how best to handle them.

Top negotiation tips

When meeting with dissenting senior managers, don't sell to them. Instead, listen.

Take time to genuinely understand their point of view, identify what the underlying blockages are and **negotiate** a mutually acceptable solution, for example:

- Work through which parts of the proposal both parties agree on, and which they don't, with the aim of finding common ground and identifying where the real sticking points are.
- Delve to understand what's behind the underlying reasons for their concerns – to the level that they are prepared to reveal – by continually asking 'What's concerning you?' until their answer makes sense.
- Identify the facts, data or evidence that they would need to see to be convinced, and agree how to source those facts – for example, through new customer research, analysis of sales data, or proven internal or external case studies.
- Identify the conditions that would need to change for them to be comfortable – for example, 'If we achieve a 20 percent market share, then would you be happy to proceed?'
- Give them time to review the plan and talk with others in the business – then follow up with a second meeting once you've both had time to think it through further.
- Negotiate to find a win-win solution.

Typically, I use the one-page Executive Summary storyline as the basis for these discussions, talking them through:

- *The business context* – outlining why it's important for the team to take time to consider the recommendation and be actively involved in the decision-making.
- *The recommendation* – asking them what their point of view is and why. If they're not overly hostile and it seems beneficial, I might anonymously disclose what others think and why, and ask for their point of view. If they're hostile, I probe to understand their point of view.
- *The resolution* – pinpointing where both parties agree and disagree, and probing what they would need to see to change their point of view, for example, new data or facts, or changes in market conditions.

- *The issues* – proactively broaching issues that you think might concern them, to gauge where they stand.
- *The next steps* – agreeing on the data or facts you'll source, including who they will talk with to help resolve the issue, who else you should talk with or what else you should do, as well as when you'll next meet and what you'll be covering in that meeting.

When conducting these meetings, it's important that the senior managers feel able to speak openly – which is partly why I prefer to conduct them face-to-face and one-on-one.

To show respect for their point of view, take care to listen and understand where they are coming from. Ask probing questions and summarise for clarification. For example, show that you are listening by repeating back what they say to you, using statements like "So, to summarise, what you're saying . . ." or 'If I hear you correctly . . .'

Delve to really understand where they're coming from. Use statements like 'So what's really worrying you about this is . . .'

Look for common ground that you can agree on, by asking questions like 'What elements of this plan are you comfortable with?' or making statements like 'So, it's fair to say that we agree on . . .'

Isolate the key point of disagreement by asking 'So is the key difference between us . . .?'

Look for ways to resolve their issues. Ask, for example, 'What can I say or show you that would convince you?' or 'What data would you need to see for you to be convinced?'

Be straight, by saying, 'This is an important issue for the company and so puts us in a difficult position.'

Never sell to them, argue with them or tell them that they are wrong.

Don't make lots of statements, hide behind charts or bamboozle them with data.

Let them get their issues out on the table and explain where they're coming from.

And be absolutely clear in your communication, in particular the key points of disagreements and agreed next steps, to ensure that there are no unnecessary misunderstandings.

If the emotions and concerns are aired in the first meeting, the second meeting is likely to go more smoothly.

Step 3: Escalate

In the fact-finding meeting, it's possible you will hit a stalemate due to conflicting objectives or insurmountable concerns. If there's clearly no room for negotiation, give them time to raise their issues with their peers to assess whether there's a resolution and to evaluate whether others have a similar view to them – or whether they are a lone voice.

If they are a lone voice, then they will pick their battles wisely – choosing to go into battle only if they feel strongly enough. In other words, giving senior managers space to reflect can sometimes make the issue go away.

If that doesn't work, the next step is to **escalate** up the line for your and their bosses to debate it out. This means recognising that higher-level politics makes it impossible for the issue to be resolved at your level.

Be straight in your discussions, let them know that you're going to escalate it – for example, 'If we can't resolve it between us then I'm afraid we will have to escalate it up to . . .'

In essence, if a senior person doesn't want to play ball, then it's the responsibility of the business to resolve it, not you.

Step 4: Retreat

If your bosses can't resolve the issue, there may well be good reasons as to why this isn't the best time to proceed – possibly reasons that you'll never know about or understand.

For example, senior management may not be aligned on the best way forward – requiring more time to reach a common point of view. Or the organisation may not be ready – there may be other projects that need to happen before this one, or the necessary resources may not be in place yet. Or the company may think, or even know, that this is right thing to do but doesn't want to tackle this issue now – the perceived risk may be seen as greater than the potential upside. I have seen senior managers agree that something needs to happen, but then take two to three years or more to summon up the courage to take the hit.

Sometimes senior management will only make the leap when there's a trigger that encourages them to do so. This could be an external change, such as a significant drop in sales or profit, or a consumer backlash. Or it could be an internal change, such as new proof that demonstrates how compelling the case is, or a new CEO who is keen to champion the cause, or completion of a major project freeing up resources.

In these situations, recognise that the current timing isn't right and **retreat**. Sometimes the team should turn its attention elsewhere. At other times, it's worth assessing what needs to change for the timing to be right and to continue to collect the facts and data needed to build the case so that the team will be more prepared when choosing to raise the issue again.

When the going gets really tough

In conversations such as these, the going can get particularly tough, and over the years I've found two techniques to be especially helpful – I call these 'Dance Baby Dance' and 'Shoot Me in the Heart'.

Let's start with Dance Baby Dance.

When meeting a senior manager for the first time, I've sometimes found that they begin the meeting by testing how confident I am in my recommendation. In essence, they fire a series of questions at me at rapid speed to see if I flinch.

Are all of the questions in my comfort zone, or do any bamboozle me?

Do I answer all of the questions confidently, or do any fluster me?

I call this scenario Dance Baby Dance – imagining that they are firing bullets at my feet and thus forcing me to dance – and I've found that if I hold my ground and answer confidently, they soon visibly relax.

To illustrate, when selling in a piece of complex data analysis on 'what drives customer behaviour', a Board member opened the conversation with a series of questions on exactly which statistical techniques we had used and why – lasting a good fifteen minutes of the hour-long meeting. The questions came in rapid succession and were complex in nature. Once he saw that we knew our subject and had considered and discounted a number of options for sound, logical reasons, he visibly relaxed – and we successfully sold in the findings and 'so whats' of the data analysis.

Similarly, when I was a brand manager, I had to redo every piece of packaging copy for more than thirty Olay stock keeping units (SKUs). When I took them to the marketing director for approval, his opening question was whether he would find even one mistake when he read through them that night. Without hesitation, I answered that he would find no mistakes. Because of my confident reply, he signed the paperwork then and there, without any further checking.

The second technique, Shoot Me in the Heart, can be helpful when under pressure. Occasionally, a senior manager may be so unhappy about a recommendation that they will proactively attack. When this happens, I've noticed that my natural physical response is to close in on myself – I tend to cross my arms, drop my shoulders and hunch forward in my chair, in essence, protecting my body. This physical response can be read as a sign of nervousness – which then encourages even more attack. In contrast, I've found that if I open up my body when under attack – by making myself bigger, throwing my shoulders wider, and sitting back in my chair in a more relaxed way, with my arms open and either alongside my body or placed on the arms of the chair – I am better able to hold my ground.

When I do this, two things seem to happen. Firstly, I feel more relaxed and confident and my nervousness reduces. In a sense, by physically relaxing, my mind seems to mentally relax too, making me less on the defensive. Secondly, my 'attacker' is visibly surprised by the move – they expect me to be cowed but instead I have given them a 'clear shot at my heart' – implying that I have something to feel confident about, and thus they should engage.

I call this Shoot Me in the Heart and have found it incredibly effective at turning an aggressive meeting into a constructive one.

C: Presenting with the end in mind on the day itself

As mentioned earlier in this chapter, the ideal for any team is to secure Board agreement to the recommendation prior to the Board meeting itself, so that getting it approved in the boardroom will be more of a formality that takes minutes rather than hours.

Prior to the Board meeting

If the case is contentious, syndicate the **final** recommendation, storyline and, where appropriate, the presentation deck with any senior managers who had concerns, with the aim of pre-selling the final recommendation before the presentation day itself. Prior to the Board meeting, set up a short meeting or call with each of these senior managers, to ask if you have their support, and why or why not, and if there is anything else you can do before the final meeting to alleviate their concerns.

If reservations or concerns still exist, let the Board members who are actively supporting the recommendation know so that they can either address the issue with the relevant individuals before the meeting, or at least, are pre-warned, thus reducing the risk of any nasty surprises on the day.

Before the meeting, try to look at the recommendation through the eyes of each Board member and be prepared for questions that might arise on the day.

For example, the finance team is tasked with ensuring that any profit targets that have been promised to the shareholders are delivered. If a project under-delivers in its first year, confidence can quickly be dented and investment in other projects curtailed. Those in the finance team often see their role as the 'conscience' of the company and are quick to identify holes in the business case, especially when reviewing more creative projects. The finance team is likely to focus on the short-term cost, the likely risk of the project not delivering and what is being done during the launch phase to mitigate the risk.

Teams that are heavily tied up in the manufacturing, selling and servicing of the core business are likely to be concerned about the high level of distraction that a new product or service launch could create. Therefore, the production, sales and technology teams may well focus on how to strike the right balance between supporting the products that are the mainstay of today's business versus backing the new products that will undoubtedly eat up more time during the launch phase.

At the Board meeting

Traditionally, I have been a nervous presenter – seeking reassurance by following the script, which in turn makes me nervous that I might leave something out.

Over time, I've learned how to eliminate presentation day nerves. For me, the trick is to focus on why senior management needs to engage and what we want agreement to. By knowing this, it matters less whether the script or meeting discussion goes off-piste, as you can always bring the discussion back to what really matters – namely *why the Board needs to engage and the key asks you want agreed.*

On the presentation day itself, focus on what you want your audience to agree to and what you can say to convince them.

Use their time efficiently to get agreement and buy-in by putting yourself in their mindset, thinking and talking in their language and seeing the issue from their point of view.

Ask if they have read the deck and, if so, whether they need further clarification on the recommendation and rationale. If they do, this could be a good time to talk through the one-page storyline.

Ask whether they'd like to discuss the implications and issues before making a decision – and use the relevant pages in the presentation deck to aid the discussion.

Then focus on why they should engage and what you want them to agree to – ensuring that the 'reasons to progress' are compelling and that the 'asks' are tangible. Demonstrate how the project is important for the company, as well as for each of them personally as part of the leadership team.

If cross-functional support is needed to deliver the project, then use the Board meeting to create a sense of shared responsibility – by asking relevant Board members whether they are happy to provide the necessary support. For example, can the digital team support the product, service or advertising launch with a seamless online experience that encourages customers to buy? Can the data team provide the customer leads needed to run the advertising? Can the sales and call centre teams provide the support needed to handle the incremental demand? If cross-functional teams don't provide the necessary support, it can really harm the project – and so the Board meeting can be a great forum to achieve cross-functional buy-in early on.

Senior management also wants to see marketers who have the confidence to say, 'I can deliver the company £X million using £Y million of investment money' (rather than, 'I might be able to') and 'If you agree to this investment then I will be accountable for making sure it delivers'. Knowing someone truly believes in the project and will do whatever it takes to make it work can help to build the confidence of the senior team.

When the debate is drawing to a close, ask for their agreement to proceed as well as their buy-in to the key 'so whats'. These should include the timeline, costs, work plan, immediate next steps and any outstanding issues still to be addressed. Pause to ensure that you have their agreement – and then clarify what you will do over the coming weeks and what they will see next to keep everyone on-board.

After the Board meeting

Marketers should be sanguine if their projects are not prioritised. It doesn't mean that they've failed. It may be the case that there are more compelling projects on the table right now, or that the business is investing in too many projects like these and so is keen not to take on another. Or perhaps the business doesn't think that the recommendation is strong enough and needs more work.

It's best that tough decisions are made at this stage, rather than launching and then spending the next three years regretting it, or launching and then slashing funds half-way through, creating a self-fulfilling prophecy of project failure.

Whatever the outcome, marketers should write up and circulate the meeting notes within twenty-four hours of the meeting, including the meeting purpose, attendee list, key agreements, proposed next steps and what the Board will see next.

If the project is approved, marketing needs to keep the Board on-board, by being on top of the delivery from day one – proactively tracking in-market performance, addressing issues and managing risks as soon as they come up – thus maintaining Board confidence. 'Keeping the Board on-board' is something we look at in more detail in the next chapter.

In summary

To get the Board members on-board, it's important to win over their hearts as well as their minds – showing them how important the project will be for the company and for each of them as part of the team.

To achieve this, marketers should engage Board members as allies throughout the problem-solving process. They should syndicate the one-page storyline hypothesis among senior managers in an early stage 'listening and problem-solving' rather than 'selling' meeting – with the aim of getting senior managers' input on what the 'right answer' is, identifying and addressing any concerns or 'showstoppers', and accessing any support data that will help make the case.

They should not shy away from challenging conversations with the Board members, but instead look for ways to handle them effectively. For instance:

- At the start of the project, marketers should *rationalise* using a logical, compelling recommendation, supported with a robust business case.
- If that doesn't work, they should assess if there is any emotional complexity – if so, they should arrange a pre-meeting and try to *negotiate* a win-win solution that is mutually acceptable to both parties.
- If they can't negotiate a win-win solution, they should *escalate* up – letting their bosses resolve it.

- If their bosses can't resolve it then *retreat*, enabling the team to choose the right moment to raise the issue again while actively continuing to build the fact base in preparation for that day.

They should present with the end in mind on the presentation day itself. For example:

- Prior to the Board meeting, they should:
    - Syndicate the final recommendation, storyline and presentation deck with senior managers, with the aim of pre-selling the final recommendation before the presentation.
    - Anticipate any questions or concerns that might be raised, by looking at the recommendation through the eyes of each Board member.

- On the presentation day itself, they should:
    - Focus on why the Board needs to engage and the key asks they want agreed.
    - Use the Board meeting to achieve cross-functional buy-in and a sense of shared responsibility.
    - Outline key agreements and proposed next steps to ensure that everyone is clear and aligned.

- After the Board meeting, they should:
    - Be sanguine if their project is not prioritised.
    - Write up and circulate meeting agreements and proposed next steps.

By winning over senior managers' hearts and minds, marketers can get Board agreement to proceed. In the next chapter, we look at how to keep the Board members on-board by maintaining their confidence once in-market.

Chapter 11

Winning the Board members' confidence

"I am a man of fixed and unbending principles, the first of which is to be flexible at all times."

Senator Everett Dirksen

To protect and manage a company successfully, the Board's primary focus is to optimise short- and long-term shareholder return, with the aim of maintaining a steadily growing share price. Understandably, the Board is keen to avoid anything that might trigger a fall in the share price and actively looks for ways to maximise the net present value of new initiatives, while simultaneously managing the risk of projects not delivering.

For the Board, delivering targets is sacrosanct. If a project under-delivers in its first year, confidence can quickly be eroded and future investment curtailed. In cases where underperformance is high, investment in other projects may need to be sacrificed to guarantee that overall company targets are met.

Yet, as great entrepreneurs know, not all of their decisions will be 'right'. It's likely to be their own money that they are spending. So being on top of how well the investment is performing and recognising and killing bad initiatives or activities quickly before they jeopardise profits or cause the business to collapse is key. As the saying on Wall Street goes, great moneymakers 'cut their losses short and let their winners run'.

Consequently, once they've done the hard work of convincing the Board to invest, marketers need to maintain the Board's confidence by managing the company's money in a financially responsible way.

They need to demonstrate what the investment money is trying to achieve, and how – and, if it is underperforming once in-market, quickly course correct to minimise the risk of the project not delivering. Investing in pre-agreed stages or tranches and tracking and reporting in-market performance from day one are key. This close monitoring should help to ensure that the project hits its short- and longer-term objectives (or if necessary, that the objectives are revised to be more realistic) which in turn helps to minimise the risk of underperformance, causing budgets to be cut after year one and the overall project to fail.

They also need to recognise and learn from their in-market successes *and* failures.

For example, great marketers recognise that a new brand, product, service or advertising launch is only the beginning. They go out into the marketplace on day one to identify 'early wins' that they can take to the Board to start to build confidence that the investment is working – as well as identify what isn't working well and needs to be fixed, thus ensuring that every pound spent on the launch is optimised.

Similarly, improved technology and analytics is enabling marketers to better identify which communications activities are most effective at driving short- and longer-term growth and so should be invested in for growth, and which are underperforming and so should be eliminated. Consequently, leading-edge companies are investing in building systematic 'test & learn' programmes, supported by 'rapid campaign testing', to deliver this.

In this chapter, we look at some of the ways that marketers can engage with the Board once they've started to invest in-market to help manage the inherent business risks and maintain Board confidence. These include:

A   Embracing failure as much as success.
B   Investing in pre-agreed tranches and monitoring performance from day one.
C   Recognising that the launch is only the beginning – and identifying early wins and emerging issues early on.
D   Optimising in-market performance through 'test & learn'.

Let's look at each of these in turn.

A: Embracing failure as much as success

Failure, as well as success, is an inherent part of our natural world – and a huge learning opportunity for those who embrace it.

At its most fundamental level, humans have evolved into what we are today, due to a continuous 'test & learn' process called 'natural selection'. Individuals with traits that are most suited to the environment that they are in are more likely to survive, reproduce and pass these genes onto their offspring. Over time, the weaker traits gradually die out and the stronger traits dominate, creating 'natural selection' or 'survival of the fittest'.

The same is true in business.

At an individual level, many successful people have failed many times before they have succeeded. Take Thomas Edison, who failed nearly ten thousand times to create a commercially viable electric light bulb. In his view, it was the accumulated knowledge developed from nearly ten thousand failed attempts that ultimately led to his success. As he famously said, "I have not failed. I've just found 10,000 ways that won't work."

J. K. Rowling's first Harry Potter book was sent to and rejected by twelve publishers before the eight-year-old daughter of the editor of Bloomsbury Publishing read it and convinced her dad that it had potential. Even then, J. K. Rowling was warned to "get a day job as she would never make any money writing children's books".[1]

Similarly, Michael Jordan said of his years as a professional basketball player, "I've missed more than 9,000 shots in my career. I've lost almost 300 games. 26 times, I've been trusted to take the game winning shot and missed. I've failed over and over and over again in my life. And that is why I succeed."[2]

At a company level, companies embrace and learn from day-to-day failure to improve their overall performance.

An example of this is Toyota Motor Company's Production System, which continually learns and improves from small day-to-day failures. When a problem on the production line occurs, the affected machinery stops immediately (preventing defective products from being produced) and the team use the 'andon' device (the problem display board) to immediately identify and fix the issue. Toyota uses these tiny failures to learn how to improve its overall productivity levels, leading to greater processing capacity.[3]

Essentially, learning from failure is key to our growth as a race, as individuals and as companies.

As Matthew Syed writes in his book *Black Box Thinking*, "Failure is rich in learning opportunities – it is showing us that the world is in a sense some way different to the way that we imagined. These failures are inevitable because the world is complex and we will never fully understand its subtleties."[4]

Given the psychological nature of marketing, this couldn't be more relevant. By testing and learning in the real world what works well and what works less well, we can better understand what motivates our customers and what we can say and do to engage them.

Yet people avoid failure.

On the one hand, failure is a good thing. We recognise that everyone fails and that failure is a natural part of the learning process.

Yet on the other hand, we are conditioned from a young age that failure is 'bad' and a sign of weakness. It signifies that we have screwed up or are stupid.

So to avoid failure, we do one of two things.

We either deny failure – we ignore it, bury it, or see it as a one-off anomaly. Many people can't admit their mistakes to themselves let alone to their bosses and to the Board.

Or, we avoid failure – we put our head in the sand rather than take a risk, to the point that we are so scared of messing up that we don't even try.

This human aversion to failure is further exacerbated by the corporate aversion to failure.

In business, successes and failures happen all of the time – they are part of the natural learning curve and an inevitable part of our everyday interaction with a complex world. Yet when failures happen, senior executives can often be quick to pin the blame on someone – both so that they are seen to have dealt with the issue efficiently as well as convey to others that mistakes will not be tolerated.

In fact, this issue is so prevalent that, according to a Harvard Business School report, executives believe that only 2 percent to 5 percent of the failures in their organisations are 'truly blameworthy'. Yet 70 percent to 90 percent of them were treated as blameworthy, making this a huge lost opportunity for company learning.[5]

Interestingly, in Dr. Carol Dweck's book *Mindset*, Dweck shows how successful people tend to act in a counter-intuitive way, by embracing rather than shying away from failure.[6]

For example, she tracked the two-year performance of students after they transitioned up into junior high school – a notoriously tougher learning environment. By doing this, she showed that students with what they call a 'fixed mindset' – a belief that their basic qualities such as character, talent and intelligence are largely fixed – view failure as proof that they don't have the characteristics needed to succeed and never will, and so avoid situations in which they might fail. In her experiment, students with a 'fixed mindset' showed an immediate drop-off in grades when they transitioned up into the new school, and these grades slowly but surely dropped further over the next two years.

In contrast, those with what they call a 'growth mindset' – a belief that most basic qualities can be developed through hard work – embrace failure as a learning opportunity, and are more likely to keep trying until they succeed. In her experiment, those with a 'growth mindset' showed an increase in grades over the next two years.

In her words, "When the two groups had entered junior high, their past records were indistinguishable. In the more benign environment of grade school, they'd earned the same grades and achievement test scores. Only when they hit the challenge of junior high did they begin to pull apart."

Human nature and corporate culture can make failure feel, at best, uncomfortable and, at worst, unacceptable. If we admit failure, will we be pilloried in front of our peers, marginalised or even fired?

The best marketers embrace failure alongside success. They understand that they can learn at least as much when they get it wrong as when they get it right. And they use failure to find new, bigger, bolder ways to go to market and become more creative. Conversely, as the philosopher Karl Popper said, "True ignorance is not the absence of knowledge but the refusal to acquire it."

There are a number of leading-edge companies that are increasingly recognising the competitive edge that 'embracing failure' can give them – including two in the entertainment industry.

King.com (the inventors of the hugely successful social media game, Candy Crush) soft launches a number of online games every year, with the aim of quickly and cheaply identifying those with strong potential for further investment. For example, between April 2011 and July 2012, only six titles from a portfolio of 160 went on to full launch, with two achieving Top Ten status within the year. Effectively, the company avoids investing high levels of resources in a game until it is pretty sure that the game will succeed. As the CEO, Riccardo Zacconi, says, "Innovation requires experimentation, and experimentation also implies failure, but we fail fast and cheaply."[7]

Similarly, as co-founder of Pixar, the creators of animated films such as *Toy Story, Finding Nemo, Monsters Inc.* and *Up*, Ed Catmull attests, "Early on, all of our movies suck." New ideas are rarely perfect at the outset – and so Catmull encourages his team to pull them apart again and again, until they have created the next great story. For example, when the team presented its first storyline for Pixar's film *Up*, it featured a castle in the sky inhabited by people who were at war with people on the ground. This version didn't work – and neither did the next two versions. But by constantly challenging the idea, the team was able to transform a weak story into one that won two Academy Awards and was nominated for three more, including Best Picture. Ultimately, Catmull says, "to be a truly creative company, you must start things that might fail."[8]

B: Investing in pre-agreed tranches and monitoring performance from day one

Once the Board agrees to invest, marketers need to demonstrate that they are managing the company's investment money responsibly.

To assess whether the project is succeeding or failing, and thus will deliver what was promised to the Board, marketers need a sense of what they're trying to achieve and how – and an ability to measure how well the investment money is performing once in-market.

So how can marketers achieve this?

Defining which metrics to track

To help maintain Board confidence that the investment will deliver the promised business growth, marketers should track how well their investment money is performing from day one of the launch and, if it is under-delivering, quickly course correct.

At the outset, the marketing team should get Board agreement to a succinct set of short- and longer-term customer, brand, advertising and business metrics, and the associated targets that need to be met to be successful.

To achieve this, the team should use the business model assessment, outlined in Chapter 9, to help define which customer behaviour metrics need to change and accordingly which customer, brand, advertising and business metrics (or key performance indicators) to track. For example, if project success relies on existing customers buying and using our product more frequently, then metrics should include relevant 'purchase frequency' and 'usage frequency' measures. Similarly, marketers should show how the investment would successfully deliver bottom-line growth, by showing how the customer, brand and advertising metrics ladder up to relevant business metrics, such as revenue and profit.

These metrics should be developed early on in conjunction with the finance team to ensure that they include the key measures that are needed at the Board level to fully assess project performance.

They should be 'outcome driven' (what we have achieved with the spend) rather than 'input driven' (*not* what we bought with the spend). For example, they should show 'actual audience viewing rates' rather than 'reach and frequency ratings'.

If the desired customer outcomes can't be measured, then the team should use relevant proxy metrics or 'lead indicators' – namely metrics that are known to correlate well with the desired outcome and can be measured in a timely way. For example, if we want to achieve an increase in longer-term customer preference, then metrics such as 'dwell time' on the website and number of 'Facebook likes' may act as relevant proxies, by indicating whether the campaign is building short-term preference.

The marketing team should then work with the finance team to size the required level of change across each of the core metrics, to deliver the required business growth. This includes an assessment of where we are today and where we need to be (or what needs to be achieved) at specific time points in the future.

Balancing 'money now' versus 'money later'

A perennial problem for Boards is successfully balancing the need for 'money now' versus 'money later'. Over recent years, companies have become more fixated on short-term measures, given how important it is for investment money to quickly deliver results and how much easier it is to track short-term measures.

But, in reality, Boards need to achieve the right balance of short-, mid- and longer-term initiatives to balance immediate sales needs with longer-term customer engagement and brand health.

Marketers can help Boards to balance 'money now' versus 'money later'. They can be effective business stewards, helping the business to recognise the need to successfully balance the delivery of both its short-term sales goals and its longer-term brand health goals.

Short-term initiatives are often used to deliver immediate sales uplifts and are measured using short-term metrics that move quickly, such as 'advertising recall', 'click-through rates' and 'cost per click'.

Mid-term initiatives can be effective at building customer engagement and can be measured by relevant customer engagement metrics, such as 'the number of times a customer visits a website', 'the number of pages that they view' and 'the amount of dwell time that they spend on the site'.

Longer-term initiatives can be effective at maintaining or building brand health and are measured by metrics that shift more slowly, such as 'top of mind brand awareness', 'brand consideration', 'brand preference' and relevant 'brand image' scores.

For example, Coca-Cola balances the need to build longer-term customer loyalty and drive sales, as it recognises that the creation of strong long-term customer relationships drives sustainable sales growth. As Silke Muenster, Coca-Cola's director of knowledge and insights, said, "We know that we would only have sustainable growth if we are able to build relationships with our consumers. These relationships convert into sales." To measure customer loyalty, Coca-Cola uses a proprietary tracking tool to measure 'Brand Love' – a metric that according to Muenster is now "as important as market share" to the firm.[9]

Ideally, a company such as Coca-Cola would also track short-term metrics that are good proxies for its longer-term 'Brand Love' metric – namely 'lead indicators' that can be measured in the short term and are known to correlate highly with the longer-term metric. In this case, good short-term proxies might include 'positive brand sentiment', 'more visits to the website', 'more dwell time on the website' and 'more Facebook shares'.

Armed with this knowledge, the team can keep the Board updated on how well the project is performing – maintaining Board confidence if the project is going well or enabling the Board to help resolve any emerging issues early on if it is underperforming.

Tracking in-market performance from day one

Once the core metrics are agreed, the team should summarise these key metrics in a scorecard that can be completed and distributed in a timely way. This can be used to keep everyone focused on the most important metrics and updated on how well the investment is performing to ensure no nasty surprises.

The primary metrics that are included in a scorecard are typically:

- In-market activity, such as advertising and promotion levels, distribution levels and pricing.
- Absolute performance, such as sales revenue and profit.
- Relative performance versus competitors, such as volume and value market share levels.
- Consumer metrics, such as the number of new users, customer retention and products per customer.
- Brand metrics, such as awareness, consideration, enquire, trial, repeat, recommend.

- Advertising metrics, including both offline metrics such as 'advertising recognition' and 'brand recall', and online metrics such as 'click-through rate' (CTR), 'cost per lead' (CPL) and 'dwell time'.

Many of these measures are typically shown over time and versus competitors to reveal growth trends.

The scorecard should contain fewer, rather than more, metrics. Firstly, this helps to ensure that the metrics can be easily and quickly gathered and enables the team to fill in and distribute the data quickly – with emerging issues recognised and addressed promptly, rather than 'after the event'. Secondly, it helps to focus the mind on the metrics that really matter, and reduce any complexity that might arise from conflicting data due to a wealth of metrics being tracked.

Once the scorecard is set up, the team should put in place a tracking process that identifies how to accurately and efficiently fill in each metric. It's important that any data collected is *as unbiased and representative* as possible, with a large enough base size to ensure that it's statistically robust. It should be collected as quickly as possible to ensure that any emerging issues are identified and addressed early on.

At the outset, the team should ideally review the scorecard weekly, if not daily, depending on which metrics are being tracked. An analyst should be responsible for collecting, collating and synthesising the data, as well as summarising the conclusions and 'so whats' for the Board.

Given that multi-channel advertising campaigns rarely work in a linear way, the analyst should triangulate the scorecard results from all angles – going beyond the obvious to uncover what is really going on. Importantly, if an in-market issue is identified early on, then it's crucial that the team is alerted immediately so that the issue can be dealt with as quickly as possible.

These scorecard metrics should be monitored over time to ensure that each is still valid and that no new relevant metrics have emerged that should be tracked alongside or instead of these. If the situation has changed, the scorecard metrics should be flexed accordingly.

Investing in pre-agreed stages or tranches

Marketers should demonstrate to the Board how they are mitigating project risk wherever possible. Investing in stages or tranches once key targets have been met, with a Board review at the end of each stage to ensure that the initiative is on track, demonstrates to the Board that marketers are investing in a financially responsible way.

This way, each tranche can be optimised based on previous learnings, increasing its chance of future success. It also allows commercially savvy marketers to quickly identify which activities are performing well and should be invested in more and those that are not and should be killed off.

This means adopting a 'test & learn' approach from day one, acknowledging that part of the launch plan and product and service offer will not hit the mark and will need to be optimised.

In practice, the marketing team should lay out the business case, detailing the investment it plans to spend over the coming three years and what it expects this investment to deliver for the business – then divide this three-year business case into stages, each with a clear set of dates (or stage gates).

For each stage, the team should outline what level of investment it wishes to invest over that period, defining what it expects to spend each tranche of investment on, what it expects each tranche of investment to achieve, when it will be asking the Board for the next tranche of investment money and what the business performance should look like for the Board to warrant it. Then, if the launch is significantly either over- or underperforming, the dates or stage gates, investment levels and what the investment is spent on can be adjusted appropriately.

It should also track the impact of any new project launches on overall cash flow. For example, if a marketing team is launching a number of initiatives simultaneously, then the negative impact on overall cash flow may be considerable.

Once in-market, the team should immediately start building confidence, both internally and externally, by communicating 'early wins'.

This can be done by sending out regular communication updates to the day-to-day team and senior management on how the latest tranche of investment money is performing, highlighting:

- The growth achieved to date.
- The investment spend to date.
- How growth and spend compares versus target key performance indicators.
- What's working well and why.
- What's not working so well and how it's being fixed.

At the end of each investment stage, the team should arrange regular Board updates to review the scorecard performance, highlight any emerging issues, and decide and agree how best to address these issues.

To course correct quickly, each Board update should be held as soon as the scorecard has been completed. For example, the scorecard should be sent out overnight, giving the Board members time to review it and team members the opportunity to update their Board member representative, with the regular Board update scheduled the following day.

It's important for the team to be frank with senior management about what's working and not working well, so that they together, as a team, can problem solve and quickly course correct any issues.

C: Recognising that the launch is only the beginning, and identifying early wins and emerging issues early on

No launch is perfect.

A team, based on what it knows, launches what it thinks is the optimal product or service but, in reality, not even the most lauded marketing team in the world can predict whether a product or service will succeed until it actually launches. Nor is it likely to get everything right on day one of the launch – there are always aspects that can be improved.

These may be issues that were in the team's control, for example, poor display units that hide the most attractive products, advertising that is poorly branded or frontline staff who don't know how to sell a new product.

Or they may be issues that were beyond the team's control, for example, competitors might come into the market to deliberately spoil the launch by loading people up with their brand, using three for ones (as Fairy did in the Persil Washing Up Liquid launch) or dropping free full-size bottles through people's doors (as Creamsilk did during the Pantene launch test market in Carlisle). Or people might respond differently to what was predicted in market research, where they said that they would be 'interested in buying a product within the range' yet, in the real world, lack the incentive to switch.

As Richard Branson said, when asked how to build a business from scratch,

> As you prepare for launch day, you must ensure that you're going to be nimble enough to cope with unforeseen problems and to take advantage of any valuable opportunities that arise. A stall or cart offers some advantages in terms of flexibility, because if you notice that a particular type of product is doing especially well, you can more easily transfer your energy and funds to developing that area of the business than a large company ever could. This may mean modifying your original idea, which can be difficult – many businesses fail because their founders are too headstrong to adjust course.[10]

Being 'nimble' is key.

Savvy marketers are out in the marketplace from day one of the launch, looking for 'early wins' that they can take to the Board to start building confidence that the investment is working.

Equally, they acknowledge the likelihood that part of the launch plan might not be 'right' and that elements of it will need to be optimised. So they are also out there looking for what isn't working well and needs to be fixed, with the aim of fixing those issues immediately to ensure that every pound spent on the launch is optimised.

They can do this by 'being customers themselves' and by observing customers in-store, talking with customers when out and about or in qualitative research groups, and talking with people in the trade or frontline staff, to assess how well the launch is going.

To illustrate, when a fast-moving consumer goods company launched a new cosmetics brand in a test market, the marketing team went out on day one to watch how people shopped the in-store fixture and ran focus groups in the first week of the launch to understand how well the launch was working. The team quickly realised that the on-shelf product layout was confusing, identified weaker-than-expected branding in the advertising and were able to fix these issues immediately to ensure a successful launch.

Another effective way to get immediate, helpful customer feedback is to watch what people do so that you can see exactly which aspects people are engaging with. For example:

- *Watch what people buy.* Those products that sell easily with little additional push or support are the ones that are offering people something that they really want.
- *Watch how people behave.* The search words they enter, pages they click on or products they enquire about will tell you what's on their mind and help you identify other products or services you can offer that they might want to buy.
- *Watch what people share.* Giving people product or service information that they can share with others not only helps advertise your brand to people who are likely to be in your relevant target market, but also tells you what people think is important enough to share with others.
- *Ask your customers what they like.* People who like your brand are often keen to tell you why, giving you ideas on what to say to 'non-users' to convince them to try it. Conversely, those who have a problem with your brand are also keen to let you know about it, enabling you to identify issues that you might have otherwise missed.

Confetti, the online wedding portal, was not only effective at creating a viral community that people wanted to be part of, but was also well-attuned to what was and wasn't working, and fast to exit activities that were underperforming.

Recognising how much brides-to-be like talking about weddings, Confetti built a number of viral components into its website that could be shared with friends – who were, by and large, people of a similar age and who were likely to be getting married in the near future. One of the strongest of these was its 'Save-the-date' page that new brides-to-be used to ask friends to reserve their wedding dates in their diaries and, in doing so, were cost-efficiently advertising Confetti to their friends. Another example was the 'Wedding Gift List' page that brought wedding guests to the Confetti website.

Confetti also identified that brides-to-be keenly sought top tips on 'how to make wedding receptions fun and interactive'. In response, its range of Confetti pocket cameras for 'the big day' was not only a huge hit but also acted as an advertising tool whenever these cameras were used at weddings or when people visited the website to review the photos.

Similarly, by offering a range of thirty to fifty wedding stationery designs online, people could select three free samples – giving immediate feedback on which designs were most popular and which were not well liked, enabling the marketing team to eliminate half of the designs within weeks of the launch – an example of a fast, effective cull of an initiative that wasn't pulling its weight.

There is an immense amount of data and information out there that savvy marketers can tap into and leverage – and this level will only increase going forward.

D: Optimising in-market performance through 'test & learn'

Improved technology and analytics is enabling marketers to better identify which communications activities are most effective at driving short- and longer-term growth – thus enabling them to more quickly focus on the winners and cull the losers.

This means identifying which marketing and communication activities are most effective at driving business performance, investing in those that perform best and quickly eliminating those that are underperforming. Doing this proactively demonstrates to the Board that marketers are spending their marketing investment wisely.

Entrepreneurs tend to be good at this. Prompted by the fact that it's often their own money they're spending, they are more open-minded to thinking that they may have got it wrong. They test new initiatives at a small scale to identify the ones that are working, before significantly investing in them – and they quickly recognise and kill bad initiatives to ensure that they stay afloat.

Yet in reality, this can be difficult. At times, it can be incredibly tough to isolate the different marketing activities to fully understand how individually each is performing.

But it can be even tougher to admit that an idea is poor and that the company should stop investing in it. It's a brave marketer who ditches their latest creative campaign and replaces it with an old one because it achieved a higher ROI – yet doing so could be the difference between success and failure.

To overcome this, marketers need to *think more like entrepreneurs*, viewing every pound of the investment money as if it were coming out of their own pocket, and as a 'learning opportunity' that will help identify what does and what doesn't work well.

They should recognise that it's impossible to get everything right. Some of the activities they choose to invest in will work well, and others will underperform, consuming rather than contributing to profits.

It's important to not waste marketing investment on poorly performing activities that not only eat up valuable resources – both the investment money and team brainpower needed to try to make them work – but also stop the stars from shining. If half of the team time and investment is focused on communicating something that fundamentally won't catch on, then the stars that *would have succeeded* are being deprived of the team time and investment they need. It makes better business sense to get rid of communication clutter and single-mindedly focus investment on the stars that are likely to shine.

In essence, marketers need the honesty to admit when they have failed, the curiosity to learn from their mistakes and the tenacity to keep testing. This in turn should deliver the results that were promised.

To identify the winners and losers (and essentially where to focus their spend) leading-edge companies are investing in building:

1   'Test & learn' programmes that systematically test each marketing and communications activity, to identify which to continue or increase investment in, and which to kill.
2   'Rapid campaign testing' that enables communications activities to be tested and optimised in bite-size tranches, with further spend only invested once the in-market activity is proven to work.
3   A culture that enables people to 'fail fast' and encourages everyone to continuously 'test & learn'.

Let's look at each in turn.

1. Setting up a 'test & learn' programme

Marketers can quickly and cost-efficiently test & learn *qualitatively* – by getting out in the real world and talking with people.

For example, they can ask new customers during the signing up process why they joined and what encouraged them to join today.

They can use events to talk with loyal customers and sceptics to better understand what engages people and what's turning people off.

They can ask their sales and call centre people what customers are looking for and what convinces them to buy or makes them hesitate.

They can ask people in the trade what customers are saying about the products – both what's attracting them to the range and what's stopping them from buying. They can watch how people are shopping the category when in-store – what they look at and consider when at the shelf.

These are all typically quick and highly cost-efficient ways to identify what's working well and why, and improve marketing investment performance.

Today's leading-edge companies are also measuring the impact of different communication activities *quantitatively*. In essence, they are looking for ways to achieve 'marginal gains' across every element of the marketing communication mix – by breaking down the communication investment into its small, component parts, rigorously testing which elements are and aren't working, and finding ways to improve each small element.

The concept of 'marginal gains' was made famous by the general manager and performance director of Team Sky, Sir Dave Brailsford, when he used it to build Great Britain's professional cycling team into one that could win the Tour de France. In explanation, he described it as "the one percent margin for improvement in everything we do" – in essence, if every tiny part is improved by just one percent, then all of those small gains will add up to something remarkable. The team looked for one percent gains across each and every element of the training experience, including the more obvious elements (such as the nutrition of riders, the ergonomics of the bike seat and the weight of the tyres) but also the less obvious ones (such as the optimal pillow for sleep, the most effective type of massage gel and how to minimise the risk of hand infection).

The outcome? Team Sky dramatically turned around the performance of the team and famously won the Tour de France within three years – well within its target of five – and, to prove that it wasn't a one-off, they repeated this remarkable feat the following year.[11]

Marketers are emulating Sir Dave Brailsford's approach by using 'test & learn' to achieve 'marginal gains' in as many elements along the customer journey as possible – for example, by looking for ways to achieve +1 percent more click-throughs, or +1 percent more likes, or +1 percent more seconds of dwell time on the website. If they achieve marginal gains across a high number of elements, then the overall performance of the communications campaign will be exponentially higher.

To set up an effective quantitative 'test & learn' approach, marketers need to first create a testing plan by identifying the key questions they want to test, defining which metrics to track, and setting aside a 'test & learn' budget that they are comfortable to invest – for example, 20 percent of total marketing communication spend.

Next, they should set up an active customer engagement programme looking for opportunities to engage with people and learning from each interaction they have with the brand. This 'test & learn' programme should test the performance of different campaigns, moving from a few large campaigns to frequent 'rapid-fire' testing, as well as benchmark performance versus category norms.

Marketers can then commission sales response curves that aggregate the tests to better isolate the effect of different marketing activities. By aggregating the curves, they can identify the optimal spend level and budget allocation, creating a 'What if' scenario planning tool that can be used to test different options.

Then they should create a database of test scores to understand what 'good' looks like.

By doing this, marketers can continuously focus future spend on the most effective activities and drop those that underperform – as well as develop relevant scenario planning models that can be implemented if conditions change.

2. Using 'rapid optimisation' to generate faster feedback loops

Improved technology and analytics has paved the way for leading-edge companies to increasingly invest in rapid in-flight optimisation. This generates faster feedback loops – enabling companies to more quickly and accurately measure how well each piece of communications activity is performing.

If a campaign is performing well, they can commit more funds to it. If not, they can either stop investing in it or try to optimise it. Either way, this enables marketers to use only a small level of marketing spend to assess how well a new campaign is performing before deciding whether to commit more – which in turn helps them more quickly identify and invest in high-performing activities, and more efficiently recognise and kill underperforming ones.

Here's how it can work in practice.

- Companies can test a new image on a homepage within one to two days.
- They can test different website formats by showing different formats to different groups of website visitors. For example, Google optimised the colour of its toolbar by randomly assigning visitors to forty test groups, each of which saw a different toolbar shade. Through trial and error, Google was able to identify which toolbar shade of blue generated higher click-through rates.[12]
- They can show different banner adverts to different customer segments, with click-through and engagement rates measured early on to identify which messages are most effective and therefore should be rolled out – much as a food retailer did when testing which food recipes had greatest resonance with its target customers when advertised online.
- They can use live API data feeds from platforms such as Twitter to immediately measure the level of interest in, and sentiment towards, an advert in real time – and prioritise those adverts with greatest resonance.
- They can track the level of mentions on platforms such as Twitter to assess the ideal time to place an advert. For example, are there better days of the week or times of day to advertise? And what does the predicted weekend temperature level need to be to make it worthwhile advertising summer barbecue ingredients?
- They can also use Twitter to conduct regional tests. For example, they can test the power of different messages by placing different adverts in different regions and tracking the volume of mentions in each. Or they can test the relevance of different adverts in different regions by analysing the types of mentions in each region – for instance, are there some regions that are more interested in drinking cider, or in drinking cider that is low calorie or low alcohol?
- They can hand select which customers see a television advert, by using the Sky channel to show the advert only to households within their target market. For example, a brand such as Mercedes could target advertising

to 100,000 households who would be open to buying a Mercedes C-Class by sending them traditional direct mail, alongside a targeted television advert using Sky TV's AdSmart platform. If interested, the recipients can then book a test drive by responding to the direct mail or via their Skybox.

- They can send a series of search and display adverts and e-mails to an individual, testing which series of messages best moves people from awareness, to consideration, to conversion – much as Discover Iceland did when encouraging people to consider holidaying in Iceland.
- They can test their way to creating a seamless multi-channel experience across offline and online channels – for example, TV that encourages people to go to the website, a landing page that encourages people to sign up and a loyalty card that tracks whether someone purchased anything in-store in the coming days – much as John Lewis spearheaded as part of its desire to be an omni-channel retailer.

When done well, 'rapid optimisation' enables a new marketing campaign to be briefed in on Monday, approved on Tuesday, placed in-market on Wednesday, assessed (in terms of in-market performance) on Thursday, adapted on Friday, then placed again on Saturday.

This is delivered by having day-to-day brand teams in place that include both creatives (such as copywriters and designers) alongside research and data analysts all focused on the same objective – creating, testing and optimising new campaigns, as quickly as possible.

One word of caution is to ensure that the time frame used to test any piece of activity is realistic. For example, measuring the impact of an advert on new car sales within a week or even a month is probably unrealistic, given the lengthy sales cycle within this industry. Within a week, the team may be able to measure an uplift in website visits, and within a month an uplift in the number of test drives – but a significant uplift in actual car sales is probably not going to happen.

3. Instilling a 'test & learn' mindset

The biggest barrier to 'test & learn' isn't the technology but the culture.

In business, successes and failures happen all of the time – they are part of the natural learning curve and an inevitable part of our everyday interaction with a complex world.

Yet people don't want to fail. Most of us view failure negatively and as a sign of weakness. We prefer not to analyse how well an activity has performed, fearful of being exposed as having screwed up or made a mistake. Additionally, companies encourage their people to 'not fail' – or at least to not admit to it. They promote a blame culture, penalising their people when bad decisions are made and things go wrong, and creating an environment where people are less willing to challenge the existing norms and make real change.

As Syed writes in *Black Box Thinking*, "When we are testing assumptions, we are pushing out the frontiers of our knowledge about what works and what doesn't. Penalising these mistakes has a simple outcome – it destroys innovation and enlightened risk-taking. In short, blame undermines the information vital for meaningful adaptation. It obscures the complexity of our world, deluding us into thinking that we understand our environment when we should be learning from it."[13]

Leading-edge companies are increasingly recognising the huge business opportunity that comes from encouraging their people to 'fail fast' by allowing them to test new ideas, quickly learn from their failures and optimise their content accordingly. Working in this way means marketing teams can think bigger and more boldly – daring to venture into new territories to find new, more cost-efficient ways to go to market – as well as quickly identify and prioritise great ideas, and learn from and eliminate poor ones.

However, this requires moving away from 'blame' and giving people more autonomy to try new things and make mistakes.

More and more companies are trying to find the right balance between 'a blame culture' and 'an anything goes' culture – and, in doing so, are moving away from 'leading by command' to 'leading by example', delegating power to people to generate great ideas.

These companies are empowering people to get closer to the business, and to drive customer-centric change across the whole customer experience.

They are encouraging people to build momentum – by starting something and learning from it, rather than not starting something at all.

They are creating an agile working environment that is 'always on' – rewarding people who continuously challenge the status quo, and are curious and open-minded about what might and might not work.

They are enabling people to analyse why activities succeeded or failed – by taking the time to fully assess what really happened and why, and finding in-market data and evidence to prove their case.

They are encouraging people to capture and share their successes *and* failures – and are sharing these examples on big-scale learning platforms to inspire and guide others.

The size of the opportunity is significant.

Leading companies are eliminating up to half of their communication activities due to poor in-market performance. This can double the effectiveness of a marketing budget, highlighting why it's important for any marketer to be actively looking for ways to improve the effectiveness of their marketing spend. However, as we know, one of the hardest things is admitting defeat and making the tough to decision to get out.

In the words of Richard Branson when asked what an entrepreneur was, "Entrepreneurs must not only cope with failure, but welcome it. There's no shame in admitting that something isn't working and going back to the drawing board – we've done our fair share of that at Virgin. This ability to bounce back will make the difference, allowing you and your team to apply yourselves to new goals wholeheartedly, without looking back."[14]

In summary

Once they've done the hard work of convincing the Board to invest, marketers need to maintain the Board's confidence by managing the company's money in a financially responsible way.

It's important to adopt a 'growth mindset' – believing that 'practice makes perfect' and embracing failure as an inevitable learning opportunity.

Once in-market, it's important to manage the company's money responsibly by:

- Defining which metrics to track.
- Helping the company to balance 'money now' versus 'money later'.
- Tracking in-market performance and course correcting from day one.
- Investing in pre-agreed stages or tranches.

This close monitoring should help to ensure that the project hits its short- and longer-term objectives – or, if necessary, that the objectives are revised to be more realistic – which in turn helps to minimise the risk of underperformance causing budgets to be cut after year one, and the overall project failing.

It's important to recognise that a new brand, product, service or advertising launch is only the beginning and to be out in the marketplace from day one, to identify 'early wins' and 'emerging issues' early on.

And it's important to continually 'test & learn' by:

- Setting up a 'test & learn' programme.
- Using 'rapid optimisation' to generate faster feedback loops.
- Instilling a 'test & learn' mindset.

This enables the team to test new initiatives at a small scale – to identify the ones that are most effective at driving business performance before significantly investing in them, as well as to recognise and quickly eliminate those that are underperforming.

Doing this proactively demonstrates to the Board that the team are optimising every pound of marketing investment, which in turn helps to build Board confidence that the company's money is being invested wisely.

Notes

1 "Best Sellers Initially Rejected," *www.litrejections.com*, http://www.litrejections.com/best-sellers-initially-rejected/, accessed October 2016.
2 Forbes, "Thoughts on the Business of Life," *www.forbes.com*, http://www.forbes.com/quotes/11194/, accessed October 2016.

3 Toyota Global, "Toyota Production System," www.toyota-global.com/company/vision_philosophy/toyota_production_system/, accessed October 2016.
4 Matthew Syed, *Black Box Thinking* (London: John Murray), 33.
5 Todd Mundt and Amy C. Edmondson, "Strategies for Learning from Failure," *Harvard Business Review*, April 2011.
6 Dr. Carol S. Dweck, *Mindset* (New York: Random House Inc., 2006; London: Robinson, 2012), 6, 7 and 57.
7 Steve Peterson, "King.com Interview: CEO Riccardo Zacconi," July 2012, www.gamesindustry.biz/articles/2012–07–20-king-com-interview-ceo-riccardo-zacconi.
8 Nicole Laskowski, "Pixar President on Why Building a Fail Fast Culture Is Hard," October 2015, http://searchcio.techtarget.com/opinion/Pixar-president-on-why-building-a-fail-fast-culture-is-hard.
9 Warc, "Coca-Cola Focuses on Brand Love," March 2010, www.warc.com/LatestNews/News/Coca-Cola_focuses_on_%22brand_love%22.news?ID=26428.
10 Richard Branson, "A Foundation Built on Flexibility and Fun," January 2014, www.thenassauguardian.com/component/content/article/67-richard-branson/44545-a-foundation-built-on-flexibility-and-fun.
11 James Clear, "The Coach Improved Every Tiny Thing by One Percent and Here's What Happened," 2016, http://jamesclear.com/marginal-gains.
12 Matthew Syed, *Black Box Thinking*, 98–199.
13 Ibid., 246.
14 Branson, "Entrepreneur: A Bold Brand," www.thenassauguardian.com/index.php?option=com_content&view=article&id=44046&Itemid=2.

Bibliography

"Best Sellers Initially Rejected." *www.litrejections.com*, October 2016. www.litrejections.com/best-sellers-initially-rejected/.

Branson, Richard. "Entrepreneur: A Bold Brand." December 2013. www.thenassauguardian.com/index.php?option=com_content&view=article&id=44046&Itemid=2.

Branson, Richard. "A Foundation Built on Flexibility and Fun." January 2014. www.thenassauguardian.com/component/content/article/67-richard-branson/44545-a-foundation-built-on-flexibility-and-fun.

Clear, James. "The Coach Improved Every Tiny Thing by One Percent and Here's What Happened." 2016. http://jamesclear.com/marginal-gains.

Dweck, Carol S. Dr. *Mindset*. New York: Random House Inc., 2006; London: Robinson, 2012.

Forbes. "Thoughts on the Business of Life." *www.forbes.com*, October 2016. www.forbes.com/quotes/11194/.

Laskowski, Nicole. "Pixar President on Why Building a Fail Fast Culture Is Hard." October 2015. http://searchcio.techtarget.com/opinion/Pixar-president-on-why-building-a-fail-fast-culture-is-hard.

Mundt, Todd and Amy C. Edmondson. "Strategies for Learning from Failure." *Harvard Business Review*, April 2011.

Peterson, Steve. "King.com Interview: CEO Riccardo Zacconi." July 2012. www.gamesindustry.biz/articles/2012–07–20-king-com-interview-ceo-riccardo-zacconi.

Syed, Matthew. *Black Box Thinking*. London: John Murray, 2015.

Toyota Global. "Toyota Production System." October 2016. www.toyota-global.com/company/vision_philosophy/toyota_production_system/.

Warc. "Coca-Cola Focuses on Brand Love." March 2010. www.warc.com/LatestNews/News/Coca-Cola_focuses_on_%22brand_love%22.news?ID=26428.

Index

Note: Page numbers in italics indicate figures